Engineering Paradise

by

David Gardiner

MERILANG PRESS
Bodyfuddau
Trawsfynydd
Gwynedd
LL41 4UW

This is a work of fiction, not an historical document, and although some of the incidents described are based upon real events that took place in Belfast and elsewhere in the 1960s no attempt has been made to achieve historical accuracy with regard to the details or the chronology of the events forming the background to this novel.

Copyright © David Gardiner 2011
Cover photograph © Sam Styles 2011

A CIP catalogue record for this book is available from the British Library

ISBN: 978-0-9569379-0-2

ISBN 978-0-9569379-0-2

9 780956 937902

Acknowledgements

My sincere thanks to Aliya Whiteley, John Griffiths, Omma Velada, Mike Shearing, Godfrey Boyle, Jean Duggleby, Mavis Turner and David Turner for reading and commenting upon earlier drafts of this manuscript, and to those attending the 2010 UKAway writers' holiday and the members of the UKAuthors.com writers' website for providing helpful feedback on individual chapters.

Thanks also to Daffni Percival of Merilang Press for her unfailing encouragement and assistance during the preparation of this work for publication.

Sincere thanks also to Becky Simpson for setting to music some of the words of the original songs quoted in this book, and to Lesley Gore for her kind permission to reproduce lines from her 1963 recording *You Don't Own Me* (lyrics by John Madara and David White).

The Holocaust has shown us that the creation of hell on earth is just a matter of engineering. The creation of an earthly paradise is an engineering problem also.

Stafford Beer (1926 – 2002)

Contents

Prologue

"G'night, Danny."

It was the old woman who ran the bamboo snack booth at the top end of the beach, selling fried rice and grilled fish and local beer, where everything was a US dollar – unless you didn't have a US dollar, of course, in which case it was whatever you had. Maria wasn't very hot on business accountancy.

"'Night, Maria. Didn't see you in there in the bushes."

"Thought I'd better wait for you and tell you. That ol' Irish guy with the suit's been poking around your cabin again."

"Has he? Thanks for letting me know. What does he look like?"

"Old."

"I'm old."

"Older'n you."

"Pretty damn old then. Thanks Maria."

She got up wearily from the log she had been sitting on, pulled the strap of her shoulder bag over her neck, and trudged up the sandy path towards the palm trees and the lights of the village. Soon her shape was lost among the tree shadows, her footsteps drowned out by the gentle waves and the relentless trill of the cicadas, like dried beans shaken furiously in a biscuit tin.

Danny could smell a tropical storm on the way. Hadn't had a big one since last year's Wet Season. Wasn't going to hold off much longer. He pushed open the door of his cabin. The bottom of it scraped along the wooden floor. Sagging on its hinges a bit. He should mend it some time.

Too dark to see very much inside. He flung his straw hat on the mattress and pulled the lever to switch the battery from the solar panel chargers back to the distribution box. That done he turned on the light. The low energy tube flickered reluctantly into life.

With a start Danny realised that there was someone sitting on the wicker chair by the side of the mattress. Like Maria had said, he was old. And not dressed for the tropics. Gaunt and pale, with a couple of days growth of grey stubble and a few wispy strings of matching grey hair, trimmed neatly around his ears. He was holding something in his right hand, hidden under the drapes of one of Danny's old sarongs. The yellow one with the picture of the coconut crab. He remained completely still, not even blinking his narrow eyes as Danny surveyed him. He could almost have been a corpse.

"Long time, Danny," he said at last.

"Yes Seamus. Long time. I've been expecting you of course. Do you want to get it over with?"

He shrugged. "Why so impatient?"

"Oh, I don't know. What's the point of dragging it out?"

There was another pause. "Why don't you sit down?"

Danny sat.

"You haven't lost your Irish accent. I think I have. They tell me you run the local radio station here?"

"It gives me something to do."

More seconds passed.

"Do you ever think about the old times?"

"Of course I do."

Chapter One
Interview with Fr. Walsh

"Danny Gallagher."

The name rebounded from the cold green plaster of the corridor. Danny felt a shiver run down his neck. The words were not so much shouted as projected, in the manner of a skilled stage actor, so as to precisely fill every cubic inch of the enclosed space.

"What are you doing here at this time of day?"

"My mother had one of her turns, Father."

There was a pause while the priest absorbed the information. "And that made you twenty-five minutes late?"

"Yes, Father." The smell of stale school milk seeped into Danny's nostrils. In the distance he could hear the muffled chant of a class reciting the familiar gibberish of The Lord's Prayer in Irish:

Ár nAthair atá ar neamh,
go naofar d'ainm
Go dtaga do ríocht
Go ndéantar do thoil
ar an talamh mar a dhéantar ar neamh...

"Have you got a note?"

"No, Father."

"Come into my office. I've been meaning to have a talk with you anyway."

Danny wiped a bead of sweat from the bridge of his nose and walked towards the still figure. The priest opened the office door as Danny reached him and with dignified slowness walked ahead of Danny into the room and sat behind his large mahogany desk with its green leather inlay. The window, like most of the windows in the gloomy Victorian building, was small and high, and admitted only a narrow shaft of sunlight that touched one corner of Father Walsh's desk. Within it tiny dust motes floated endlessly downwards. On the wall behind the desk, between the two tall bookcases, the red flame of an oil lamp glowed on a small shelf in front of a 'sacred heart', a garish picture of Jesus with an exposed heart in the middle of his chest. Neatly propped against the side of the desk was a thin bamboo cane with its end curved into the shape of a handle. It held Danny's attention like the sight of the gallows to a man on Death Row. In front of the desk were two simple wooden chairs. As Father Walsh sat down Danny sat also.

"Did I ask you to sit down?"

"No, Father." Danny sprang to attention.

The elderly priest scanned the boy from top to bottom. "How long have you been with us now, Gallagher?"

"Three and a half years, Father."

"So you're fifteen?"

"Very nearly, Father."

"Is that a hole in the leg of your trousers?"

Danny tried to cover it with his hand. "Yes, Father. It got burned with a soldering iron."

"And what's that on the shoulder of your jacket?"

"I think it's pigeon..."

"Pigeon guano. That's what it's called in polite society. Does your father keep pigeons?"

"No, Father. I think I got it at a friend's house."

"Hugh Laverty?"

"Yes, Father."

The priest continued his inspection. "What is the colour of the shirt that we wear at this school?"

"White, Father."

"And what is the colour of your shirt, young Mr Gallagher?"

"Blue, Father. I... couldn't find a white one when my mother took her bad turn..."

"I see. And would you like to give me your opinion of the shoes that you are presently wearing?"

"They're a bit dirty, Father."

"I agree. In fact I would say, extremely dirty. Unacceptably dirty is a description that I might apply. Do you by any chance have shoe polish in your house?"

"Yes, Father."

"May I suggest that you apply some before you come to this school again?"

"Yes, Father."

Father Walsh picked up a black address-book from his desk and thumbed through it. When he found what he wanted he cranked out a number on the rotary dial of his antiquated desk telephone. The voice with which he spoke into the device could scarcely have been recognised as belonging to the same person. "Oh, good morning Dr Gallagher. Sorry to disturb you. It's Father Walsh at the School. I have your son here and he tells me that Mrs Gallagher is unwell this morning... oh, I'm very sorry to hear that... yes, I understand. We shall include her in our lunchtime prayers. Thank you, Doctor." He put down the phone.

"May I go to Science now, Father?"

Walsh gave him a cold look. "Sit down, boy." Use of the term "boy" suggested trouble. Danny obeyed.

Walsh paused for a few moments.

"Your family background is somewhat different to that of the other boys at this school." The priest spoke slowly to lend theatrical weight to the words. "You may see this as a burden. Perhaps the children of artisans victimise or tease you. I don't know. But having the background that you do is in fact an enormous opportunity and privilege. You come from a home where learning is respected and encouraged. You are surrounded by highly educated adults. You live in a world of books and newspapers, art, culture, intelligent conversation. Isn't that so?"

"Yes, Father." Danny didn't really recognise this picture, but if it was the one Father Walsh wanted to believe in then it was fine with him. His own perception of his home life was of something more akin to a boxing ring, in which the two contestants continuously chased each other around in circles looking for a gap in the ropes.

"Your privileged life brings with it great responsibilities," Father Walsh continued. "To the other boys here, you represent a kind of role model. Education, after all, is the product on offer. You come from an educated and professional family. The boys look to you for an example. How you dress, how you speak, how you behave. These things matter more in your case than in the case of the other boys. Do you understand what I'm saying?"

"Yes, Father."

"That is why I find it necessary to point out to you those areas in which you are not setting the example that you should be. What is that in your pocket, boy?" The priest made a beckoning gesture for Danny to hand it over.

The sudden jump in the flow of Father Walsh's monologue made Danny start. He drew the object from his trouser pocket, standing out of his chair to do so. "It's a valve, Father," he explained in a meek voice, placing it in Walsh's outstretched hand.

"One of those glass tubes out of a wireless set?"

"Yes, Father."

The priest twirled it between his fingers and looked at the metal components inside. "And what would this do if you had a fall in the playground?"

"Probably break, Father."

"Exactly so. And then what would happen? Shards of glass in your leg. All kinds of sharp pieces of metal sticking into you. Heaven knows what chemicals injected deep down under your skin."

"I don't think it contains any chemicals, Father."

"Don't you, indeed?" The priest slipped the offending object into the side drawer of his desk. "You may have it back when school is over. Why did you bring it to school anyway?"

"To give to somebody, Father. Somebody who's trying to make a radio set."

"Ah, yes. Radio sets. Quite the radio expert, aren't you?"

"I read *Practical Wireless*, Father. I make radio sets as a hobby."

Father Walsh paused again, looking Danny straight in the eye. "So I am informed." He opened another, lower, drawer and took from it a small red lapel badge bearing the face of a Russian astronaut and placed it on the desk. "This was confiscated from a boy in Father McCormack's class. The boy said that he got it from you."

"Yes, Father. It's a Yuri Gagarin badge. I got them from Radio Moscow. Yuri Gagarin was the first man in space..."

"I know who Yuri Gagarin is. But do you know what Russia is? What the Soviet Union stands for?" Danny was out of his depth and did not answer. "It's a godless country where the Roman Catholic Church is banned, and anybody who practices their religion is thrown in gaol! No religion is allowed except the worship of the state and the Communist Party. People get dragged from their beds in the middle of the night and thrown in prison cells. More often than not taken out and shot without a trial. The newspapers and radio and TV stations are all controlled by the state and anybody who disagrees with the government is executed. People can't leave the country or travel abroad. Everybody has a number and the secret police watch all the people in the country, day and night, just looking for any excuse to drag them out and shoot them. And if we didn't have our own atom bombs in the West to defend ourselves with they'd have atom-bombed us all and taken over the whole world years ago. Do you want to live in a country like that?"

"No, Father."

"Why are you distributing the badges, then?"

"They're just about Yuri Gagarin, Father. About flying in space..."

"They're Communist propaganda, boy! An attempt to corrupt the minds of Ireland's young. Do you even know what the writing on the bottom says?"

Danny picked up the badge and, with some difficulty, read out the Russian words: "'Hayuk za mir', Father."

"I know what it says! But do you know what the words mean?"

"They have two meanings, Father. Like a kind of pun. 'Science for peace' and 'Science for the world'."

"Are you trying to be a smart Alec?"

"No, Father."

The priest grabbed the offending badge and tossed it back into the drawer.

"I don't want to hear that you've been distributing anything like this ever again. This is a liberal institution but the line has to be drawn somewhere. If I hear about anything like this coming from you again you're out of this school on your ear. I don't care who you are or who your father is. A line has to be drawn. Do I make myself clear?"

"Yes, Father."

"Now, go and join your science class. And let that be an end to it."

15

Chapter Two
Dr. Gallagher's Reaction

"He threatened our son with expulsion! That's what he did. That old fart Walsh, whose family runs the chip shop in Bundoran. And you want me to just sit back and take it?"

"Let the boy alone, Kieran. Don't draw attention to him. If you go in there kicking up a fuss they'll crucify him in the playground. They do anyway, but it'll get ten times worse. Can't you remember when you were a teenager yourself?" She put the plate down in front of her enraged husband. The delicious aroma of fried steak and onions drifted up to Danny's nostrils.

"Kicking up a fuss? I should get the RUC onto that place. It's like something out of Dickens. It should be closed down. Common assault with a cane every five minutes. Science teachers that think the world was made in six days by an old man with a white beard. Indoctrination into fairy tales and superstition. Refusal to permit discussion of contrary views. Teaching lies about socialism and world politics. Teaching the boys to hate Protestants. That place is stuck in the Middle Ages, like the whole damned Catholic Church. There must be a Grammar School somewhere in Belfast that isn't run by mindless buffoons with crosses on strings around their necks."

"It's all right, Dad," Danny pleaded, "I don't mind. It was only a dressing-down. I didn't get the cane. St. Benedict's isn't such a bad school... all my friends are there."

His mother totally ignored the interjection. "Now don't be silly, Kieran. This is a Catholic family whether we believe in God or not. You send the boy to a Protestant school and he'll like as not get his head kicked in. You know that as well as I do."

"Jesus Christ! Will the Middle Ages never come to an end in this place?"

He cut up his meat and conveyed a bite-sized chunk to his mouth. "That's good beef. Is that from McKenna's shop?"

"No. It's from a new butcher on Leeson Street. They're called Posners. I think they're Jewish. They don't sell any pork products."

"Moses was no fool. The pig is the host to the same tapeworm species that infects humans. If I was Moses I'd have made that rule too. But I'd have added that they should review it every thousand years or so." The phone rang on the dresser behind him. "Bloody phone." He reached over and lifted the receiver.

"Gallagher speaking. What can I do for you?... I see. Yes, 'discharge' is exactly the right term... is that so?... Yes, you can get a discharge for a number of reasons... A green discharge, yes, that's one of the most popular colours. I was just about to eat my dinner, Mr Rice, how about you?... I see... Yes, I understand... Now let me stop you there, Mr Rice, because I have to confess to a disgraceful gap in the medical training provided by Trinity College Dublin. You see, they completely neglected to teach us how to diagnose on the telephone. I'm afraid you're going to have to come in to the surgery in the morning, or the evening session on Wednesday if you have to go to work... Yes, I think it would be safe to leave it until Wednesday... Yes, I've heard of that treatment before, but I'm afraid I have to inform you that I am aware of no evidence of the clinical benefit of contact with religious relics, apart, that is, from the placebo effect... Yes, that's when you fool yourself into believing that something's doing you good and so it does... Yes... No... If you want advice regarding the spiritual realm you could consult my older brother, John Seamus Gallagher, DD, SJ. We call him 'Witchdoctor Gallagher' in the family, in order to distinguish him from myself... No, to the best of my knowledge he is presently in Ecuador, attempting to make the people there as ignorant and superstitious as himself... No, you were correct the first time, I did indeed mean to imply that the whole thing was a load of bullshit. You may quote that as my professional opinion, should the occasion arise... Yes, Mr Rice, a small Scotch is an excellent idea. You could drink to your own health and mine. Now, my dinner is getting cold. Will it be okay if I eat it?... Thank you. Goodbye, Mr Rice." He replaced the receiver. "Neanderthals," he said under his breath.

Danny's mother eyed him grimly as he turned back to the dinner table. "I never thought I'd hear you say that a small Scotch was a good idea."

"There's a difference between a small one and the tumblerfuls that you put down your throat."

"Don't listen to him, Danny. All I ever take is a wee drop at night so that I can get some sleep."

"You know, sometimes I wonder if I'm the only one in the whole rotten city of Belfast who lives in the real world."

At this his wife smiled. "They say that when you think everybody's mad except yourself you're a prime candidate for the funny-farm."

For a few precious moments everybody ate in silence. Then the telephone rang again. "Gallagher speaking. What can I do for you?... Your wife, Mr Conroy? Isn't she able to come to the phone herself?... No, I'm sorry, I'm not at liberty to discuss anything to do with another patient... No, Mr Conroy, I can't even confirm or deny whether or not she has been to see me... I do understand that she is your wife. I'm afraid that it doesn't make any difference. In fact as far as I am concerned it wouldn't make any difference if it was your conjoined twin that you were talking about. It's exactly the same as the seal of the confessional, Mr Conroy. It's something that doctors don't do. Full stop. No need to even think about it. That makes life a lot simpler...You are exactly right, it is indeed part of the Hypocratic oath. Solemn declaration, in my case. I can quote you the relevant section if you like, in Greek, Latin or English. ...Yes, Mr Conroy. I'm sorry that I wasn't able to help you on this occasion. Goodbye." He replaced the receiver and returned to his meal.

"But you don't believe in God, do you Dad?" Danny enquired with his mouth full. "So even if you took the oath, you wouldn't have to keep it..."

"Now that's a good example of what I was talking about just now," he said, addressing his wife rather than Danny. "They put the idea into the boys' heads that the only reason to keep your word is so that you don't end up as the main course at some kind of supernatural barbecue in Middle Earth. Do you think I'm someone who goes around telling lies and breaking my promises, Danny?"

"No, Dad. The opposite. You never do anything like that."

"And why do you think I don't?"

Danny considered the question. It was a hard one. If there's no God, and no hell, and nobody's watching, what's the point of telling the truth and keeping your word? "Is it for my sake?" Danny suggested at last. "To give me a good example?"

"No Danny. It's not for your sake. Or for your mother's sake. It's for my sake. For my sake and nobody else's. Does that make it any clearer?"

Danny remained puzzled. "I think what your father means..." Danny's mother began.

"Let the boy think it out himself," his father interrupted. "He's old enough to understand things like that now. He'll never learn to think for himself if you don't let him have a try."

Danny put down his knife and fork. He could see that some kind of answer was expected of him, but he had that familiar feeling that he was out of his depth. At least he wasn't going to get a cane across the knuckles if he got it wrong. He thought hard. "I suppose..." he ventured at last, "...that if you tell lies and don't keep your promises you end up not liking yourself very much, or respecting yourself..."

"What did I tell you? That boy's a son of mine all right!"

There was nothing Danny valued more than his father's praise. He felt his cheeks tingle with his small rush of pride.

"And that's why I want you to wear that Yuri Gagarin badge all the time, except when you're at school," his father added minutes later, as if it were a continuation of the same sentence. "They can control what you do to some extent when you're within the walls of the school, and as your mother says, it would be stupid to get yourself victimised by the prehistoric types that inhabit that place, but once you're outside those school gates your life is your own and there isn't a damned thing they can do to you. Let them try it and they'll have me and the RUC to contend with."

"I don't mind, Dad. It's only a badge. It's no big deal."

"You'll wear the badge when I tell you to. And have you got a spare one – for me?"

"You're daft, Kieran. You can't do that. It'll get into the *Irish News*. They'll say we're Communists and burn us out."

"I'm not ashamed for people to know that I'm a socialist. What do you think I went to Spain for when I was young?"

"That was different. That was fighting the Fascists. Everybody agreed with that."

"But it's wrong to fight the intellectual Fascists of the Catholic Church? If we don't take a stand, what happens when the next person with a mind gets into that school? Let them get away with it once and they'll be twice as quick to stamp down on the next person, and the one after that. We don't have thought control just yet in Catholic schools, and I'm not going to do anything to make it easier for them to achieve it. Will you get me that badge, Danny?"

"I wasn't trying to do anything political, Dad. I was just interested in Yuri Gagarin and space travel. I just wrote to Radio Moscow…"

"The badge, son. Where is the badge?"

Moments later, Danny's father stood in front of the full-height hall mirror admiring the small red badge which stood out like an open wound on the lapel of his light grey jacket. "Solidarity, son. Brotherhood with the ignorant and oppressed masses of the world. *Liberté, égalité, fraternité*. Ask them in your French class what those words mean, Danny."

Chapter Three
A Small Family Crisis

Danny arrived back at the end of his long walk from school as the afternoon was darkening into evening, and put down his scruffy cloth hold-all to open the front door. As he did so he felt the first few drops of rain on the side of his face. He rummaged in his pocket for the key.

Danny always walked to and from St. Benedict's. He had cycled to school when his family had first come to live in Belfast, but after having one bicycle stolen and a second one wrecked, no doubt by somebody angry at its being chained to a post and difficult to steal, he had made the decision that he would walk instead, and before long he was finding that he actually enjoyed the solitude of the early morning stroll, and the opportunity to break his journey at friends' houses in the afternoons.

To his annoyance, although he turned the key, the door wouldn't open. He tried to shake it on its hinges to confirm that it had been bolted from the inside.

He stabbed the front door bell, listening carefully at the letterbox to make sure it was working. There was no response. He tried again. Nothing.

"Mammy!" he shouted through the brass letterbox. "It's Danny! Can you open the door please?"

Bernard, who was in the year below him at school and lived in the house across the road, stared at him from the downstairs window with consummate interest and no pretence of concealment. Bernard knew as well as he did what it meant when she bolted the door. Embarrassment was added to Danny's annoyance. He lifted the flap of the letterbox again and shouted even louder: "It's me, Mammy! Can you open the door, please?"

He waited again. Still no response. A strengthening spray of rain was blowing into his face now and he carefully removed the blue plastic mac from the top of his hold-all and put it on. There was no telling how long this might take.

A black Austin car passed by on the road behind him, its tyres hissing faintly on the wet tarmac. He watched it move past the young trees that rose a few feet above their protective metal cages on the pavements, and the rows of tidy semidetached brick houses, differing from one another only in the designs of their front gardens and the makes and colours of the cars parked in their driveways. It all oozed respectability, like the news shots of the 'quiet neighbourhood', where nobody would ever have expected the murderer to reside.

The rain was getting heavier. It seemed to release a musty smell from Danny's mac. He stood in as close to the front door as he could and tried shouting through the letterbox one more time. Across the road, Bernard was clearly enjoying the show. Locked out in the pouring rain! That would be something to tell the other boys in the morning.

The minutes ticked by and nothing happened. Danny considered the option of running to the phone box at the bottom of the street and using it to tell her he was outside. In a doctor's house the phone was the most important thing of all. To fail to answer it was unthinkable, although it had happened once or twice with his mother. A missed call could be a lost life, as his father had told her time and time again.

He decided on balance that he didn't want to give Bernard the pleasure of watching him do that. Instead he tried the side door leading to the back yard. To his relief it was open. At least his attempts at communicating with his mother would now be unobserved.

He found a dry spot for his hold-all under the back door porch and peered in through the kitchen window. The inner door leading to the small dining room was open, and although he couldn't see her from this angle he reckoned that there was a good chance she was in there. He rapped on the window, gently at first, then more vigorously. Why couldn't he have normal parents? Why couldn't he live a normal life? He bashed the window with the side of his hand, employing a force that he hoped was just insufficient to shatter it. It sounded like the bass drum in a pop band.

At last, walking very slowly, his mother appeared at the dining room door and acknowledged his existence. She beckoned him to go around to the front again. Clearly the back door had been barricaded even more thoroughly than the front one. Resigned to providing Bernard with some further amusement he recovered his hold-all and did as he was bidden.

When at last the door was opened and he had wiped his feet and removed his mac he took a good look at his mother and tried to assess just how much she had drunk and how long ago. From the dullness of her countenance, her bare feet, the open buttons on her blouse and the dishevelled state of her hair he reckoned that the relevant row and subsequent drinking bout had taken place in the morning, shortly after his leaving for school, and she had been sleeping it off for the rest of the day. "Where's himself?" he asked in the most neutral tone he could muster.

"That's a daft question. How the hell should I know? And if he thinks he's coming back here he has another think coming."

"It's his house, Mammy. It's where he lives. Where else is there for him to go?" He accompanied her back to the kitchen where she put water in the electric kettle and switched it on. "I'll make the coffee," he offered.

"Tea. I don't want coffee."

"I think coffee is what you need, Mammy."

"You don't know anything about what I need. You're getting just like him."

She returned to her soft chair in the dining room and slumped into it. Danny followed her and discreetly removed the empty bottle and the glass. "Have you had anything to eat today?" he asked. The lack of a reply told him that she hadn't. "I'll do a bit of bacon and egg. Would you like that?"

"I don't know what food's in," she murmured, which was the equivalent of a yes. He slipped the bottle into the kitchen trash and set about the task of creating a meal for one. It occurred to him that she didn't seem to get hangovers any more. A few years ago, food would have been the last thing on her mind at a time like this.

"What was it you had words about this time?" he enquired, feigning a polite interest that he hoped wouldn't make her clam up.

"You wouldn't understand."

"I'm not a kid, you know. I can understand more than you think."

"You don't know what it's like to live with him."

25

"I thought I did live with him." The delicious aroma of cooking bacon began to fill the room. That, in Danny's estimation, should be enough to cheer anybody up.

"I hate this place, Danny," she told him very quietly.

"This road?"

"This city. This stinking country. I want to get away from here. Somewhere civilized, where a doctor and his wife have some kind of social standing."

Danny could see that she wanted to talk and didn't interrupt.

"I had another letter from your Auntie Maud in Selly Oak yesterday. She'd love us all to come over. Birmingham is a hundred years ahead of this place. Medicine is completely different over there. It's a proper profession. They have big group practices in brand new modern buildings, with secretaries and maybe the nurse visiting three or four times a week, and antenatal clinics, and dieticians and physios and all kinds of things going on. Everything is done by appointment – no first come, first served – and you're only on call maybe one or two nights a week. The rest of the time you're doing fixed shifts like an office worker. And sometimes the doctors sort of specialize – like maybe one of them takes on the antenatal and maternity end, and another does the paediatrics, and another one chronic illness, and maybe another one the more psychiatric stuff… like a mini hospital. And there's none of this fighting to get names on your list, the total income from the whole practice is shared out equally. You get proper holidays and you know exactly what's going to be in your pay cheque at the end of the month… and there's no religion over there. Everyone's Church of England. It would be a step into the modern world for him, Danny, that's what it would be. Instead of being the mug trying to run a one-man band like his father did."

Danny turned it over in his mind. "I can see why it wouldn't appeal to him," he said cautiously, hoping not to offend. "I mean, he could have been a hospital doctor if he wanted to. That was what his teachers wanted him to do. But it's not in his nature, is it? He likes to be his own boss – he'd never fit in with a team like that. He wants to do everything his own way. I just can't see him going for it, to be honest…"

"You're always taking his side, aren't you? Always undermining me. Doing me down." She had got to her feet and was buttoning up her blouse and trying to find her second sandal by rifling through the discarded remains of the Sunday newspapers with her toe.

"That's nonsense, Ma. Anyway, who said anything about sides? We're a family, aren't we? There's no 'sides'." He handed her the cup of tea and returned his attention to the frying-pan. "Was that what the row was about then? Moving to Birmingham?"

Her hesitation suggested that it was a bit more serious than that. "Your da got a phone call last night," she reluctantly explained. "Mrs Whittaker has died."

"Died?"

It was hardly unexpected, Mrs Whittaker had been very ill for a long time, but Danny knew that there was something special about her. His father's relationship with Mrs Whittaker was never spoken about directly. Nobody ever put a name to it. But a sure way to plunge Danny's mother into a foul mood was for Danny's father to say he was going to see Mrs Whittaker and he might be back late.

And now she was dead. That would be a big blow. Danny almost let the bacon burn thinking about it.

Infidelity? He couldn't relate a word like that to his father. Probably just a gentle friendship – the intellectual stimulation that he couldn't get from his wife. Whatever bond it was that they had, it had been severed now by death. For the first time that he could remember, Danny felt sorry for his father.

Chapter Four
Mrs Whittaker's Funeral

Danny heard the unmistakable sound of his father's car pulling up on the front driveway. His mother put down her knife and fork. "Jesus, it's himself, and I don't think I bolted the front door when I let you in!"

"What's the point of bolting the front door, Ma? This is where he lives. He's not going to go away." He took her plate and dumped the remains of the meal into the bin before adding the plate to the dirty cutlery in the sink, while she buttoned her sleeves, cleared the weekend newspapers from the floor and opened the curtains.

"What do I look like, Danny?" she asked as the sound of the engine died.

"Your hair could do with a brush."

She went to the kitchen sink, wet her hands and stroked her unruly hair down. Danny handed her a tea towel and she delicately dried off her hair, then both her hands, before replacing the cloth neatly on the rail. She tucked a dangling flap of her blouse under the waist of her slacks and tried to straighten-up the line of buttons down the front. As she finished they heard the sound of the front door opening.

Danny's father, still wearing his outdoor jacket, looked into the kitchen. He was pale and had a wounded, far away expression that Danny hadn't seen before. He looked at his wife but spoke to Danny. "Hello Danny. Is that bacon I smell?"

"Yes, Dad. I was a bit hungry when I got back from school. Would you like some too?"

He shook his head and walked back towards the hall. Danny followed. Out of his mother's earshot, Danny spoke quietly while his father hung up his coat. "I heard about Mrs Whittaker."

He made his way to the front sitting room and lowered himself heavily into the sofa before he replied. "The funeral's on Thursday. Would you like to come with me?"

Danny was taken aback. "To the funeral? But I didn't know Mrs Whittaker…"

"No, of course not. You're right. Stupid idea." Danny had never seen his father look so defeated and subdued. He sat down beside him, which was something he would not normally do. If his father was a different kind of man he might have taken his hand.

For a few moments his father simply looked straight ahead and didn't speak. Danny was silent too. When his father eventually did speak his voice was so low that Danny could only just make out the words. "I feel a terrible fraud, Danny. My job is supposed to be the preservation of life, and there wasn't a damn thing I could do for her. Not a damned thing. A gentle, intelligent woman, who put all her trust in me. And I let her down."

Danny didn't know what to say. This was a side of his father that he had never seen before. There was something else, beyond the arrogance and cynicism, the supreme contempt for the stupidity and incompetence of others. He wasn't Superman after all.

What would his father have said in his position? Of course. Danny put on a stern voice. "Quite right. It's disgraceful that you can't make your patients live forever."

He had captured his father's tone perfectly. A weak smile flickered across his face. "If there really is a God up there, I don't know how he sleeps at night."

For another few moments, neither of them spoke.

"Actually, I've changed my mind, Dad. I do want to go to the funeral."

His father patted the back of his hand twice. "I'd better write a note for Father Walsh." It was the first physical contact with him that Danny could ever remember.

Kieran heard the handle of the door of the spare room rattle loudly. He recognised it as his wife's version of knocking. Then the door creaked open.

"What are you doing in there, Kieran?"

He shrugged uncomfortably. "Oh, I was afraid I mightn't sleep too well tonight. I didn't want to disturb you."

To his considerable surprise she started to make her way over to the bed and pulled the covers back to climb in. "It's a bit narrow for two," he said, not in a tone of protest but rather one of surprise.

"I'm sorry for... The way I've been, about Mrs. Whittaker." She cuddled up to his back and put her arm around his chest. "I thought maybe you wouldn't want to sleep on your own tonight," she said very quietly.

"No. Maybe not. I think you're right." He put his hand over hers and said nothing more.

The rain had only just let up so the ground was still saturated. The little funeral party kept carefully to the gravel path down the centre of the churchyard, stringing out into a crocodile to do so. Her husband and her two children were a lot younger than Danny had realised. The girl looked about eight and the boy was a couple of years younger than himself. It seemed wrong for somebody far younger than his mother or father to be dying. It made him feel very uncomfortable. Mr Whittaker was nothing like Danny had pictured him either. For some reason he had imagined him as a rough, uneducated man with big hands and tree-trunk arms and a cigarette hanging out of his mouth. Somebody she had married by mistake, for all the wrong reasons. Somebody to provide a perfect foil to his father, a man Danny's father would have called a Neanderthal. In fact he was tall and dignified, with finely sculpted, almost Roman features and just a trace of grey in his neat, somewhat curly, dark hair.

He glanced at Danny's father several times during the course of the service and the interment ceremony at the graveside. Danny found himself trying to work out what was behind the glances. Contained in them was the hint of a shared intimacy. Did Mr Whittaker know about his wife and her doctor? What was there to know anyway?

The wake was held in the big front room of the Whittaker's house. It was an elegant Regency style room, with a fine grand piano at one end and framed musical scores and pictures of composers on the walls. The funeral party by no means filled it. Towards the end of the gathering, when they had all had a sandwich or two and a drink (even Danny ventured a glass of expensive-looking claret) Mr Whittaker took his father aside and they had a brief conversation, which Danny couldn't hear. He could see that his father was shaking his head, saying no to something, but Mr Whittaker would not accept the no. He saw his father's resistance break down. They separated and Danny walked up to him and looked at him expectantly. "What was that all about?" he whispered.

"A bit of foolishness. He wants to give me her violin. Daft bugger. It's worth a fortune. It was her most treasured possession. I told them there's nobody in our family that's even musical. He wouldn't have it. He's giving it to me, like it or not."

Danny turned away so that his father wouldn't see him wipe his eyes. So maybe that was what they did. Maybe she played the violin for him. He waited to make sure his voice wouldn't betray what he was feeling. "It doesn't sound as if Mr Whittaker thinks you did a bad job. What does he do for a living?"

"He plays the oboe in the Ulster Orchestra. You'd think he'd have the sense to pass the fiddle on to one of the children, wouldn't you?"

"No, Dad. I wouldn't think that, actually."

He paused for a moment, wondered if he should risk the question. "What did she play for you?"

"Lots of things. My favourite was *The Last Rose of Summer*. That's… sort of what she was to me, I suppose. Anyway, that was my favourite."

The actual whereabouts of the violin was something that Danny's father kept to himself in the months and years that followed. Danny speculated that this might be because he was scared that his wife would destroy it if she found it. It was something that both of them put to the backs of their minds and never spoke about.

For the rest of his life, however, whenever he heard *The Last Rose of Summer* Danny thought of his father and Mrs Whittaker, and of everyone's mortality, including his own.

Chapter Five
A Visit to Wee Hughie's

It was a sunny day and Danny didn't have too much homework to do, so on the long walk home from school he decided to make a detour, down one of the familiar back streets off Falls Road, and pay a visit to Wee Hughie. Wee Hughie had been the first person in Danny's new school to befriend him when his family had moved to Belfast from Ballyrowan in County Donegal. The friendship had lasted well, although Wee Hughie's school career had not matched Danny's, and in truth Danny was beginning to tire of him a little. He was in the lowest set now, and towards the bottom of his class, and the area that they had in common seemed ever-diminishing. He had a talent for football and he could draw a respectable picture in the art class, but he was never going to be an academic. It was of no concern to Danny, but he didn't emphasise their friendship to his parents.

It was Wee Hughie's mother who opened the door. She was severely overweight, with greasy-looking lank black hair, a reddish colouration to her face, and big pores on her nose like an old man. As always she was wearing one of her unnecessarily tight floral dresses, accompanied by a blue and white check apron, neither of which did anything for her appearance, but mothers were under no obligation to be attractive. "Is Hughie at home, Mrs Laverty?" Danny inquired.

"Aye. He's up with the pigeons at the back. Do you want to come through?"

"Thank you, Mrs Laverty."

He knew his way very well: up the stairs, and instead of turning right towards the bathroom and the three small bedrooms, straight ahead across the landing, stooping to go through the tall open window to the flat roof of the rear extension. Even before he got to the shed the smell of Connor's pigeons assaulted his nose. It was a unique smell that, once experienced, could never be mistaken or forgotten. A mixture of the mustiness of old damp buildings and something pungent, like rotting eggs or ammonia. There seemed to be no way to get rid of it from the improvised pigeon accommodation, despite Connor's best efforts to change the straw regularly and keep it clean.

The pigeon loft was in reality a small and much-repaired wooden garden shed, now relocated on to the felt-covered flat roof, its original door replaced by a large oblong frame with chicken-wire stretched across it. Inside, the birds resided in individual wooden cages stacked up on a bench, each of them about eighteen inches in every dimension, with similar chicken-wire individual doors.

When Danny had first known Wee Hughie the pigeon loft and its occupants had been a novelty and a source of endless fascination; now its appeal was wearing thin, and the unpleasantness of the smell was beginning to dominate the experience of each visit. Wee Hughie was in the shed using a small plastic trowel to fill the birds' feeding troughs from a bucket of grain, while his seven-year-old brother Pedro looked on.

"Hiya, Danny," Wee Hughie greeted him warmly. You haven't been around for a while."

Hughie was always referred to as 'Wee' for the obvious reason that he was very short for his age. Hardly much taller than Pedro. Danny towered over both, so that, thankfully, he could see everything Hughie was doing with the pigeons and conduct his conversation without needing to come too close to the shed. "Exams," he said by way of explanation, "a lot of extra homework. You know how it is."

"They're not puttin' me in for nothin' this year," Wee Hughie announced happily. "There's about six of us in the class that's goin' to do an extra year. Waste of time if you ask me. I'd rather get out of it an' do somethin' interestin'. Maybe motor mechanics like Connor, or go an' work in the zoo. I'd like to work in the zoo."

"The zoo. Yeah. That would be good. I thought Connor said we weren't to feed the pigeons any more?"

"He's not around an' I'm only givin' them a wee bit. Me an' Pedro likes to watch them eating."

"Connor said you'll make them too fat for racing."

"I know what Connor said. What does Connor know? Connor's not my boss." He closed the cage door and put away the bucket and the trowel. Wiping his hands together in the manner of someone who

34

has done a good and satisfying job, he emerged from the shed and closed the door. "Hey! Danny! Have ye seen Connor's new motor bike?" At the mention of the bike Pedro's face lit up.

"No. I heard he'd got one though."

"Come on. I'll show ye."

Hughie and his brother hurried to the far end of the roof, and took the improvised wooden steps down to the back yard. Connor's bike was big and black and, while obviously not new, well cleaned and polished-up, with gleaming twin chrome exhausts and chrome sides to the fuel tank, which bore the familiar Honda badge. Danny felt an immediate surge of envy. "Bloody hell! Bet it can do the ton!"

"'Course it can, easy," Hughie assured him. "It's a three-hundred cc four-stroke. It's called the Honda Dream. Leaves the old BSA standing. Let me show you something else..." Hughie glanced around guiltily and produced a small screwdriver from his trouser pocket. "The ignition switch is worn," he whispered. "You can turn it on with anything."

Within a few seconds the engine was surging up and down in response to Hughie's twisting of the throttle, from a gentle purr to a full-throated roar. Pedro literally jumped up and down with glee.

"That's brilliant, Hughie, but Connor'll murder you if he catches you."

"Aye, but he has to catch me first. He's workin' late tonight, won't be back for hours yet." He switched the engine off and removed the screwdriver from the ignition. Pedro calmed down.

Hughie glanced around again with an even more guilty expression. He spoke in a lower whisper than before. "Do ye want to see something really good, Danny?" Danny glanced around conspiratorially and drew closer.

"What?"

Hughie seemed genuinely nervous. "Ye'll have to come upstairs again. It's in Connor's room."

Wee Hughie led the procession consisting of himself, Danny and Pedro in by the back door, past the kitchen where his mother was doing something at the sink, through to the hallway and back up the staircase to the middle bedroom, which Danny knew was Connor's, although he had never been in it. Hughie opened the door cautiously and beckoned them in.

The first thing that Danny noticed was a six-foot wide green, white and orange flag, emblem of the Irish Republic, pinned to the wall behind Connor's bed in a way that suggested it was blowing in the wind. Adorning the other walls were posters of James Connolly and Pádric Pearse, heroes of the 1916 uprising in Southern Ireland through which the south had, in the rhetoric of the Republican movement, "gained its freedom". There were also framed reproductions of Southern Ireland's Declaration of Independence, old black-and-white photographs of the siege of the General Post Office building in Dublin, and one of what Danny took to be an English firing squad executing a captured Irish rebel.

Danny had no interest in politics but it had been drummed into him long and hard by the priests at St Benedict's that the men who had risen up and driven out the English in the second decade of the century were more or less saints, and it was only a matter of time before similar heroes would rise in the north to drive the English out of there too. The notion of rising and driving out the English was an important part of the folklore of the Roman Catholics of Northern Ireland, the equivalent of the 'revolution' patiently awaited by socialists of many shades across the channel in England. The message was endlessly reinforced by dozens of 'rebel songs' about how wonderful and glorious it was to die for Ireland, and indeed Connor was well known for singing them to his own guitar accompaniment. Danny and Hughie much preferred his attempts at Elvis Presley and Cliff Richard songs, and the kind of music they watched every Thursday on *Top of the Pops*.

"Connor's well into this Republican business then?" Danny mused.

"Yer not kiddin'. Thinks about little else these days." Once again Hughie paused to look around him for imaginary spies and intruders. In a hushed voice he added: "He's gone an' done it, Danny. He's joined the Volunteers."

"Who are the Volunteers?"

"Shush! Not so loud. I'm not supposed to know about it. The IRA, for God's sake. Everybody knows who the Volunteers are."

"Oh. Yeah. I knew that," Danny assured him.

36

With a swagger, Wee Hughie went to the head of the bed and shoved his hand under the pillow, pulling out a small but heavy-looking black pistol. Danny knew nothing about guns, but it didn't look like a toy. "It's a Makarov," Hughie said under his breath. "Russian semi-automatic. Fires eight nine-millimetre rounds, from this…" he slid the magazine out of the handle and gave it to Danny. It was a flat black metal container with cut-outs in its sides through which you could see the brass-coloured bullets. Danny was certain that this was a genuine weapon. He suddenly felt acutely uncomfortable but tried not to show it. He handed the lethal trinket back to Hughie, who slid it back into the handle, where it made a satisfying click. He aimed the device at the centre of Danny's forehead and said "Bang!"

"For Christ's sake Hughie! That thing's real. Are you trying to kill me? What's Connor going to do with it anyway?"

Hughie replaced it under the pillow. "Personal protection. He reckons that if the Prods find out he's in the Volunteers they'll send somebody around to murder him in his bed. All the Volunteers get given one. It's part of the deal."

Danny was genuinely shocked. Apart from the ones that members of the police force, the Royal Ulster Constabulary, occasionally wore in their hip holsters, held firmly in place with a buckled leather strap, he had never seen a real handgun before.

"It's against the law to have that," Danny warned him. "He'll go to prison if they find it."

"Don't ye think he knows that? He's a Volunteer – he's sworn that he'll give his life for Ireland if he has to. Goin' to prison would be nothin'. In fact, between you an' me, I think he'd love it."

Danny knew exactly what he meant. And Hughie would love it too, he realised. What could confer more kudos in a Belfast Catholic boys' school than having a brother in gaol for membership of the IRA? He could see what his father meant when he said, as he so often did, that everybody in Belfast was certifiably nuts.

Chapter Six
The Pirate Radio Station

Danny's bedroom was the smallest of the three in the house. He had chosen it, leaving the middle-sized one beside it as a spare room for guests, as well as for the many nights when his father and mother slept apart. What he liked about his room was that it was at the end of the corridor, out of the way of his parents and relatively cut off from whatever might be going on in the rest of the house, so that he could have territory to himself, and make a certain amount of noise without disturbing them. It also overlooked the long back garden, which had been his mother's pride and joy when they first moved to Belfast, but was now overgrown to the extent that it was becoming difficult to see where the paths and flowerbeds had originally been.

For Danny the significance of the long sweep of waste ground was that it ended in a couple of old tall pear trees, separating it from the gardens of other houses on the next road. Although the trees were chocked with bindweed and no longer produced fruit, one of them provided a perfect anchorage point for the far end of the long aerial wire that entered his bedroom through the wall, protected by a special Perspex sleeve designed to minimise signal leakage into the brickwork. It was quite a professional setup of which Danny was justifiably proud.

A long improvised table running down one whole wall of the room held Danny's assortment of home-made radios and electronic gadgets, a bulky Dansette record player in a two-tone red-and-beige felt covered wooden cabinet, and his modest record collection, as well as some books, tools and test equipment. Dominating the table was an elderly but still functional oscilloscope with a circular screen, which was Danny's pride and joy. When it was switched on it produced a graphic representation in green of various electrical changes measured against time. It allowed Danny to 'see' subtle electronic phenomena taking place in copper wires, and modify and tune his home-made equipment according to what was revealed. It was a window into a hidden world that fascinated him, logical and predictable as it was, a total contrast to the madness and irrationality that seemed to surround him everywhere else. The magnolia painted walls sported a large cork notice board with the usual scraps of paper held in place by drawing pins, and next to that a hardboard-backed world map in 'interrupted' projection, giving it the appearance of a big blue-and-white letter 'M' with an extra foot. The map was divided into regions and territories, each of which was inscribed with the Amateur Radio prefix that the region had been allocated by international agreement. Danny had pushed a large number of coloured pins into the map, showing some of the locations of the radio amateurs whose transmissions he had been able to receive on one or another of his home-made radios. Their actual call-signs he recorded in a log book, together with times, dates and comments on such matters as mode of modulation and signal strength. Alongside the map was a large circular electric wall clock which kept superbly accurate time.

Danny had started studying for his own Radio Amateur's Licence, which involved passing an examination in radio theory and regulations, as well as a test in sending and receiving Morse Code, but he had yet to go through this admission procedure. For the next few months work for school exams would have to take precedence – his father would never allow him to waste his time on exams connected with his hobby when there were others on the horizon that would determine his future.

Newly added to Danny's wall was a large colour poster of the offshore pirate radio vessel *MV Caroline*, named after President Kennedy's daughter, and presently anchored three-and-a-half miles off Felixstowe in Suffolk, and therefore in international waters and beyond British law. The poster announced the station's transmission wavelength of 199 metres, Medium Wave. Its output of continuous pop music, some of it from groups that were never heard on any other radio station, was hosted by disc jockeys such as Roger Scott, Simon Dee and Terry Walker, names that were as familiar to Danny and his friends as those of the Northern Ireland Prime Minister or Pope Paul VI. It wasn't really the music that interested Danny, and, except in the late evening, the station's signal was almost inaudible in Belfast, it was the romance of broadcasting itself that quickened his pulse – the whole notion of doing something technically demanding and either illegal or at least 'non-legal', yet harmful to no one and pleasurable to many. If he were completely honest with himself it was probably the technical challenge of getting a broadcast transmitter to work properly that appealed to him most of all.

Danny felt an enormous contentment when he sat at this table and tuned across the Amateur Radio bands to see what he could pick up, or made some modification to the circuitry of one of his creations. He felt a sense of achievement when a unit that he had constructed from individual components, fed by an aerial that he had rigged with his own hands, allowed him to hear a conversation between two fellow-enthusiasts, one in Auckland, perhaps, and the other in Kuala Lumpur. It was a pleasure that few of his friends could really under-stand, far less share, and its solitary nature often worried his mother, but this was simply the way that Danny wanted to spend his free time. Problems in electronics and circuit design were the kind of problems that he enjoyed solving. This was Danny's private world.

At the moment he busied himself removing the aerial lead from one of his short wave radios, a bare-chassis affair with an aluminium front panel and the valves and components in plain sight behind it, and connecting it instead to his latest project. This was housed in the grey steel box of an old hospital radio-paging system that his father had taken home and passed on to him when the hospital had installed a new one. On its front panel it sported a meter for measuring current and a number of graduated pointer knobs, all of which Danny had retained in his new design, as well as the internal power supply and the original large type 807 output valve, to which he had assigned new duties. This was now a Medium Wave broadcast transmitter, something for which no licence was available to private individuals anywhere in the British Isles, or indeed Europe.

He connected a lead from his small battery-powered microphone mixer and switched on both the transmitter and the Dansette. Patient-ly, he waited for the valves in both units to warm up, while he adjusted the position of the desk microphone, all the while keeping an eye on the exact time on the wall-clock. At exactly seven o'clock he threw the main switch on the front panel of the transmitter and made a very fine adjustment to the circuitry that matched the aerial to the output impedance of the unit.

Danny always felt a bit foolish at this stage of his experiments, but somewhat elated as well. He spoke slowly and quietly, in a self-consciously clear and precise voice. "This is a test transmission from Kingston Radio, Calico Jack speaking. Hello Hughie. I hope you're receiving this loud and clear. Tonight I want to do a level test on the modulator. I'm going to turn the audio level up in stages, then back down in stages, and I'll give a reference number for each setting. I want you to note down when the sound becomes distorted, and when it becomes too quiet for comfortable listening. I'll do it with the microphone setting first, then the setting for the music. While I'm testing the music I'll keep the microphone live and let you know..." Danny's detailed instructions to Wee Hughie went on for some minutes, then he conducted the two tests very carefully, and ended the transmission with a few minutes of the theme tune he had chosen for his station, Duane Eddy's *Ghost Riders in the Sky*, fading it down to silence to end the transmission.

Danny checked his watch. He had been on for seventeen minutes. Quite long enough for a determined engineer from the Post Office Radio Services Department to get a fix on his location, but he had no reason to believe that they knew of his existence. He was careful to vary the times of the test transmissions and not to interfere with television or any other services, which would be a sure way to bring down the wrath of the authorities. The truth was, nobody quite knew which pirate stations were offshore (and therefore untouchable) and which were schoolboy setups like his, and unless he caused a problem to somebody there was very little likelihood that they would go to the trouble of closing him down. Or at least that was what Danny always told himself at times like this. If the Post Office officials were to one day ring the doorbell, his parents would not be well pleased, and he would begin his university career with a criminal record. Strict observance of the laws of the English overlords, however, was not considered a duty by any of the people he associated with, even the priests at St. Benedicts.

Chapter Seven
Report of a Death

Danny was disappointed to discover that Hughie was not at school. He was not in his usual seat at morning assembly to hear Father Walsh's long diatribe about the use of bad language and taking the name of Our Lord Jesus Christ in vain, and he was nowhere to be seen in the playground at lunchtime either. In itself this was not unusual. Hughie often 'bunked off', especially if the weather was good, so that he could go to see Connor in the garage where he worked, or down to the shipyards to watch the big cranes and the men with the welding torches, or perhaps up into the fields at the foot of Cave Hill to look for frogs and newts, and maybe sneak into the zoo over an unguarded rear fence. But today Hughie was supposed to report to Danny regarding last night's test of the transmitter, and if he wasn't coming in to school he should at least have had the courtesy to let Danny know. They were friends, after all, they weren't supposed to just ignore each other's requests. Danny felt a little aggrieved but presumed that there must be a good reason for Hughie's absence. Maybe Pedro was sick, or his dad (though supposedly on the run for political offences) had come in drunk and smashed the place up again. Hughie's life was not lived to the same level of routine and predictability as his own, even allowing for his mother's drinking habits.

French was Danny's worst school subject, but he loved the French conversation periods, which provided a chance to ogle Mlle Grenier, the shapely *Aide Française*, hardly much older than the boys she was teaching, with straight dark brown hair, soft shapely breasts that wobbled slightly inside her blouse as she moved and spoke, and short skirts that showed off her heavenly legs. When it was the regular priest taking the French lesson Danny would amuse himself by drawing circuit diagrams or cartoon faces on the back pages of his jotter, but when it was Mlle Grenier his gaze never left her. Unfortunately she lacked any concept of keeping order in her class, or retaining the attention of the boys. One or two of them in the front row might speak to her, but against the babble of random conversations going on at the same time, those further back could hear almost nothing. Her first name, Danny knew, was Claudette. He had won this piece of information by memorising a complete and correct French sentence by which to ask her. That sentence represented pretty much the full extent of his knowledge of the language. He did however have plans to translate and memorise the French for "May we go somewhere together after school?", although in his heart he knew that he would never have the courage to say it to her.

Right now he was lost in a deep reverie, fantasising that he and Claudette had just sat down together in the back row of the Queens Film Theatre in Botanic Avenue to see a risqué French film, and his arm was beginning to creep around the back of her seat. The daydream was ruined by a firm rap on the classroom door, and Miss Munsen, the middle-aged and stern-faced school secretary, whose appearance could not have contrasted more with Claudette's, strode in and exchanged a few quiet and clipped words with her in English. It had never occurred to Danny that Claudette could even speak the language, it was a secret that she had guarded well.

Her authority now established, Miss Munsen addressed the class. "Be quiet!" The boys obeyed. "Father Walsh sent me to tell you that you have to go to the assembly hall straight away, and take all your belongings with you. You're to walk in an orderly fashion, not run, and when you get there you should sit wherever you normally would for morning assembly. Father Walsh will be there in a few minutes. He doesn't want to hear any talking in the hall or to see anybody out of their seat. That's all."

As soon as she had finished a loud babble of conversation broke out all around the room, as boys put forward theories as to what the reason might be for calling everyone back to the assembly hall. Could it be some kind of fire drill? Were the state inspectors in the school? Was there a major problem with the water or the gas or the lavatories or god-knows-what that meant the school would have to be closed and everybody sent home? Why else would Father Walsh have asked them to take all their belongings with them to the hall?

Claudette refused to abandon her façade of speaking no English. "*Quittez la pièce calmement, s'il vous plaît* ," she instructed, standing back so as not to be knocked over in the stampede.

Danny always sat behind Wee Hughie in the assembly hall. He couldn't sit alongside him because the classes were required to sit separately in their designated rows. This time, the seat in front of him remained empty as boys surged in from the two sides of the hall, chattering loudly and pushing each other to and fro to get to their places. Eventually, they settled down and the talking diminished to a low rumble.

To Danny's surprise, Carew the janitor started carrying piles of stacked chairs on to the stage and arranging them in a semicircle around the dais. Something very unusual was going on. The volume of the talking increased slightly, and became louder still when the teachers walked on to the stage in a long line and each took one of the chairs in the semicircle. Finally Father Walsh himself walked on to the stage and up to the dais. The talking rapidly faded to an expectant silence.

"In the name of the Father, and of the Son, and of the Holy Ghost," he began, touching his temple, chest and right and left shoulders to make the sign of the cross as he did so. This ritual served to confer an air of importance on whatever he was about to say. He paused for dramatic effect and scanned the faces of the first few rows.

"Boys," he began, in that seemingly quiet voice that nevertheless filled every recess of the large hall, "I have stood here many times in the years that I have been head teacher of this school to announce proud and happy events. The examination successes of our senior pupils. The successes in life of old boys of the school. The honours awarded to our athletics team and our hurlers. The vocations to the priesthood of boys I have known and taught.

"Today, I stand here to make what I think is the saddest announcement it has ever been my misfortune to have to make, to you or to anyone else. Today, I have to inform you of the death of one of your fellow pupils. Not as a result of an illness or any normal misadventure that we might all understand, like a road accident or a fall, dreadful though such a thing would be. Today, I have to tell you that

Hugh Laverty in Father McCrory's Year Five class, was killed in a tragic accident involving a firearm at his home." There was a surge of chattering, which Walsh allowed to continue for a few seconds before silencing the room again with a downward hand gesture.

"It is natural that you should be thirsty for details of this terrible event. I will pass on to you as much as I know. The weapon, I have been informed, was an automatic hand gun illegally held by Hugh's older brother Connor. The accident happened early this morning, before Hugh's mother was out of bed. Connor had left the house early for some reason, and was not involved in the incident. There were only two people in the room when it happened, Hugh and his younger brother Pedro."

At this point, Danny's brain stopped processing incoming information. The events of a few days ago began to play back in his mind. Hughie proudly brandishing the gun, aiming it at Danny's head, and shouting "Bang!" His little brother Pedro watching, drinking it all in. Danny felt a coldness that had nothing to do with temperature. A sickness invaded the depths of his stomach and the room that he was sitting in became dim and far away. The voice of Father Walsh began to enter his consciousness once again.

"...The school will not be opening tomorrow or any day next week. We're not sure yet when Hugh's funeral is going to be, but there is a requiem Mass planned for tomorrow week, Saturday the sixteenth, and we shall assemble here at nine o'clock in neat and clean school uniform ready to join the procession..." Walsh's voice droned on. Holy communion for everyone. All the practical details. Danny paid no attention.

"Now please rise for a prayer..."

In Danny's head, his own words of a few days ago began to replay: "For Christ's sake Hughie! That thing's real." At that instant it seemed like the only real thing in the entire world.

Chapter Eight
A Media Funeral

The death of Wee Hughie was on the TV news. Not just the Northern Ireland news, although it got more coverage there, but the main six o'clock national news from the BBC as well. Danny and his parents gathered around the set in the front room to watch it in sad fascination. The reporter spoke his piece to camera from in front of the gates of St.Benedict's.

"In a tragic accident today, Hugh Laverty, a fourteen-year-old pupil at this Roman Catholic Boys' Grammar School in West Belfast, was shot dead in his home by a handgun that his seven-year-old brother was playing with. The younger boy can not be named for legal reasons. Police have arrested the boys' older brother Connor Laverty, who is an apprentice motor mechanic with the British Leyland Central Service Department in York Street, Belfast. The arrested man is not thought to have been involved directly in the incident, but has been charged with possession of an unlicensed firearm and ammunition, and also with membership of an illegal organisation. In a bizarre written statement, handed to newsmen outside his house as he was taken away, Connor Laverty said that his brother had not died in vain, but was the first casualty in something that he called 'the Second Irish War of Liberation'.

"It's not yet clear whether the authorities intend to invoke the controversial Northern Ireland Special Powers Act, under which anyone accused of a terrorist offence can be kept in prison indefinitely without trial. This legislation is still in force, but has not been used by the Northern Ireland Government since April 1962.

"Connor's mother, who has asked that we respect her privacy, said through her lawyer that she considers her son misguided and irrational, and that she had no idea that he had been concealing firearms in the house or was a member of any illegal organisation. The dead boy's younger brother was today admitted to the children's ward of the Mater Hospital in Crumlin Road, Belfast, suffering from what was described as 'shock and psychological trauma'. No date for

Mr Laverty's trial, if indeed there is to be one, has been announced as yet.

"This is Liam Flynn for BBC Television, in West Belfast."

His father got up and switched the set off. "Hughie was a good friend of yours, wasn't he?"

"Yes. I was in his house only last Friday."

"Did you know anything about this gun business?"

"No. Well, not really. Connor used to boast about being in the Republican movement. Used to sing rebel songs, and put up posters of IRA heroes. That kind of thing." Danny wondered if his father could tell how uncomfortable these questions were making him.

His father shook his head sadly as he lowered himself back into his chair. "We've never come this close to The Troubles before."

"They're patients of yours, aren't they, Dad? That whole family." His father did not reply. "Is young Pedro really bad? Do you think he'll ever talk again?" His father looked at him. There was no need to say anything. Danny understood the seal of confidentiality as well as he did. "No, I thought you probably wouldn't be able to say."

"Guns, Danny, are machines designed to cause death. If you'd seen as many of them as I did in Spain, and the results of their use, you'd know what obscene things they are. There is nothing good to be said about them. They have no redeeming features. Anybody who would allow a seven-year-old to play with a loaded gun deserves locking-up forever. I hope that's what he gets."

Danny's mother merely crossed her arms. "Your dinner'll be ready in about half an hour," she said, rising from her seat to make her way to the kitchen.

Mrs Whittaker's funeral was the first one that Danny had ever attended. Now, in the same month, this was his second one.

It was a huge affair. At the head was an imposing flower-decked Rolls Royce hearse, followed by another enormous black limousine containing the immediate family members. Walking behind the second car, a priest in white and gold vestments waved an ornate smoking censer on a chain, leading seven white-and-red-robed altar boys in military formation, the first of them carrying a tall silver crucifix. Behind them, six more priests in dark suits and dog-collars, teachers at St Benedict's, walked side by side in a solemn rank. Next came seemingly endless jumbled ranks of schoolchildren in uniform, of whom Danny was one, policed by strategically placed teachers. After this came the main bulk of the mourners – hundreds or perhaps thousands of them in dark clothing, walking in random bunches between the further thousands of casual onlookers in their everyday outfits who lined the pavements. Two sets of TV cameras on the backs of pickup trucks crawled along within the crowd at different positions, while reporters with smaller hand-held cameras that flashed every now and again pushed their way through the people on the pavements and the procession itself to find the best positions for photographs. Walking slowly down Glen Road in a ragged column with his fellow St. Benedict's pupils, Danny had his first inkling of what it was like to take part in history, to feel himself an actor in some huge and sinister drama written by others, a member of the chorus in the Greek tragedy whether he wanted to be or not. Two phrases kept repeating in his head, "The Second Irish War of Liberation" and "For Christ's sake Hughie! That thing's real."

When the front of the mighty procession had passed through the ornate stone archway into Milltown Cemetery the column came to a complete halt. Danny was a couple of hundred yards from the gates, and the high walls prevented him from seeing what was happening inside. He had no idea what was causing the delay, but bearing in mind the number of people now being funnelled through the relatively narrow cemetery gates it was not particularly surprising. The pause lasted several minutes. He transferred his weight from one foot to the other and stretched his toes.

Lost in his thoughts, Danny was startled by what sounded like a substantial explosion beyond the cemetery walls. Disorder broke out in the ranks of the schoolchildren. The older boys rushed to the gates and jostled each other in an attempt to see what had happened. The priests and teachers angrily shepherded them back into line.

From boy to boy down the columns, word was passed as to what the noise had been. "IRA men," he heard those in front of him announce in an excited whisper. "Balaclavas and everything. They fired a volley over the coffin."

The TV news had still photographs of the incident that evening. Their truck-mounted cameras had been outside the gates, further back than Danny, and had seen nothing. The armed men, they said, had appeared from nowhere wearing their black knitted Balaclava helmets, fired hand guns, and melted into the crowd as suddenly as they had appeared. Nobody had managed to identify any of them. Hardly surprising, Danny thought to himself, since the ability to identify IRA gunmen might prove detrimental to your health.

Danny couldn't help feeling excited. IRA men firing guns over the coffin of your best mate. He seemed to be living through an episode of *Z Cars* or *Danger Man*. And if Wee Hughie had really been his best mate, why did he feel so little for him? He felt a flicker of guilt at his *lack* of feeling.

Maybe it was because he couldn't quite take it seriously. Part of him knew that it was all real and appalling, but another part of him refused to believe that it was actually happening. This wasn't the kind of stuff that went on in real life. He would surely waken up in a minute or two and Wee Hughie would be alive and well, and it would be time to go to school, and everything would be completely normal again. But that awful hollow feeling in his stomach told him otherwise.

Chapter Nine
Danny Pays a Social Call

There was really no way out of it. Father Leonard had marched the entire class to St. Matthew's Church for them to go to Confession ready for receiving Communion at the Requiem Mass for Wee Hughie in the morning. They would all be marching to the altar like a military column, it was not optional.

What if a person had nothing to tell, Danny asked himself, or what if he had something so bad that he needed to work up the courage, and didn't want to tell it just at this moment? Even though he didn't believe in all this stuff he could see that Father Leonard had no right to force people to take part in a ritual as intimate as this if they didn't want to.

He looked at the vacant faces of the boys patiently waiting beside him in the seated queue to go into the cubicle, and wondered what he was going to confess. There were only two of them ahead of him now. He'd better come up with something. Impure thoughts? The priests liked that one. Taking Our Lord's name in vain. Yes, he could use that one. Eating meat on a Friday? He had a vague recollection that somebody had told him that that wasn't a sin any more. Telling lies and breaking promises. That really was a sin. Even his father thought so, in his twisted atheistic way. But somehow he felt that he couldn't bring himself to use that one. It wouldn't be true.

The seconds ticked by. Cormac Dynan, the big thin gawky boy with the thick glasses, came out of the confessional and it was Danny's turn. There could be no shirking it now. He stepped into the dark little space, about the size and shape of a telephone kiosk, and knelt on the pad by the wire grid with his face to the square hatch. In a few seconds the little door slid open and he was looking through the wire screen into the dimly-lit face of a priest he didn't know.

"Bless me, Father, for I have sinned," he began automatically. "It's three weeks since my last Confession."

"And what sins have you committed since then, my child?" The priest had an unusual accent, a sort of cross between Northern Irish and English.

"I've taken the Lord's name in vain three times... and I've had impure thoughts six times..."

"Did you touch yourself when you had these thoughts?"

"No, Father. And..."

"Yes, my son?"

Danny hadn't expected to hear himself say what followed. It just seemed to come out. It was something he needed to tell someone. "I don't know if it's a sin, Father, but I could have said something... to the police... about a gun... and I didn't... and..."

"Are you talking about the death of Hugh Laverty?"

"Yes, Father."

"There was something you knew about it, but you didn't say? Is that right?"

"Yes, Father. Kind of. I knew that Connor had a gun... and I knew that Pedro had seen it..."

"Go on."

"Well, that's it, really. Hughie had been playing with the gun, which he should never have done, and Pedro had seen him do it. I knew about that, I'd seen it happen, and I didn't say anything."

"I see. And did you know where Connor got the gun?"

The question seemed odd. "From the Volunteers. The IRA, like he said when he got caught."

"Did you know the name of the person in the IRA who had given him the gun?"

Danny suddenly felt very uncomfortable. These questions were inappropriate. It was his own confession the priest was supposed to be hearing, not Connor's or Hughie's. And what did people's names have to do with it, even if Danny knew them? "No, Father."

"Did Connor tell you the names of any of the people he was involved with?"

Danny did not reply. The conversation was taking a very sinister direction. What he wanted to say was: What has it got to do with you? But he said nothing. After a few moments the priest seemed to decide that he should move on.

"Say five Our Fathers and five Hail Marys." He lifted his hand and made the sign of the cross in the air between them, after which he began to recite the absolution prayer in Latin. He quickly finished and told Danny that his sins were forgiven, Danny left without another word.

For the rest of the morning, Danny was unable to get the inquisitive priest out of his head. There was something deeply unnerving about what had happened.

In the playground he ran into Bernard O'Shea, the boy who lived just across the road from him and was in the year group behind his. Now that Hughie had gone Danny had no real "best friend" at the school, but he needed to unburden himself to somebody, and Bernard would do.

"Hello Bernie. Did they make your class go to confession this morning?"

Bernie nodded. "Yeah. We've only just got back. There's some classes still down there."

"Did you get that new priest, with the English accent?"

Bernie nodded. "Aye. What about him?"

Danny took the younger boy aside and explained to him how the priest had seemed so out of line, asked such strange questions. Bernard listened with rapt attention. "I just thought it seemed a bit odd," Danny finished. "What do you think?"

Bernard's young face took on an expression of acute concern. "It's very fishy, Danny. I think you should tell someone."

"You mean one of the teachers?"

"Naw, don't be silly. One of the Volunteers. Leave it with me."

"You're joking!"

"Like hell I'm joking. You say nothing more to anybody an' I'll find out if the Volunteers want to talk to you."

Danny smiled. This little kid who was only in his fourth year at the school was obviously putting on a show, talking big. "Aye, okay Bernie. I'll wait and see what the Volunteers have to say about it."

Danny wouldn't have given the matter another thought. Little boys were always trying to impress with their talk of having powerful friends in important places. But when a large black car drew up alongside him the following morning, just as he was beginning his long walk to St. Matthew's Church, he knew instantly that Bernie had not been boasting. There were two young men in green pullovers and sunglasses in the car, one driving and one in the back seat. The rear passenger opened the door to block Danny's path. "Good morning, Danny," he said politely.

Danny stopped. He felt himself tense-up. He remained silent.

"Don't be scared. Big Jim Harrison just wants a word with you, that's all. It won't take very long."

"Big Jim Harrison the IRA man?" Danny asked hoarsely.

"Who said anything about Big Jim being an IRA man? Did I say anything about that, Rory?"

"Not a thing, Finbar," the driver assured him.

"He's just somebody who'd like to meet you. Just being sociable." He beckoned Danny into the car and Danny obeyed. The car did not move off at once.

"I'm afraid I'm going to have to ask you to wear this," the man explained in a carefully-controlled reassuring voice, wrapping a piece of musty-smelling cloth around Danny's eyes. "What you don't know you can't talk about, am I right?"

No more words were exchanged during the journey, which seemed to Danny to take quite a long time and involve much stopping and starting, sharp corners and heavy braking. The sounds of the city traffic gradually faded, and only the gentle hum of the engine remained. There was a long stretch of smooth road surface, then a sharp right-hand corner and they were rumbling over pot holes. At last the car stopped, and Danny heard the two men open their doors.

"This way, Danny." The man who had been sitting beside him helped him out of the car, holding his head down so that he wouldn't hit it on the doorframe. Then they walked hand-in-hand along a gravel surface and through an outer and then an inner doorway. "Young Danny Gallagher to see you, Jim," he heard his escort announce.

"Good man," came a quieter, more refined voice that he had not heard before. "Leave us, but wait outside."

Danny felt gentle hands untie the blindfold, and he was looking up into the pleasant face of a tall middle-aged man in jeans and a matching loose denim shirt. His brown hair was streaked with grey and a bit too long, and he was in need of a shave, but Danny would not have given him a second glance on the streets of Belfast. "Are you really Big Jim Harrison?" he asked in awe.

The man nodded. "Sit down." Danny looked around. He was in the parlour of what looked like a small farmhouse, with an open turf-burning fireplace that hadn't been used for some time, and a porcelain clock on the mantelpiece above it indicating some minutes after noon, which he was certain was wrong. The heavy curtains were drawn and all the light came from a naked bulb dangling from the exact centre of the ceiling. The furniture was traditional and well-used. Danny took one of the two soft chairs by the fireplace.

"What have you heard about me then?" the man asked, taking the chair opposite.

"Well, that you're the head of the IRA," Danny blurted out, hoping that it wasn't the wrong thing to say.

"I'm the commander for Belfast," his host explained in a matter-of-fact manner, "the top command is in Dublin. What are your thoughts about the Volunteers then, Danny?"

"I don't really know anything about them," Danny admitted, an audible tremor in his voice.

Chapter Ten
A Talk with Big Jim

Big Jim looked him in the eye and Danny flinched. "You were right to tell us about that priest," he said with a disarming smile. Danny had already picked up the Southern Irish musicality of his host's accent. This and his affable smile seemed to defuse the tension of the situation. "The first thing I want to do is say thanks."

"I didn't know I was telling you. I thought I was just telling Bernie, Mr Harrison."

"Please call me Jim. We don't stand on formality in the movement. That's very honest of you. Bernie is a friend of ours. We have a lot of friends. We'd like to be able to think of you as a friend too. That's one of the reasons I wanted to meet you."

Danny doubted if he could bring himself to think of Jim Harrison as a friend, or call him by his first name. The man in front of him wasn't just a lot older than himself, he was a Belfast legend. People might doubt if he really existed, but everybody knew his name. "What does that entail?" he asked, trying not to sound timid and boyish.

"Nothing much. Just keeping your eyes and ears open like you did yesterday. Letting us know if you come across anything suspicious. Maybe doing the odd little favour if the occasion arises. Most of all, keeping your mouth shut. I'm sure I don't have to emphasise how important that is. You're a bright lad."

Harrison waited but Danny could think of nothing to say. "In return," the big man went on, "we would be happy to do the odd favour for you. You'd be surprised at all the different ways we could help – how influential our network can be. We owe you one right now, Danny. We don't forget our friends – or our enemies."

Danny still said nothing. Harrison smiled pleasantly. "Is it a deal, then?"

"I'm not clear, Mr… Jim. What exactly is the deal?"

Harrison laughed. "You're a cautious little bastard, aren't you? I like that. You're quite right. I'm not making myself clear. All I'm

57

saying is, you scratch my back and I'll scratch yours. At the moment people seem to think that you know something about the Volunteers. In fact you know nothing, any more than Connor does. That's good. That's what we want people to think. Every time somebody approaches you, they give themselves away. You pass on the fact that they approached you, we've nailed another informer. That's all we want. Simple, isn't it?"

Danny nodded. "So... that priest was an informer?"

"Who could be better placed to ferret out information?"

"You know who he is then?"

"We know who he says he is. And now we know what he's up to. We've had our eye on him for a while. We're pretty sure he's not what he pretends to be. If you had absolution from him you'd better go to Confession again somewhere else. I'm pretty sure that man's no priest."

"That's okay. I don't believe in any of that stuff anyway."

"Oh, of course not. Your father. Still an auld atheist, is he?"

"He is, but that's not why I don't believe in it. I've thought it out for myself. It's not scientific."

This seemed to amuse Harrison quite a lot. "Well, I'm no great theologian myself, and no great scientist either. I just say my prayers morning and night and hope that the man upstairs isn't watching me too closely. I'll have to book a double appointment when my time comes to give an account of myself. I've got a lot to explain."

"Do you know my father then?"

"Used to know him very well. I knew him in Spain. And years before that too, when he was chairman of the debating society at Trinity College Dublin. Old times. Did he ever mention me?"

"I don't think so."

"How is he getting along?"

"He's very well, Mr... Jim."

"That's another of the reasons I got you out here. I wanted to take a look at Kieran Gallagher's son. He's a very exceptional man, your father. I always admired him. To tell you the truth, I was always a bit jealous of him."

"Why was that?"

58

Harrison shrugged. "I think most people who knew him were. There seemed to be no limits to what the man knew and what he could do. He made the rest of us feel like eejits. Even his professors in Trinity were scared that he'd show them up."

Danny had often felt the same kind of things about his father. It was strange to hear it coming from a man like Harrison.

"Has he talked to you about his family? About how he got into Trinity?"

"No, never." Danny was feeling a lot more relaxed now. Jim Harrison was a pleasant and articulate man. This wasn't what an IRA gunman was supposed to be like at all.

"He and I were exactly the same age. Students at the same time, him in Dublin and me in Belfast, but we often ran into one another at the debates. We were on the same circuit. He was the one I could never beat, whatever the subject, whatever the motion, for or against, if he was on the other team I knew I was beaten before I started.

"I was a law student. My family paid part of the fees and the rest came from a trade union scholarship. There was no free University and fat grant cheques back then. But his education never cost his family a penny. He got what they called a State Exhibition. There were only four or five of them for the whole of County Donegal. The family had spent every penny they could afford on the first son, John – they put him through Maynooth Seminary in County Kildare to become a priest, and then the Jesuits got hold of him and paid for him to go to The National and do a Doctor of Divinity. The parents thought the sun shone out of his arse, but the truth was, the younger son, your father, was three times as bright. But inside the family, John was always the blue-eyed boy, no matter what your father did. I think that put him off his own family and probably off religion too. But who knows? I don't suppose you're interested in this auld stuff at all. It's all water long under the bridge."

"No, it's very interesting actually. I never knew any of that."

"You've got big shoes to fill, young Danny. Now, back to our deal. You report to Bernie. He'll report to somebody else, and that somebody else will report to me. That's how it works. There's always a chain. The less each individual knows, the less they can let slip. Oh, and nothing is too trivial to report. I really mean nothing.

Somebody gives you a funny look, asks you a funny question, does something you wouldn't have expected – tell Bernie. Let other people decide whether it's significant or not. There's no such thing as too much information. Is that clear?"

Danny nodded.

"Now. Is there anything we can do for you? Anything at all?"

Danny thought for a moment. "I've got kind of interested in pirate radio lately. I've built a transmitter – I've been wondering if I could get away with broadcasting – maybe one programme a week. An hour on a Sunday afternoon – a DJ show. Something like that. But of course it isn't entirely legal…"

"We've got people in the Post Office hierarchy. What will your radio station be called?"

"Well, I've been calling it Kingston Radio. The *Kingston* was a pirate ship. Calico Jack was the captain."

"Okay. Kingston Radio is never going to be investigated or closed down. You have my word."

"Really? Are you certain? Is it as simple as that?"

"Yes, Danny. It's as simple as that."

Danny thought for a moment. "If it's as simple as that, couldn't you have got Connor off that firearms charge?"

Harrison let out a breath of exasperation. "Connor Laverty. He's a good boy, but not the sharpest tool in the box. Did you hear what he said about his dead brother being the first casualty in the Second Irish War of Independence or something? What kind of twisted logic is that? Beats me. But believe it or not, Connor got exactly what he wanted, and so did we, in a way."

"But they say they might use the Special Powers Act against him. He might never get out."

"Connor will get out when Northern Ireland gets its freedom, and that isn't as far away as you might think. To tell you the truth, I hope they do use the Act against him. A young boy like that held without trial would be worth a hundred recruits a day to the Volunteers. What matters in the modern world, Danny, is how things come across in the media. A good-looking young martyr is a gift to the movement. It's all a matter of the way the public perceives things. Hearts and minds, Danny. Connor is doing more for the movement now than he could in three lifetimes on the outside. And if we can get somebody to write a song about him he'll be as happy as a puppy with a pound of sausages.

"Make no mistake, Danny. I've been through all this before. I know what I'm doing. Our day is going to come. And it won't be very long. When it comes, you'll be glad that you and your dad are with us."

"With you? Well, I don't know about that. Dad won't have anything to do with a movement that uses guns. And I think your brand of socialism isn't the same as his…"

"Danny, let me quote you something that Fidel Castro said about a different revolution. He said that there are many sides to every question, but there are only two sides to a barricade. He was right. When the crunch comes, the niceties won't matter. We'll all be on the same side then.

"Now I'm afraid I'll have to say goodbye. And I'll have to put the blindfold on you again. It's for everybody's protection, yours included. I've enjoyed our little chat. And if ever you need to talk to me again – I mean to me personally – tell Bernie and it will be arranged." He rose and replaced Danny's blindfold. "And I'd like to say remember me to your father, but that wouldn't do, I'm afraid. You can't talk to anybody about this meeting. This meeting didn't happen. You'll be back in time for your Requiem Mass. Look after yourself, Danny."

Chapter Eleven
Danny Goes to Douglas

Danny felt a great sense of relief now that the examinations were over. Ever since he had walked out of the big intimidating hall, with the last answer booklet sealed into its brown envelope, people had been asking him how he thought he had done. Danny had told them that he thought he had passed in most subjects but distinguished himself in none. Those who knew him less well than his parents, like aunties and friends of the family, interpreted this as false modesty. Danny knew that his father had no romantic illusions about his abilities and would accept his assessment as honest and probably accurate. "Never mind, Danny," he had once remarked, believing himself to be offering words of comfort. "It's not your fault. It's called 'regression to the mean'."

Weary from the effort of clearing out his locker and the long walk back from school, he put down his battered and now bloated hold-all in the front porch before he came through the inner doorway. It crossed his mind that he would need something a bit slicker than that if he was to keep up appearances as a senior. Something made of leather, more like a brief-case. More grown-up.

His mother heard him arrive and came through to the hallway to meet him. He noticed that her complexion was jaundiced and her eyes slightly rheumy, like an old woman's. Another of her turns on the way, he knew the signs. "Hello son. Isn't it great that you've got all the summer in front of you before you have to go back to that place?" He nodded. Summer holidays were all very fine, but about half way through the break the envelope with his results was going to arrive. That prospect spoiled the anticipation of the long carefree days. "Have you any plans about what you would like to do?"

He considered the question as he followed her back into the kitchen. Get as far away from this house as I can, had been his first thought. But it needed to be made a bit more precise. "You remember that time we all went to the Isle of Man – I think I was about ten?"

"Of course I do. What about it?"

"I think I'd like to go back there – on my own. Maybe stay for a while. Get a summer job."

"A summer job? Are you serious? What could you do?"

He thought quickly. "I could work in a shop… or I could do an office job… or work in a hotel…"

"You need skills for all those things. You need to be able to add up and work the till in a shop, and give the right change. You need to be able to type to work in an office. I suppose you could answer the phone in a hotel, but I don't know what else you'd be any good at. I can't see you sticking any of those things very long either, even if you could find somebody to employ you. A seaside place in the summer will be flooded with students looking for a wee job and a free holiday. You'll be right down at the bottom of the list."

"Thanks for the vote of confidence, Ma. The Isle of Man isn't all seaside. They have farms there, and ordinary villages, with post offices and pubs and everything. And a couple of museums and things."

"Farms? What would you know about farming? Or museums, for that matter."

"Libraries. I could work in a library."

"In your dreams, Danny boy."

"Well, Ma, you asked me if I had any plans and that's my answer. I want to go to the Isle of Man. I can take the tent and the paraffin stove and camp out until I find something better. I'm nearly sixteen now, it's time I was doing things for myself." Although it was an idea that had only just occurred to Danny, and he knew that she was probably right in a lot of her objections, the more she ridiculed the plan the more determined he became to make it work. The Isle of Man was just right for him. It was almost foreign, and yet only a few hours away on the ferry.

As he followed her through to the kitchen he discreetly lowered a discarded newspaper into the waste bin to cover up the two empty bottles. She saw him out of the corner of her eye. "Those are old ones. I found them upstairs. I didn't finish two bottles in one night, for God's sake."

"Of course not, Ma. I'm just covering them up so that Dad won't see them and give you a hard time."

She put an arm around his waist and drew him close. The smell of her breath suggested that her account of finding old bottles upstairs was not entirely accurate. "You're a good boy, Danny. You've a lot more understanding than your Da. Do you know that?"

He pulled himself free. "Thanks Ma. And before you try to argue with me, I'm leaving on the ferry at the weekend. That's all there is to it."

His mother shrugged. "You'll be away from home for your sixteenth birthday if you do that." Almost at once her eyes brightened. "Can you bring me back a few things from the Duty Free?"

The Manxman was a rusty and neglected vessel, not one of the new roll-on-roll-off car ferries, but a traditional passenger ship, with deck-room for a few vehicles, which had to be winched on and off by crane. Danny had been on her before, and knew that she didn't ride a choppy sea very well. He had watched most of his fellow passengers turn green and part company with their breakfasts when he had made the crossing with his parents on that first holiday after the move to Belfast. Today however, the sea was flat calm, and the sun stung his face as he stood near the front of the throng that had gathered on the deck to watch the ship dock at the port of Douglas.

Although the capital city of the island, Douglas was small and compact, with an elegant curved beach promenade of fine white-faced four-storey Victorian hotels, and behind these on slightly higher ground, a couple of lines of shops with bright-painted fronts and red roofs, followed by a scattering of smaller, mainly white houses, rapidly giving way to green fields and narrow, barely discernable roads on the hill above the town.

But dominating everything, rising skyward from a low granite rock in the middle of the bay, was the incongruous fairytale castle with its towers and keep that made Douglas magical. Danny knew that it had been built in Victorian times as a refuge for shipwrecked sailors and to this day was stocked with fresh water and emergency rations that might keep body and soul together until help arrived. But coming as it did straight from the pages of a young child's storybook, it lifted the whole town of Douglas above the ordinary, into the realm of fantasy and dreams.

I'm in a kind of fairytale myself, Danny thought. Nobody watching me, no Father Walsh or interfering neighbours to tell my parents if I step out of line, nobody to tell me what time to go to bed or when to get up in the morning or what I should eat for my lunch. This must be what it feels like to be grown-up. Infinite possibilities. Nobody to answer to but yourself.

He was glad that he'd had the courage to go through with his impromptu plan. For the first time in his life, despite or maybe even because of the feeling of unreality that the castle generated, he seemed to be standing on the brink of the adult world.

Behind him families with young children tried to push forward, eager to be among the first to disembark, dispose of bags and suitcases and stake out their spots on the beach. Children chattered excitedly to their parents, trying to elicit promises of visits to the fairground or the Witches' Museum or the little zoo in the days to come.

Engrossed in the scene, Danny turned around casually and found himself looking straight into the face of a girl who looked slightly younger than himself, with long, straight black hair. She was wearing a skimpy, almost see-through, yellow summer dress, and carried a small rucksack tossed over one shoulder. His stare must have been very obvious, because she stuck her tongue out at him before giving him the most heart-stopping smile he had ever seen.

How, in his craziest moments, could he have considered Claudette even vaguely pretty? This was a goddess. He felt his heart pounding like Brian Bennett's drum intro on *Apache*, and a lump came to the back of his throat. A great wave of tenderness passed through him. In his (almost) sixteen years on the planet he had never seen a human face as beautiful as this, or a body so perfectly proportioned, had never been affected by the sight of another human being as profoundly as he was now. He continued to stare, tongue-tied and motionless.

She was with her parents, seemingly their only daughter, and, horror of horrors, her father was wearing the light grey suit and clerical dog-collar of a Protestant minister. She giggled at Danny and he dragged his eyes away from hers. He realised that he was physically shaking and his vision had become a little blurred. Also that a purpose had entered his life.

Danny had never shadowed anybody before, but he had seen it done in films and it looked reasonably straightforward. You hurried from one hiding place to another, keeping out of sight behind walls and lamp posts and parked cars, and the person you were following never looked around, or had the faintest inkling of what was going on. In real life it was a lot less easy. Or possibly he was useless at doing it. Many times, as he struggled along behind the little family group, staggering under the weight of his huge rucksack, the girl turned around, and even waved to him discreetly behind her parents' back. To her what was happening was clearly an enormous joke, to him it was his newly-discovered sole reason for living. Nothing else mattered any more.

Danny remembered a saying that he had heard on some trashy daytime TV show: Falling in love is like being struck by lightning. You can no more make it strike you than you can avoid it. He had not sought the lightning and he had not avoided it. The lightning had simply struck. His life had changed forever.

Even if the girl had been coy and had tried to avoid Danny's attentions he would have found a way to get to her. But in fact she made no such effort. He had only to wait an hour or so in the café across the road from her family's budget hotel, give them enough time to carry their luggage to their rooms and unpack, and she obligingly reappeared alone, wearing the same yellow dress, but with the rucksack replaced by a light beige shoulder bag from which protruded a rolled-up towel. She paused at the front entrance of the hotel and looked around.

Danny leaped to his feet, and leaving his massive back-pack on the floor of the café and his bill unpaid, ran giddily across the street to greet her. He stood in front of her, tongue-tied and suddenly feeling ridiculous, and stared at her with the expression of one afflicted with a learning disability. But she had already diagnosed his condition correctly. "Hello," she said very quietly. "Don't be scared, I won't bite. My name's Joyce – what's yours?"

Danny suddenly realised that he had been holding his breath and exhaled with a sound like a venting whale. "I'm Danny…"

"Danny. Right. Hello. Do you fancy coming down to the beach for a swim?"

"Yes. Oh God, yes."

The girl giggled. "I like you. You're funny." She took his hand and, almost entering a trance, he allowed himself to be led down the road in the direction of the beach.

"Hey! You boy!" a rough voice called from across the street. "We only accept money for coffee here. Not rucksacks!"

Danny might have supposed himself to be dreaming except that no dream had ever been as perfect as this, or ever could be. He had his first kiss in the sea, standing higher than his waist in the gentle waves, the fairytale castle out in the sea in front of him, lifting up her slender body with his right arm to reach her lips, feeling as he held her close the softness of her half-developed breasts and the hardness of her nipples beneath her swimsuit, her tongue probing softly between his teeth. He held her with infinite gentleness and care, as he would a delicate butterfly that he had rescued from a spider web to release in the garden. "God, I'm crazy about you," he whispered into her ear.

"I know, I can feel it," she whispered back. She kissed him again, wrapped her legs around his waist, and almost imperceptibly at first but with growing urgency, moved her pelvis, sometimes up and down, sometimes in a slow circular motion against his groin.

Oh my God, he mentally begged the deity in whom he did not believe, don't let me come! Not just yet. Please, not just yet. But God was not listening.

Chapter Twelve
Danny Falls in Love

Joyce tried to release herself from Danny's embrace but he resisted by hugging her a little tighter. "It's a beautiful day, Danny," she coaxed. "We're not going to lie here all afternoon, are we?" She pulled down the zip of the tent to reveal blue sea melting into blue sky.

"Just another five minutes. Please. Nothing like this has ever happened to me before. I just want to hold you for a while. Please." She relaxed back into his arms.

"Was that your very first time?"

"Couldn't you tell?"

"Well, yes, I suppose I could really. But you were good. It was nice for me too."

"Nice? How can you use a word like 'nice' about something like that? It was… miraculous. Unbelievable. I've never felt like this before in my life. Was it your first time too?"

She giggled. "Are you kidding?"

Danny decided that he didn't want to pursue that line of enquiry. "I just never knew I could feel as good as this. I think if I died right now I wouldn't have missed out on anything."

"You're sweet." She kissed him lightly on the lips.

"I don't care if you get pregnant," he said more quietly, "I would marry you. I would look after you and your baby. I would stay with you forever…"

She wriggled in his arms as though he had given her a shock. "Hey! Lighten up! Who said anything about babies? I'm not a fool you know."

"But, we didn't use any protection, did we?"

"You didn't but I did. Haven't you heard of the birth control pill?"

"The Pill. Yes, of course, my Dad's a doctor. But I thought you had to be grown-up. And married…"

"You don't have to be anything, Danny. Just female. This is 1964, not the Dark Ages. Don't you read the newspapers? Don't you know anything?"

"Oh." Danny was wounded. He knew that his impersonation of a man of the world wasn't flawless but he felt that her reaction was a little unkind. "I suppose I should have thought…"

"Relax, Danny. We can have fun together. We've got a whole week before my family goes back. But I'm not your wife – or your wife-to-be. Just be cool. Don't try to lay things on me. Okay?"

Danny nodded. He realised that he would accept her terms, whatever they were. But the thought of losing her after just a week was more than he could bear. "We can meet up again after you go back, can't we? Where do you live?"

"Bangor. You?"

"Belfast. Just off the Antrim Road. But I've got a bike. I could cycle to Bangor in a couple of hours. Maybe less."

"Maybe. Okay? Just stay cool. Take it easy. There are other things going on in my life, you know."

"Other things. You mean, other boys?"

"That's my business. We don't belong to one another. That's not what I want. I have a very busy time, apart altogether from boys. I'm doing a lot of extra classes – singing lessons, dancing lessons, acting lessons… I want to get into RADA. Do you know what RADA is?"

"It's a school for actors and actresses, isn't it?"

"Just the number one school on the planet for actors and actresses. I know I look good, and I know I've got talent. I don't intend to settle for second best. I intend to have a great career. In the movies or on the West End stage. Or maybe singing, I'm not sure yet. But the world is going to know about me, one way or another."

Danny could see with perfect clarity that this was the case. "You're amazing," he breathed.

"I like you," she said by way of reassurance, kissing him again for emphasis, "but I'm never going to be owned, by anybody. Women have lived like that for thousands of years. But my generation has a chance to do things differently. We don't have to depend on men, or be pushed around by men. We're going to have our own lives and decide what to do with our own bodies. You'd better get used to it."

70

He was stunned by the eloquence of someone so young. "I can do better than that. I can help. You're obviously right. I don't want to push you around or own you. I want to help you. I want to... be on your side." He paused to try to think out what it was he was trying to say. "What happened to me... today... showed me that life can be wonderful. Just like the heaven that the priests talk about, but real, and right here on earth. People loving one another, being close to one another, caring about one another. Maybe that doesn't have to be just one man and one woman. Maybe... it could be a whole network of people. A whole society... a whole human race. Do you know what I mean?"

"Of course I do. 'The Times They Are A'Changin''. Ask Bob Dylan. What kind of music are you into?"

Danny panicked slightly at being asked this question. Joyce's family was obviously Protestant, so if he said rebel songs, which was the first genre that came into his head, he might be putting his foot in it very badly. "I like folk music," he ventured. "All kinds of folk music."

"Really? Me too. Do you play an instrument?"

"No, I'm afraid not."

"I wish I'd brought my guitar. I could sing for you."

"Could you? Really? God, that would be fantastic. Can you sing anyway? Unaccompanied."

"Maybe. But not lying down..." she pulled herself up on to her knees and hunted around for her swimming costume, "and preferably not naked." She started to pull it on. "What would you like to hear?"

"Anything. You choose."

As soon as she had got her arms through the straps of the one-piece costume she sat in the lotus position by his side and sweetly and flawlessly sang:

Oh hard is the fortune of all womankind
She's always controlled, she's always confined
Controlled by her parents until she's a wife
A slave to her husband the rest of her life

Oh I'm just a poor girl, my fortune is sad

71

I've always been courted by the wagoner's lad
He's courted me strongly by night and by day
And now he is loading and going away...

Danny listened to the unfolding of the story of the pregnant love-sick teenager and the tearful parting with her plebeian lover, scorned and driven off by her aristocratic parents. "You're laughing at me," he protested. "But I don't care. It was beautiful. You're a brilliant singer."

"And you're a brilliant flatterer. I think we're going to get on fine." She crawled out of the tent. "I want to swim to the castle. Are you coming with me?"

"I'm afraid this is probably the last time we can get together for a while," Joyce told him with at least a hint of regret, pulling the sleeping bag up to keep her back warm. The distant and unseen sunset made everything inside the tent unnaturally red, and for Danny brought to mind brothels, scarlet women and forbidden pleasures.

"I promised myself I wouldn't ask you this," he said hesitantly, "but is there somebody else? Somebody you're going back to?"

"Why do you ask if you don't want to know? What difference does it make anyway?"

Danny could think of no sensible answer. "You're right. It doesn't make any difference. So long as... well, so long as you're not thinking of leaving me for someone else."

"Leaving you? What does that mean? When did I arrive at you, to be able to leave?"

"Oh, don't force me to say it, Joyce. You know exactly what I mean. I want to spend time with you again. Like we've done this last week."

"Go on. Say it. You want sex with me again. That's okay. It's not an insult. I want it with you again too. Now that I've got you so nicely trained, I don't want some other girl to get all the benefit."

"You never take anything seriously, do you?"

"And you need to lighten up a bit. What do you say we meet each other half way?"

He kissed her for the thousandth time. "Okay. Just so long as you do want me again. So long as I'm still somewhere on your list. I don't need the top position." It wasn't entirely true but Danny knew that it was what she wanted to hear.

"Now you're talking my language." She reached over for her clothes and started to get dressed. "This radio station you were talking about. How many people will be able to hear it?"

"Well, the signal strength's pretty good all over Belfast. The city is in a bowl basically, a bay surrounded by mountains. It's strongest towards the south west, but I can cover just about the whole of that bowl in the daytime. At night you get a lot of strong transmissions coming in from England and continental Europe. It's not so easy then."

"How about I do a programme for you. Sing a few songs, maybe, play a few records. Do a bit of flirting with the boys. I could tape it and send it to you. What do you think?"

"That sounds like a fantastic idea. All except the flirting anyway."

"I doubt if you would even realise I was doing it. I'm not always quite as direct as I was with you."

"I'm really grateful that you were. I don't know if I'd ever have had the courage to make the first move myself."

"I thought exactly the same thing. And I knew I only had a week. It's up to you, of course, but if you never make the first move, you're always going to end up with girls like me."

Danny took her hand and kissed it. "I wouldn't have any complaints about that."

She wore the same yellow dress for the return journey. It burned itself into Danny's memory and in the confusion of his bruised emotions became a symbol for unattainable female perfection. Danny waved her goodbye from the jetty, and trying to be light-hearted, blew her a kiss like the hero in a Victorian melodrama. She responded with a demure curtsy. Her parents had gone straight inside the covered deckhouse so they could do it openly.

He had to keep telling himself that they would meet again. He had her address and her phone number and she was going to send him a tape for the radio station. Why, then, did he feel so crushed? It was of course the fear that things might not work out. There were so many details that could go wrong between now and then. It would be so easy for her to write a letter and break it all off. The whole relationship was hopelessly one-sided. If only he could somehow make her feel the same way about him that he did about her. A place on the list, probably nowhere near the top. Was that enough? Was that all he had a right to hope for? Was he going to be able to live with it?

As he strolled back to the campsite behind the beach he absent-mindedly let his eyes scan the hand-scripted placards outside the news kiosk by the railway station. 'President Johnson says US military action in Vietnam now unavoidable.' 'Protests as Nelson Mandela, South African terrorist leader, begins his life sentence for sabotage.' 'Body of murdered priest found floating in River Lagan.'

Danny froze and turned back towards the kiosk. He walked to the counter and looked down at the headline in the Belfast Telegraph. Suddenly his own minor romantic anxieties were thrown into perspective. Danny felt sick and he wanted to go home.

Chapter Thirteen
Another Family Crisis

He undid the straps of his huge rucksack in the hallway and lowered it carefully, leaning it against the wall. From the top section he removed the two bottles of Old Bushmills in their Duty Free carrier bag and took them with him into the house.

"Hello, Ma! It's Danny! I'm back a bit early. Where are you?" There was no reply so he checked the kitchen and the sitting room before making his way up the stairs. "Ma? Are you in the bedroom? It's Danny."

As he approached the master bedroom his father emerged and 'shushed' him with a finger across his lips. He looked haggard and anxious. "She's not well, Danny," he said quietly, "come downstairs. What's that you've got in the bag?"

Danny's thoughts raced. He could think of no convincing lie. "It's for Ma. She wanted me to bring her back a couple of bottles."

"We've got to have a talk about that. Come into the kitchen." Danny followed him and they each took one of the wooden chairs by the kitchen table. Danny could tell that the conversation would be serious.

"Listen, Danny, I'm going to have to ask you to grow up very quickly. I have to tell you this straight, it's no good beating about the bush. Your mother's in a bad way. She's been in the Mater Hospital for the last few days – they've just discharged her. They did a liver biopsy this time – it's full-blown cirrhosis, she's gone well past the fibrosis stage. And there's abnormal kidney function and evidence of cardiomyopathy. In plain English, she's got a very simple choice. Stop drinking or die. There's no third option. I'm sorry to have to tell you this as soon as you walk in the door."

For a while neither of them spoke. "If she does stop... will she get better?"

"Not entirely. Some of the damage is irreversible. She'll have to take things very easy. But most of it is treatable. I've seen people in her condition hang on for years. But her lifestyle is going to have to change. I don't mean she has to cut down, I mean she has to stop. Right now. Not tomorrow or the day after. Now." He looked Danny in the eye but Danny said nothing. "I'm going to have to ask you to help me, Danny. She won't listen to a word I say. As soon as she's back on her feet she'll be back on the bottle. I can't keep her prisoner and watch over her every second of the day. If she wants to kill herself I can't stop her. Maybe she'll listen to you. I know you get on a lot better with her than I do. There's nothing more I can say to her. Either she thinks I'm bluffing or she just wants to die. I don't know which it is. It's beyond me. I know it's not fair to put something like this on to you at your age. God, it's your birthday in a couple of days, isn't it? But you're the last chance we've got. See if there's anything you can do."

Danny started to say something but his jaw trembled and he stopped. He thought for a bit longer. "You said you thought that maybe she wants to die. Maybe that's where we need to start. Do you think she could be doing it for some reason? I mean, do you think the drinking could be a symptom of… something else?"

His father rose before he answered and went to put the kettle on. "I'll make a drop of tea," he said absently. Danny read it as a way of escaping from the intensity of their eye contact. "I don't think I've been very successful at making your mother happy. I did try though. Harder than you might think."

"Was it my ma who wanted to come to Belfast?"

"Yes. I liked the practice in Ballyrowan. I never wanted to live in a city. Now she's saying that she wants to move to Birmingham. That's just an even bigger city. It doesn't appeal to me at all."

"She thinks we would have more money in England, doesn't she?"

"I suppose we would. But then everything costs three times as much over there."

Danny considered his father's answer. "We're not really short of money, are we?"

His father shrugged. "Would you give money to a drunk begging in the street? I wouldn't."

The words were cruel but Danny understood what his father meant. "She says she wants to be near to Auntie Maud, doesn't she?"

"She does. She forgets that when she and your Auntie Maud lived just down the road from one another all they ever did was fight.

"It's very hard to win with your mother, you know. Wherever she is, whatever she's got, she always wants something different. Then when she's got it she doesn't want it at all. She's been chasing some kind of fantasy for all the time we've been married. They were always snobs, you know, her family. I think she imagined that she'd have a big house and servants and people licking up to her and electing her onto committees, and hanging on her every word. And if she got that it wouldn't be right either. Sorry, Danny, it's not reasonable to load all this stuff onto you at your age."

"No, you're right Dad. I think the time has come to grow up." Danny waited for him to return to the kitchen table with the two cups of tea. "But if you want me to talk to her I think I need to know everything. There's more that you're not telling me, isn't there?"

His father replaced the cup he had been about to raise to his lips. "What do you mean?"

"Mrs Whittaker. I need to know what that was really all about. It was a big thing to Ma, whatever it was. Were you and Mrs Whittaker more than just friends?"

His father shrugged as though relieved that he could talk about it at last. "Yes. Years ago. Long before you were born."

"How long ago – exactly?"

"It would have been… twenty-five years ago. Maybe twenty-six."

"Twenty-five years ago. That's Spain again, isn't it?" His father nodded. "But surely she would have been too young to be in Spain?"

"She was a lot younger than me. About nineteen or twenty. She was a music student in London, but she came from Belfast originally of course. All kinds of people came to help get rid of Franco – Students, trade unionists, ordinary working people – all ages. Some of them were as old as I am now. People with a brain in their head, who could understand what Fascism was all about. A lot of people didn't take it seriously back then, you know – they thought it was just another kind of nationalism. Thought that all the things we were saying about it were just socialist propaganda. They found out pretty quickly after the war, of course. After we'd lost. It took courage to put your life on the line for something that might have turned out to be just a battle of ideologies. A conflict of ideas. But there's nothing more powerful or more dangerous than bad ideas. She understood that and I did too."

"So she was a soldier. They had female soldiers, didn't they?"

"Yes, but she couldn't fire a gun any more than I could. She came to help at the field hospital. By the end of the year she'd seen and done and learned more than most fully qualified nurses. She was a very bright girl."

"You would have liked that, wouldn't you? Somebody very bright."

A far away look had entered his father's face. "I liked everything about her. I thought she was the most beautiful creature I had seen in all my born days. I fell in love with her the minute I laid eyes on her. We weren't doing anything wrong. We were young and single, and far away from home... I'm sorry, I don't think you would understand."

"I would."

"Pardon?"

"I would. Understand."

Father and son looked at one another. A smile spread across his father's face.

"This holiday?"

Danny nodded and smiled too.

"Good god! You're only fifteen years old. I was twenty-eight the first time I got into bed with a woman. I wouldn't say boo to a goose when I was your age. Modern boys are a hell of a lot different to what we were like."

"Actually, Dad, I think it's modern girls. And it's your profession that we have to thank for it."

His father understood at once. "Yes, I suppose you're right there. So we won't be hearing the pitter-patter of tiny footsteps any time soon?"

"I hope not. Not until the right time."

His father slowly shook his head. He seemed happy and amused. "You know, sex is nothing to be embarrassed about. It's as natural a function as eating and defecation."

"More fun though."

"I think I would have to agree with that." He shook his head slowly again. "God, children grow up fast. We never did have that serious talk fathers are supposed to have with their sons, did we?"

"It's okay. I think I worked it out for myself."

"Sounds like it. Who's the lucky girl, then? Do I get to meet her? I take it it *is* a girl?"

Danny smiled. "Yes. Nothing to worry about there. Definitely a girl. She's very young. I think she might be a bit shy about coming around to meet you. You'll have to give me a bit of time to work on her."

"Young? Younger than you? For some reason I thought she would be older…"

"She's fourteen. Nearly fifteen. Her birthday is in September."

His father's eyes widened. "You need to watch yourself there, Son. That's well under age. Though I suppose your two ages are close enough for them to overlook it. I was worried for a minute that you were going to say ten. God, you're a lucky young bastard. What's she like then?"

Danny paused. "Like Mrs Whittaker was for you, twenty-five years ago. The most beautiful creature I've ever seen in my life. And she's bright. Bright as a button. And confident. She's thought about things and she knows her own mind. You and her would get on great. In fact I'll have to be careful she doesn't fall for you instead of me if I do get her to come around."

His father smiled. "I don't think a fourteen-year-old is going to fall for me. Even if I get myself a Beatles haircut."

"Do you think I need a Beatles haircut, Dad?"

His father paused before he answered. "I think what you need is a better opinion of your own worth. And it's my fault that you haven't got it. I grew up with your Uncle John, you see, and we had a sort of banter going all the time. A sort of friendly rivalry, like brothers often do. And I think I got into the habit of trying to make people feel small. Hurtful little sarcastic remarks. Put-downs. An attitude of superiority. I know I do it, even when it's completely inappropriate. I can't stop myself, it's unconscious. But I think you may have… internalised that message. And I want to say that I'm sorry. And that the image that I've given you of yourself is wrong.

You're a fine boy with loads to offer. Not just intelligence, emotional intelligence as well. And that's something I never had." He touched the strap of Danny's carrier bag. "God, I'm nearly tempted to open one of those bottles of yours myself."

"I… think I'd rather not." Danny took the bag over to the kitchen waste bin and lowered it in unopened.

"You're my son all right," his father said quietly.

"I like it when you say that."

"What? That you're my son?"

Danny nodded. "So, when you came to live in Belfast, did you know that Mrs Whittaker would be here?"

"No, of course not. I didn't even recognise the name when I got called out to see her the first time. I didn't know her as Whittaker. Then I went out – only four or five miles down the road – and there she was."

"And you were so excited about seeing her, you couldn't resist telling Ma."

"How did you know that?"

"I just guessed. I would have been the same. When I've got something big on my mind I want to tell someone. Sometimes I say more than I should. It's the way I am. I think you're the same. It must be very hard for you to keep that doctors' Hippocratic oath clause."

"I'm glad of the oath. It keeps everything very simple. Absolutely black-and-white."

Danny thought about this. "Yes. I'm beginning to think that there aren't many things in life that are absolutely black-and-white." He took a sip from his cup. "Will I go up and talk to her when I finish my tea? Is she conscious?"

His father made a tipping gesture with his hand. "So-so. She's got a lot of medication in her system and she's very weak. She may not answer but she can hear all right."

"I'll do my best. This really is our last chance, isn't it?"

His father nodded. "No question."

Chapter Fourteen
A Minor Triumph

Carrying a large envelope and some blank sheets of paper, Danny entered the bedroom without knocking. His mother looked tiny in the middle of the king-size bed, the covers barely showing a bulge where she lay. Her complexion was a deep and unnatural yellow, her flickering eyes sunken to the bottom of two pits of wrinkled and darkened skin. The room was filled with a putrid smell of illness.

Her appearance shocked him. Although the individual symptoms were familiar, Danny had never before seen them all present at the same time, and to such an extreme degree. He tried not to feel sorry for her, but to harness his anger instead.

"Hello Ma. Yes, it's me – I'm back early. I wasn't expecting to find you like this. I had some good news that I wanted to tell you." He sat on the side of the bed and looked down at her. Her head turned to follow his movements. She tried to say something but it was indistinct. Danny's name, perhaps.

He continued in a quiet, controlled voice. "I know you can't talk very much at the moment. It doesn't matter. What I want you to do is listen." She opened her eyes a little wider and looked into his. He could tell that she had picked up the new sharpness in his voice – that he had her full attention.

"I've grown up a lot since the last time you saw me, even though it was only a couple of weeks ago. I've had a talk with Dad and gotten a few things straight. He's told me what you're doing. You're about one bottle away from the end now. Has he told you that? Of course he has. Well I think it's time you and I had a serious talk.

"I can see perfectly well why you're doing this. What better way to punish a husband who's a dedicated doctor than to die of some stupid easily avoidable illness? It's a high price to pay, but if that's your choice, then so be it. I'll respect it. But one thing I do resent, and that's the way you've involved me in it. All the bottles you've sent me out for since I started to look old enough to buy it, all the empties you've got me to hide, all the lies you've got me to tell Dad. If you want to kill yourself, then kill yourself, but don't involve me. Okay?

"The other thing is, I want a proper suicide note. I've brought you the pen and paper and I want you to write it as soon as you're fit enough, and seal it inside this envelope. It isn't for me, it's for your grandchildren. It's only fair that they get to hear your side of the story as well as mine. Mine won't be very flattering."

A shocked expression came to her face and she tried once again to speak, but Danny interrupted.

"Yes, Ma. Grandchildren. Why not? Have you thought about that? That's my news. I've met a girl. A beautiful girl. I mean film-star beautiful. And we've started a relationship. It probably won't come to anything, she's right out of my class in every way, but I'm going to give it my best shot, and if she won't have me... well, I know I'm no great catch, but I think there's going to be somebody out there who will. Because you see I know what kind of life I want now. I don't want to be a priest like Uncle John and I don't want to grow old on my own like Auntie Maud. I want a family. Not a sham marriage like you and Dad. I want to live with a pretty girl who'll sleep in the same bed and give me a hug when I come home from work and ask me what kind of day I've had. I want her to hold my hand when we walk down the road and I want us to do a whole lot of things together, like going on holiday and going to the pictures... silly, slushy, boring, ordinary things. That's what I want. The same things that ninety per cent of the human race wants. And I want to be a father, and I want to watch my children grow up, and I want them to love their parents and see how happy we are together. Straight out of some trashy Barbara Cartland novel. I'm sorry that it isn't unusual or exciting, and I'm sorry that you don't want to have any part in it, but fair enough. That's your decision.

"And that's why I want the note. Because I'm telling you right now that if I have a daughter I'm not going to give her your name and I don't want her to be anything like you. But I don't want my children to hate you just because I probably will. I want them to hear your side of the story and make up their own minds. I want to be fair. So you write that note and seal that envelope and I'll give it to your first grandchild as soon as it's old enough to understand. That's not too much to ask, is it?

"Goodbye, Ma."

Her eyes were wide and unblinking now, and fixed on his.

He placed the paper and the envelope carefully on the bedside table and took the ballpoint pen from his vest pocket to put on top of them like a paperweight. Then he turned and left, shutting the door quietly behind him.

Danny and his father had little to say to one another that evening. Danny wasn't required to give an account of what had passed between himself and his mother. His father asked him to go down to the chip shop to buy something to eat, and after their meal Danny heated some soup from a tin, which his father took up to his wife. He returned almost at once.

"Did she say anything?"

His father shook his head. "She seemed… a bit different, though. More alert."

"I did the best I could," Danny told him.

"I know you did, Son."

It took Danny a long time to get to sleep. When he did he dreamed of when he was very young in Ballyrowan, his mother dropping him off at the tiny Sisters of Mercy Primary School that had just two classrooms, the bottles of free school milk with their aluminium foil caps, the smell it produced when it was spilled and began to go off, the drone of young children's voices reciting meaningless prayers in Irish, the chimes of the town clock measuring off the day in quarter hours. The simplicity and peace and familiarity of it all.

Recent events had left him exhausted, and he slept until his father woke him up and pulled back the curtains to reveal a dazzling sun that had already risen above the brittle overgrown hulks of the dead pear trees at the bottom of the garden.

Danny turned away from its brilliance and rubbed his eyes.

"You did it, Son," his father announced with obvious delight and admiration. "You damn well did it. She's asleep, but she left me this note."

83

Danny saw that his father was holding the envelope that he had left with his mother the evening before, as well as a sheet of paper that now contained blocks of his mother's spidery handwriting.

"That wasn't for you, Dad," Danny protested.

"Why not? It was addressed to me. Do you want to read it?" He handed the sheet to Danny, who sat up and read:

Dear Kieran,
I have been very stupid and done myself and this family a great deal of harm. But that harm ends right now.

There are two bottles in a big tin box under the sink. Two or maybe three more on top of the wardrobe in the spare room, in the middle of a pile of old blankets. I want you to get all of them and pour them down the sink. Please take the money out of my handbag as well.

You told me a long time ago that there was some kind of clinic where I could get help. I want you to get me into it as soon as you can.

I can hardly believe how much of a fool I have been. Please forgive me if you can. All this madness ends here. I promise. I love you both.

It was just signed 'Ma'.

Danny looked at his father. Between them was a wordless understanding and delight. "I've got to be going to open the surgery," his father said under his breath as he left.

Chapter Fifteen
Birth of Kingston Radio

Danny arrived home after his long walk and received a pleasant surprise. There was a small package addressed to him that must have come in the morning post. His mother was in the clinic now so his father must have taken it in and left it on the hall table for him to find. He looked at the postmark. Bangor!

With a thumping heart he hurried up the stairs and straight to his bedroom at the back of the house. He locked the door and took a screwdriver from his desk drawer to tear through the carefully applied strips of Sellotape holding it together. Inside was a small plastic reel of magnetic recording tape and a note.

> *Dear Danny,*
> *This is my first tape for the radio station, as promised. I'll be listening for it this Sunday on the big radiogram with the outside aerial. I've just put a few songs on this. I couldn't really do the links because you need to be able to fade the microphone up and down on top of the music and I don't know how to do that. Maybe you could do that bit for me? I've done a little bit of talking at the end. I hope it's okay. It's mostly just me singing and playing the guitar. I've included one song that I wrote myself. It's the last one.*
>
> *Is there any way that we could get the listeners to write in? We can't give out our addresses, can we? Can you think of a way to do it?*
>
> *If you want to come out to Bangor to see me on Saturday week I think the house will be empty. My mum will be away and Daddy has a big wedding so he'll be out of the house from*

about 10 in the morning to at least 4 in the
afternoon. You know the address. Phone me
before you set out to be on the safe side.
Love,
Joyce.

At the bottom of the note was a whole line of 'X's representing kisses. Danny read them out to himself. Kiss, kiss, kiss, kiss…

Life was good. Very good. He switched on his tape recorder and carefully threaded the leader of Joyce's tape through the various metal guides to the take-up reel. He pressed 'play'.

"Hello everybody. My name is Joyce and I would like to sing for you and play my guitar. This first one is a traditional song called *The Orange Maid of Sligo*."

Danny's heart sank. He pressed the 'pause' button. An Orange song? A song from Northern Ireland's Protest tradition, on a station protected by the IRA? This possibility had simply never occurred to him.

Who could he ask? Where could he go to for advice? He remained motionless for a long time, wrestling with the seemingly insoluble problem. At last his shoulders slumped and he exhaled. He could think of no answer. He might as well listen to the song. He released the pause button.

The guitar intro was flawless. In spite of his agonising dilemma he smiled at the sound of her voice. It was utterly enchanting.

On Ben Bulben's green and lofty height
The evening sun was setting bright
Gave out a ray of golden light
Around the Bay of Sligo

A tiny craft with glancing oar
And spreading sail the wind before
It blew the tiny craft ashore
Unto the Bay of Sligo

And at the bow there sat a girl

With rosy cheeks and flaxen curl
Her tender beauty like a pearl
The Orange Maid of Sligo

So far so good, he thought. Nothing political there. Maybe it would be okay.

And glancing o'er the vessel's side
She saw upon the water's tide
An orange lily, her golden pride
Upon the Bay of Sligo

Oh dear. Problems. Serious problems.

Make haste, make haste and save that flower
I prize it more than rose or bower
No traitor must take it within his power
Around the Bay of Sligo

Getting worse. Getting much worse.

An Orange youth sprang o'er the prow
Retrieved the flower and with a bow
Bestowed it on her gentle brow
The Orange Maid of Sligo

And soon she was his bonny bride
And oft they spoke at eventide
About that lily's golden pride
Around the Bay of Sligo

Come all true blues and fill your glass
A brighter toast could never pass
We'll drink unto that bonny lass
The Orange Maid of Sligo

Danny pressed the 'stop' button. It was one of the most captivating performances of a folk song that he had ever heard. And in his present circumstances, probably one of the most dangerous. He decided to save the rest of the tape for later. He switched off the machine. There was only one person whose opinion counted. Although it was hardly a serious enough matter to take to the Commander of the Belfast Brigade of the IRA, the chilling memory of the murdered priest came back to him. The worst thing he could do was fail to keep Big Jim Harrison informed. Harrison had taken great trouble to stress to him that no detail was too small, that it was for others and not him to decide what was significant and what was not.

He cleared a space on the long table where he was sitting and fished around in his new leather case for a suitable piece of paper. He ended up tearing a page of lined paper from an exercise book. He found a pen. Bernie across the road could get the note delivered for him. Should he begin 'Dear Mr Harrison' or 'Dear Jim'? He decided 'Dear Jim' sounded friendlier. That was how Big Jim had asked to be addressed. He had talked about friendship. This was a letter from one friend to another. A simple request for guidance.

Danny could hardly believe how rapidly Big Jim's reply came back. It was hand delivered to the house by Bernie in a plain light blue envelope the following evening about teatime. He took it up to his room to read, and locked the door behind him.

Opening the letter was a surreal moment. Somebody who was talked about in whispers among the Catholic population of Belfast, somebody outside the law like a real Calico Jack, had written a letter to him.

It was on good quality Basildon Bond notepaper and it was hand written. Somehow Danny had known that it would be. It was probably something he should keep to show to his grandchildren. Big Jim Harrison's handwriting was medium-sized and extremely neat.

Dear Danny,
Good to hear from you. Thanks for keeping me
informed.

Congratulations on the new girlfriend. It'll be a long time, I think, before I'm going to have time for that side of life again myself. I hope the two of you are very happy together. Maybe I'll get to meet her some day, but let's be honest, it isn't all that likely at the moment.

You ask me if it's all right to play music from the Protestant Irish tradition on your radio station. Let me explain something to you. The Republican movement is not the enemy of the Protestant people of Northern Ireland. When Ireland becomes one nation they are still going to be here and there has to be a place for them, under justice and with all their rights and traditions fully respected. The Protestants in the South of Ireland were not discriminated against when the South got its freedom. Many of them have remained prosperous business people and indeed a lot of them are now in the government at the highest level. There is no reason why Protestant men and women should not support the Republican movement out of motives of patriotism and love of social justice. Irish Protestants are Irish too. The Republican movement is not a sectarian movement. If we have enemies they are class enemies – those who would keep the poor and exploited in their place and the power in their own hands. There are Protestant people in Northern Ireland who are victims of this evil British regime every bit as much as any Catholic.

I'm sorry, I got a bit carried away there. The answer to your question is: play whatever music you want to play. Go out with girls of any religion you like. Help us to show people by our example that they have nothing to fear from the new Ireland that's just around the corner. Get them on side, Danny. Show them we're not monsters or bigots. Your instincts in this matter are obviously good.

Remember we're trying to build a society that will
be just and right for everybody.
  Good luck to you, your family, your girlfriend,
and your radio station.
  Jim.

Danny punched the air. "Yes!" he switched on the tape recorder, waited a few seconds for the valves to warm up, and pressed 'play'. Joyce's sweet voice addressed him. "I hope you liked that. This next song is modern – it's on Lesley Gore's latest LP, and let's just say, this song must have been written with me in mind. It's called, *You Don't Own Me*.

The performance, as ever, was impeccable. But Danny's mood of elation melted away as he listened to the words:

You don't own me, I'm not just one of your many toys
You don't own me, don't say I can't go with other boys
Don't tell me what to do
Don't tell me what to say

Please, when I go out with you
Don't put me on display,
'Cause You don't own me, don't try to change me in any way
You don't own me, don't tie me down 'cause I'd never stay

I don't tell you what to say
I don't tell you what to do
So just let me be myself
That's all I ask of you

I'm young and I love to be young
I'm free and I love to be free
To live my life the way I want
To say and do whatever I please

In the remaining verses the sentiments were repeated. Danny stopped the tape again when the song came to an end. He folded up Jim Harrison's letter and put it in the drawer of his bedside table.

Why did she have to keep reminding him of all that? He had accepted it. Intellectually he believed that she was right. Emotionally, he didn't want to be just one name on the list. He did want to own her. That was exactly what he wanted. His Joyce. His girlfriend. And in return he would be hers. That was how it was supposed to work, wasn't it? The words of the song repeated in his head. You don't own me, don't tie me down 'cause I'd never stay. She could hardly be clearer with him than that. People were changing. Human relationships were changing. Bob Dylan was singing songs about it. He had better adapt. After all, he told himself, wouldn't it be so much better if she just stayed because she wanted to stay? Not because there was some kind of rule that said she had to? Wasn't that the truest love of all? Wasn't it the highest state of acceptance that anybody could aim for?

He shrugged. Why was he torturing himself about all this stuff? He knew perfectly well he'd accept her on any terms she offered. If she wanted to sleep with a different boy every night of the week he would meekly accept his place on the rota. That was the truth of the matter. He could no more control her than the weather.

Saturday week! Think of Saturday week! That was what mattered. Ten o'clock in the morning until four o'clock in the afternoon. That wasn't a bad offer, was it?

With a start Danny suddenly realised that Saturday week was his birthday. Did she know? Had she remembered? What if his parents had planned something for him at home? He needed to talk to them right away. Tell them he was busy in the daytime. Very busy.

Chapter Sixteen
Danny's Birthday

Danny pressed 'play' for the dozenth time on the song Joyce had written herself. There was a slow guitar intro to the heart-rending melody. Each time he listened it brought tears to his eyes and made him want to take her in his arms and kiss away her sadness. This was a side of her that he hadn't even glimpsed on The Isle of Man. It made his longing for her even greater.

Mother's home from hospital and hasn't said a word
And all of them are whispering but still I overheard
How will they ever tell me and just how will I react?
I'm not old enough to understand a very simple fact

That death can come to anyone on any night or day
That nothing is forever and we all must pass away
That some will have a century and some will have an hour
And to right this great injustice is beyond our human power

I'll never know you, sister, and I'll never hear you cry
I'll never take you walking and you'll never ask me why
We'll never share a secret or a pleasure or a pain
Or go playing when it's sunny or sit in and watch the rain

And I won't be a big sister or an auntie or a friend
For a little sis to turn to when some love affair will end
And we won't grow old together and we'll never have a fight
About how to bring up children or which politician's right

And for ever more I'll wonder what you might have been to me
The adventures that we might have had that never now can be
But I always will be grateful for what I have learned from you,
How to treasure every moment, try to live enough for two.

He had tried repeatedly to keep his composure and record a simple linking announcement that would insert it into the station's first one-hour music programme for the coming Sunday afternoon. He tried again. "This is Kingston Radio, with the Captain, Calico Jack at the controls." All his other announcements had been jolly and upbeat but now the voice that came out sounded forced and uncomfortable. "I've tried to introduce this next song in some light, flippant way, but I can't. This is my friend Joyce with a song she wrote herself and I can hardly bear to listen to it. I think it's something very, very special. I think… I think Joyce has put her soul into this song. And it's the most beautiful soul you're ever likely to come across. I'm sorry I can't do her or the song justice in this introduction. It's called *Living for Two*." He stopped the tape, rewound, listened to the playback. It would have to do. At least it sounded sincere. He couldn't go on changing it indefinitely.

He switched off the recorder to give himself a break. Including *Living for Two* he had nearly forty-five minutes on tape now. He had an idea about how to fill the final quarter hour. Bernie across the road had a big record collection and would be happy, he was sure, to do a DJ spot for the tape. He would have modern up-to-date material and he would know what he was talking about. Danny understood the technicalities but he was no expert on pop music, and in reality no broadcaster. This would be the first real properly planned transmission, Joyce and a few school friends he had alerted would be listening, and it had to be right.

Danny glanced from the wall clock to the oscilloscope screen with its horizontal inch-wide band of green light, then to the panel meter reading exactly one-hundred-and-fifty, then back to the clock. As the minute hand clicked on to the figure twelve he pressed 'play'.

The oscilloscope trace began to dance cheerfully between the correct limits as the opening chords of Duane Eddy's *Ghost Riders in the Sky* sounded out loud and clear in his headphones. The music faded down as his own recorded voice came in. "Hello land-lubbers. This is the first scheduled transmission from Kingston Radio, with your captain Calico Jack at the controls. I want to say hello to Joyce, Bernie, Fergus, Trevor…"

He removed the headphones and glanced one more time at the 'scope and the anode current reading. Exactly correct. No need for any last minute adjustment. He put down the headphones and picked up his small transistor radio, which was as yet switched off to protect it from signal overload, and left the room. He locked the door behind him and slipped the key into his pocket. Can't be too careful, he thought as he descended the stairs to the hall.

He looked at the phone on the hall table for a moment and tried to resist phoning – be cool, he told himself. It's more impressive just to come on the air like a professional broadcaster – but he needed to hear her voice. He dialled her number.

"Joyce," he whispered in response to her greeting, "are you getting it okay?"

"Great, Danny. Fantastic. Loud and clear. You're ever so clever!"

"I wish. Keep listening. All your stuff's on the tape. Bye, sweetheart."

He replaced the receiver. He felt his shoulders relax. This was it. He had a girlfriend, or a respectable share in one. He had built a radio station and got it to work. He had managed to talk his mother out of killing herself. He wasn't such a dead loss as he had once feared.

He walked out into the road, waved to Bernie who he could see in his front lounge listening to the broadcast, and started down the gentle slope towards the city. When he was a few hundred yards from the house, he switched on the radio but kept the volume low, listening to the now very familiar tape, the signal strength almost enough to damage the radio even at this range. He wondered if he could walk far enough during the one hour transmission to be able to detect a reduction.

He increased his pace down the damp, deserted road towards the little line of shops where it joined the main route into Belfast, then beyond them, down the Antrim Road, following his route to school. Left on to Lansdowne Road with its much larger parade of shops and small businesses. There was a bus shelter here, and benches where a few middle-aged shoppers relaxed with their bags and shopping trolleys by their feet. Danny joined them and took the transistor radio from his pocket to make a critical assessment of reception. The signal was still close to overload and the sound undistorted. Brilliant, he thought, couldn't be better.

He noticed that the shop before him was a large tobacconist and newsagent with the name "Paddy O'Neill" over the door. He had often bought sweets or chocolate there, or things for his mother that he didn't want to think about any more. But now he noticed for the first time that one of the two very big front windows was given over to a display of postcards advertising items for sale, bed-sit accommodation and services that required the employment of such euphemisms as 'escort' and 'massage'. The available space was only about a quarter full. As he listened to Joyce's performance of *The Wild Mountain Thyme* an idea began to form in his mind.

The bell above the door pinged as he entered the shop. He was the only customer. A rotund white-haired man with a face as crumpled as his open-neck blue shirt appeared from within and looked at him expectantly. "Would you be Paddy O'Neill?" Danny asked.

"That I would. How can I help you, lad?"

"I just wanted to make sure I was talking to the boss. I have an idea for you. A sort of proposition." The man's expression became more suspicious as he nodded. "What you're listening to is a pirate radio station." Danny placed the radio on the counter and turned the volume up fractionally. "Now we would like the listeners to be able to write in, but we can't broadcast our address over the air, as you can appreciate. But maybe you can help us there." Danny pointed to the front window. "How much do you charge to display a postcard?"

"Two shillings a week," the owner declared, conveying little interest in Danny's 'proposition'.

"Okay. Well, suppose listeners started sending you postcards with record requests and things like that on them, enclosing a two-shilling Postal Order or stamps or something. You wouldn't mind displaying the card for a week, would you?"

"No, why should I?"

"And you wouldn't know who was reading the messages. Anybody who passed by could read them."

"Of course."

"So you don't mind our giving out your address over the air, do you?"

"I suppose not. It's not illegal, is it?"

"No. Of course not. You don't know anything about the radio station. You just display cards that people send you – and collect the money. You don't know who the messages are intended for. You have no link with the radio station. For every ten cards that come in you've got another pound in the till. That's all there is to it from your point of view."

"I don't know. To be honest, it sounds a bit fishy."

"It's free advertising for the shop. Some people will deliver their cards by hand too, and probably buy something while they're in. It's an all-win situation for you. There's no downside."

"Tell you what. If they were paying three shillings for each card, the idea might appeal to me a lot more."

Danny reached across the counter and they shook hands. Kingston Radio had a mailing address.

It was Danny's birthday. His mother was still in the Mayo Clinic so he had become accustomed to getting up early enough to make breakfast for himself and his father, and doing the basic chores like the washing-up and the shopping as required. Neither of them went to such extremes as dusting or hoovering the carpets. As far as Danny could determine, such tasks were unnecessary.

This was a very special morning so he got up particularly early and had a bath, before carefully selecting a pair of stone-washed Levis and a blue-and-white check cotton shirt with short-sleeves. He looked in the mirror and flicked a comb through his hair. "All right!" he declared.

Today he would wear an apron to fry the eggs and bacon. A grease spot on this outfit would be disastrous. He checked the wall clock. Plenty of time before the 8.50 bus to Bangor. He headed down the stairs. As he passed through the hall he fancied that he could hear voices in the kitchen. His dad must have the radio on, he concluded. When he opened the kitchen door his dad was standing directly in his path, which gave him quite a start.

"Good morning Son," he greeted him. "Happy birthday. I'm afraid there's been a change of plan."

Danny's jaw dropped. "There can't be. Not today. I can't change my plans for today..."

"Well, I'm afraid you're going to have to."

His dad stood aside to reveal Joyce, seated at the kitchen table beside a large chocolate sponge cake on which burned sixteen candles. She was wearing what looked like a white school blouse and a denim skirt. A yellow band held her hair back from her face. She looked incredibly young and incredibly beautiful.

Danny was struck dumb.

"Happy birthday, Danny," she said cheerfully. "I thought I would save you the bus fare. I can stay until teatime, if that's okay."

Danny stood motionless, apart from a slight trembling of his lower lip.

"I'm afraid I won't be able to join you for long," his father announced, "I've got a lot of house calls to make. But I'm sure you'll be able to look after your guest. She's brought her guitar, in case you should get bored."

Danny's powers of speech began to return, only to be taken away again by Joyce's enthusiastic birthday kiss. He held her for at least a minute, stroking her long hair and her back, finally tracing the line of her arm and holding her hand. "Aren't you going to say anything?" she asked at last.

"I think I'm too happy to say anything," he whispered.

Chapter Seventeen
Examinations and Omens

Two weeks after his happiest ever birthday, spent largely in bed with Joyce, and with about ten days to go before St. Benedict's was due to reopen, Danny's envelope arrived. His mother was still in the Mayo Clinic, although she was now coming home for the occasional visit, but when Danny opened the imposing white envelope at the breakfast table it was just his father watching over his shoulder. He tried to assume an air of nonchalance. It was only a bunch of examination results. It didn't matter if there were some disappointments. Subjects could even be re-sat. His 'A' levels in two years time would be a lot more important anyway. Why, then, was his forehead moist and his hand shaking?

He pulled out the neatly printed sheet and unfolded it on the table. There was a column of subject names and opposite each one a number. It was an elaborate system, each subject was marked out of 400 and the pass mark was 160. Marks under 200 however were regarded as somewhat shameful. Danny ran his eyes quickly down the numbers. Only two below the wretched 200. French, sadly, was an outright fail. Irish, at 182, wasn't that much better. He was never going to be a linguist. Physics and English had both broken the 300 barrier. That was better than he had expected. But most of them hovered indifferently around the low 200s.

"That's okay, son," his father tapped him lightly on the shoulder, "I won't pretend that I didn't do better when I was your age, but you haven't let yourself down. It's a good effort."

"Thanks, Dad."

They both paused momentarily and sank into their own thoughts. Why couldn't he be a brilliant student like his father before him? He had tried. He had put in more work than most people he knew. But somehow life had not singled him out as one of its stars.

He wondered what Joyce had got, then remembered that it wasn't an examination year for her. He was going to see her again in a few days time, but after that, when they were both back at school, it would be a lot more difficult. Would she remember that he had been waiting for results? He was pretty sure that she would, her memory was excellent. Would she despise him if he had to admit to her that academically he was not going to rock the world? At the moment he was riding comparatively high in her estimation. She had heard all the Sunday broadcasts loud and clear, and that was pretty good. The far end of Belfast Lough and right around the headland, with some low hills in the way. Of course the signal wouldn't be attenuated very much travelling over water... He scolded himself for letting his thoughts drift onto technical matters.

More than half the cards in Paddy O'Neill's window were requests for signed photographs of Joyce. They had come to a special arrangement with a local chemist for multiple copies of a very suggestive head-and-shoulders beach pose, where it looked as if she was wearing no top, and another special arrangement with Paddy O'Neill to share the five shilling charge that they had set for each copy. It had upset Danny at first, especially her insistence on copying each of their names and addresses into her notebook, but he took comfort in the fact that he was getting a lot more from her than just a signed photograph, not to mention his shilling share of each one they sold. Very soon he was going to have another whole day with her in his Queen-size bed. In a proper bed he could be on top without crushing her. They hadn't been able to do that in the tent. Missionary position, he believed they called it. He wondered why. An image of her perfect naked body came to his mind. Her pert little breasts, her flat tummy, the way the whole lower half of her body flowed so gracefully from one curve into another... God, he loved being in bed with her!

He shifted around uncomfortably in his chair.

"I'll tell your mother you passed when she phones up," his dad's voice interrupted his thoughts.

"Yes. Thanks. I didn't quite pass everything though..."

"You don't need French for medicine. Good science grades are what you need. You'll have to work hard, but you'll get there."

Medicine? It hadn't occurred to him that a medical career was what was expected of him. Was that what he wanted? He was by no means sure. Did he have the brains for it? He was even less sure of that.

"Of course I may do something else," he suggested timidly, "I mean something other than medicine…"

His father paused for a moment. "Completely up to you, Son. Whatever you decide to do, I'm sure you'll make us proud."

He imagined himself as the full-time electronic engineer on a real pirate radio ship, anchored a few miles out to sea, looking after the huge transmitters twenty-four hours a day. That would be the kind of life he would love, he told himself, refusing to consider any of the downside. And Joyce could be the resident announcer, and sing requests for boys who had absolutely no way of getting at her.

Danny's first day back at school began uneventfully. The morning was taken up with a lecture from Father Walsh regarding the increased standards of maturity that would be expected of senior students, followed by a general talk from his new form master, one of the younger priests, to discuss which subjects he should drop and which ones he should study at 'A' level. The priest put him under some pressure to re-sit his two language 'O' levels, but he refused outright, repeating what his father had told him regarding their irrelevance for entry to Medical School. "Medical School?" his new form master repeated in a tone that suggested a healthy cynicism.

When he had been introduced to a few of his future teachers and all the decisions had been made, his new timetable was printed off in the office and handed over to him. It was now lunch time and the schoolyard was crowded with boys. There was no more need to stay for the afternoon, so he had a brief schoolyard chat with Bernie and some of the other boys he knew, collecting in the process a few requests for records and dedications on Kingston Radio, and set out for home.

He felt less of an outsider now among these people, coming as he did from County Donegal, and, whether he wanted to acknowledge it or not, of a slightly different social class to them as well. He had never felt in tune with the sectarian politics that occupied so much of their thoughts and lives. It seemed like a game to Danny, on a par with which football team you supported: he didn't feel it in his guts the way that they did, and this difference had been a major barrier to close school friendships.

"Brought up in some bog in Donegal with a doctor for a dad," a boy had taunted him when he was newly arrived at the school. "What the fuck would you know about anything?" It had hurt because it was basically true. He wasn't one of them. But now that had changed. He was the DJ on the pirate radio station. He had a role and a measure of respect. He was beginning to feel better accepted after just one half day in the senior school. And Father Walsh was right about the maturity thing as well. Would he have had the assertiveness to refuse point blank to re-sit exams last term? No way. Danny could feel his confidence growing, detect the first stirrings of manly independence. He knew that he had Joyce to thank for a lot of it, and his greatest anxiety was that he might somehow lose her. While she was around and he could rely on her, he could face whatever the world had to throw at him, or so he believed.

As it was still early and there was no great need to hurry home, he decided to call in on Wee Hughie's mother and see how the family was getting on. Probably because he had felt so guilty about the time Wee Hughie had shown him the gun, he had never offered his condolences or spoken to her at all since all those terrible things had happened and Connor had been taken away. Out of common courtesy he felt he should say something.

As he approached the small terrace house he saw that slogans had been spray-painted right across the front. The two foot high bright orange letters made no distinction between wall, window and front door.

"IRA SKUM" screamed the message daubed across the window and the wall. "FUCK OFF OR DIE" commanded the one that continued across the door. There was broken glass scattered in the tiny front yard – Danny guessed that a window had recently been broken and repaired. The curtains were drawn and there was no sign of life.

Although this kind of neighbourliness was not uncommon in Belfast, Danny hadn't expected to see it here. This was a Catholic district – who would go around spray-painting anti-IRA slogans where they were likely to get their heads kicked in for their trouble?

He approached the door and with some hesitation rapped three times with the brass knocker. A magnified human eye appeared for an instant at the spy-hole lens in the door, followed by a brief rattling of internal bolts, and then Mrs Laverty, her round red face compressed into a scowl and droplets of sweat on her forehead, pulled it open and took Danny's hand.

"Hello, Mrs. Laverty. I just wanted to say how sorry I am…"

"Come in, Danny," she interrupted, pulling him inside. She said nothing more until they were in the hallway with the two heavy bolts back in position securing the door.

"Did ye see the filth them bastards sprayed on the front of the house?"

"Yes, of course. Did you see who did it?"

She motioned him through to the kitchen. "No bloody chance. Three o'clock in the morning they came, put a brick through the front window as well." She lit the gas under the kettle with a match, pulling her hand away in alarm at the small explosion. "Tea'll be ready in a wee minute."

"Thanks, Mrs. Laverty – I wasn't really expecting tea. I just came to say…"

"No point saying nothin'. What's done's done – can't be changed. Pedro's in that special unit, Connor's in gaol, their da's on the run… I'm all on me own here. I'm gettin' death threats every day. I'm glad of the company. Sit down an' talk to me. That's what I need. That an' some kind've protection when he gets out."

"When who gets out?"

"Connor. Haven't ye seen the *Irish News*?" Danny shook his head. "Some shite English lawyer's got him off. He'll be out in a few days."

Danny couldn't make sense of this. "But he didn't deny being an IRA member. He made a statement…"

"Doesn't matter a fart what he said. They appointed a lawyer of their own – wouldn't let Connor take the stand. The bugger got him off! Insufficient proof. They said it was his da's gun an' he was talkin' shite about bein' in the Volunteers. Said he found the gun somewhere in the house from the time his da was in the Border Campaign in 1962. Wasn't no evidence worth fuck. You've got to prove things beyond reasonable doubt. An' the worst part of it is, they're right. He was no more an IRA man than you're a pirate. It was all in the wee bugger's head. Fuckin' fantasy! But now when he gets out the Prods'll hunt him down an' kill him. He'll be on the run for the rest of his life, just like his da. Not a titter o' wit between the two o' them. At least he would've stayed alive in gaol, an' he could've bided his time. This way he hasn't a hope in hell. They'll gun him down. An' he'll like as not take the rest of us with him. Silly little bugger... I think that kettle's hot enough now, I'll make the tea."

Danny's head was reeling from this new information. "Won't the Volunteers protect him when he gets out?"

"Why should they? He's not one of them. Just a silly wee bugger playing with his da's gun."

"He may not be one of them but he's a sympathiser. He's made that clear enough. And this is an IRA family, with the head of the household still on the run. And what about the shots fired over Wee Hughie's coffin? Connor's been in the news too. Why should they desert him now?"

Mrs Laverty paused and when she spoke all the fire had gone out of her voice. "Because he's not a martyr any more. I know how these people's minds work. He was found innocent. He's nobody now."

Danny remembered Big Jim Harrison's words: "To tell you the truth, I hope they do use the Act against him. A young boy like that held without trial would be worth a hundred recruits a day to the Volunteers". Maybe Mrs Laverty was right. Maybe the Volunteers had been outmanoeuvred, their propaganda victory snatched away from them. But he couldn't believe that they would be so cynical as to abandon Connor to his fate.

"Mrs Laverty…" Danny hesitated. "I'm not supposed to tell you this, but I do know somebody in the IRA. I can try to get Connor protection. At least I can put a word in. What day does he get out?"

She looked at him with obvious disbelief. "Don't give me any more *Boy's Own* bullshit like that. I've been listening to it all my life. I didn't come down the Lagan on a bubble."

"It's true, Mrs Laverty. I wouldn't bullshit you at a time like this. I can ask. I don't suppose they'll pay any attention to the likes of me but at least I can try."

She didn't reply. Instead she took a sip of tea and bowed her head as though withdrawing into her own thoughts.

Chapter Eighteen
An Engineering Problem

The opportunity to talk to Big Jim came sooner than Danny expected. The very next day, which happened to be a Thursday, Bernie called at about teatime to say that Big Jim wanted to see Danny again, and would send a car to pick him up after school on Friday at the junction of Lansdowne Road and Antrim Road. Friday was Danny's mother's day for coming home for her overnight visits, so he hoped the meeting with Big Jim wouldn't take too long.

At school on Friday, Danny did a lot of thinking about Connor and Mrs Laverty. He had managed to get hold of a two-day old copy of the *Irish News* from Paddy O'Neill and read the full account of the trial. The more he read about it the more half-hearted the Prosecution efforts sounded. He was fairly certain that it had been a sham, with acquittal as the intended outcome. Could the Protestant courts be as devious as that, he asked himself. Probably they could.

On the way home from school he was still turning it over in his mind when the same car that had picked him up before, with the same two young men on board, pulled up beside him on the Antrim Road. He now knew the driver's name to be Finbar and addressed him accordingly.

"You have a good memory," the young man remarked. "You'll remember how to put on the blindfold then."

Danny took the proffered piece of cloth and tied it firmly around his eyes, while the one named Rory watched to make sure he did it correctly. "Are we going to the same place?" he asked, to make conversation.

"I don't think you need to know that, Comrade," was Rory's answer. It was strange, and actually quite pleasant, to be addressed as "Comrade". But it still felt very much as though they were all playing a children's pretend game. Danny knew, of course, that this was far from pretend.

The car journey this time seemed a lot shorter, and ended in an ascent in a lift to an apartment high above ground level. Danny guessed that they were in one of the new tower block housing projects that were springing up all around Belfast, typically about twelve or thirteen stories high. When the blindfold was removed, he was pretty sure that he was right. There were Venetian blinds with their slats closed on the two large windows, and the furniture was clean and modern. Big Jim sat on a wide sofa that was cluttered with what appeared to be unopened newspapers, and a small coffee table in front of him bore the remains of a fry-up meal and an empty coffee mug. He smiled at Danny and motioned for him to sit down in the soft chair opposite.

"Hello Danny. Good to see you again. How's the family?"

Danny decided he should go a bit beyond the standard response. "Well, my mother's in the Mayo Clinic for her drinking problem, but she's making good progress, and my dad's fine."

"Ah yes. I heard about your mother. It's good that she's getting her health sorted out. And how's Joyce?"

Danny smiled. "Oh, she's great. Couldn't be better."

"Good, good. I asked you to come here because I wanted to ask for your help with a little technical problem. I think it's very much up your street. Would you like a cup of tea or anything?"

"No, it's okay, I'm fine."

"You see Danny, we need to make a withdrawal from one of the Royal Avenue banks, and we feel that we would have more… privacy if the police car radio system wasn't working at the time."

Danny couldn't help smiling. This was straight out of a Hollywood 'B' movie. Holding up a bank while the police radio system was jammed. Who could resist it?

"Now we've got some time to work on the problem, something in the region of a month in fact, and I've got one important piece of information." He reached into his inside jacket pocket and took out a folded piece of paper which he handed to Danny. "This is the frequency they use. It doesn't mean anything to me but it will to you. You'll probably need to buy things. That will need money. How much, would you estimate?"

Danny was thrown by the question. He had very little idea. "Well – I'll need to buy or make a VHF receiver that covers the right frequency range. Then I'll need to experiment a bit with transmitters… I suppose about a hundred pounds should cover it."

"Let's make it two hundred." Jim went over to a writing desk and took some twenty-pound notes from a drawer. "And anything you don't use you keep." He counted out ten of the notes and gave them to Danny, who gulped and stuffed them into his inside jacket pocket.

Jim sat down again. "There is just one thing. I'm sure you understand, we'll only get one shot at this. The jamming has to work one hundred per cent. There's no margin for error."

Danny nodded. He was surprised at how little anxiety he felt about his ability to come up with a technical solution. Electronic engineering, he knew, was his one true strength. "It'll work," he told Jim calmly, "there won't be any screw-ups."

"Good man."

It was clear that Jim wanted to terminate the interview, but Danny had something he needed to bring up. "Before I go, could I ask you about protection for Connor Laverty when he gets out of goal?" he blurted out.

Jim's countenance took on the wise benevolent seriousness of an old-school village pastor. "We know all about Connor," he assured his young friend. "We've spoken to him, and we've offered him a safe house until his case is forgotten about. But he won't take the offer. He wants to go back to his mother and his wee brother. We'll do our best, but we can't really guard that house all around the clock. Please God it'll all blow over very quickly and he'll be okay."

Danny nodded. "I suppose there's nothing more you can do."

"Not a thing."

Danny took his allotted task very seriously. The first thing, obviously, was to listen to the police radio activity and find out as much as he could about how the system worked. To do this he needed a receiver capable of covering that intriguing part of the VHF radio spectrum just below the FM broadcast stations, listed in *The Radio Amateur's Handbook* as allocated to 'mobile services'. He wrote to an advertiser in *Practical Wireless*, enclosing the substantial price demanded in the form of a Postal Order, and the device duly arrived four days later. The unit was housed in a neat black crackle-painted aluminium case about the size of a box of chocolates. It was ultra-modern in design, using the latest generation of high frequency transistors and a very sophisticated local oscillator, giving exactly the kind of pin-sharp frequency accuracy that he needed. The received frequency was displayed in illuminated red numbers in a small window on the front panel. It was a truly professional item. As soon as he switched it on and tuned to the frequency Big Jim had written down, there were the local police cars, loud and clear, receiving their directions from a base station calling itself 'Uniform'.

"Uniform to Romeo Nine," said a voice with a strong Belfast accent, "disturbance in the Long Bar on Leeson Street. Informant is Samuel Caldwell, licensee. Over."

"Romeo Nine to Uniform. On our way. ETA ten minutes. Out."

Danny was excited. He had heard of radio amateurs listening-in to the police radio before, but had never thought of trying it himself. He produced a school exercise book from his case and began to make detailed notes straight away about everything he was hearing.

The next day Danny bought himself a large street map of Belfast and pinned it over his cork notice board. He put aside an hour or so each evening after school for listening, and quickly worked out that there were three categories of car, the ones with a Romeo call-sign (which were the most numerous), the Juliet call-signs, and the November call-signs, which seemed particularly rare. His initial theory was that the letters of the phonetic alphabet represented the districts in which the cars normally patrolled, but after a careful analysis no such pattern seemed to be emerging. He decided that the letters must refer to the type of duties the cars performed: Romeo cars seemed to take the bread-and-butter calls: fights in pubs, drunks urinating in the street, domestic violence and the like; while the Juliets seemed to attend to slightly more serious matters like break-ins, knifings or shootings, which were a nightly occurrence at the very least. Danny quickly worked out the meaning of the spoken codes they used to refer to particular types of crime or event. A DIC was a Drunk In Charge, a 'skell' was a known criminal, a 'P skell' was a known political activist, a TDA was a Taking and Driving Away, LKA was Last Known Address, and so on. Within a few days, his notebook was half filled with information and he could translate practically all the car-talk without conscious effort.

On Sunday he had a brief but very welcome visit from Joyce, who could only stay a few hours as she had a dancing lesson in the afternoon. "Listen to this," he said after she had worn him out in bed, and switched on his new receiver.

"Uniform to Romeo Seven," came the familiar voice, "P skell youths with stones and bottles loitering at the corner of Albion Street and New Barnsley. Please investigate. Over."

"Romeo Seven, on our way. We may need back-up. Over."

"Roger Romeo Seven. Uniform to Romeo Two. Can you take this one as well? Over."

The conversation droned on. Joyce was fascinated. "You are clever, Danny. How did you do that?" She hugged him and kissed him fleetingly on the lips.

"Oh, I just came across their channel when I was messing around," he told her casually, holding her a little closer and stroking her silky black hair. There was nothing in the world he wanted more than to earn Joyce's admiration. "Better than The Light Programme, isn't it?"

In the next couple of days, he noticed a few technical anomalies. He was receiving all the cars at exactly the same very high signal strength, which initially made no sense at all. They were also able to talk to one another without the least difficulty. A car sitting in traffic in Belfast's main thoroughfare Royal Avenue, surrounded by high buildings and almost at sea level, was able to talk to a car in a similarly built-up town centre fifteen or twenty miles away and behind high mountains in Carrickfergus, Newtownards or Lisburn, and technically that just didn't seem possible at the wavelength of around four metres that they were using. The signal would be attenuated to zero by the local topography. Even more mysteriously, all the signals came from precisely the same direction. The answer had to be a powerful relay station somewhere high in the mountains above Belfast. He mentally christened it 'Uniform Relay' and set about working out where it could be.

The most obvious place to put it would be on top of Divis, the highest mountain overlooking the city, and the site of the main television transmitting mast. Could it share the same mast as the television stations? No, that would be technically undesirable, he decided, because the receiving equipment would be swamped by the powerful television signals. In fact you would want to site it as far away from the TV mast as possible, while still at a good elevation above the city. He bought himself the relevant sheet of the Ordnance Survey map and pinned this where the street map had been before. He carefully pinned a sheet of transparent polythene on top of it to avoid the sacrilege of writing on a map. Using the north western directional bearing that he had worked out using his home-made dipole aerial, he ruled a felt-tip-pen line on the polythene in the same direction, starting at his own house, and with pleasing precision it crossed the Divis plateau a few miles north of the TV mast. There was nothing marked there on the Ordnance Survey map, but no doubt the authorities would have insisted on that. He sketched a rough circle around the highest point that the line passed through. That had to be it. Uniform Relay. And it had to be big and visible.

The notion that the signals were relayed implied that there were two frequencies in use; the cars, he reasoned, must transmit on one frequency and receive on another. Otherwise the repeater station would block the incoming signal that it was trying to relay. Once he realised this fact everything fell into place. The system they were using was simple and straightforward, indeed almost primitive. A large unmanned relay station in the mountains picked up everything on frequency X and relayed it automatically on frequency Y. Frequency Y was the one Jim had given him. Frequency X, the cars' transmit frequency, he didn't yet know. But in a matter of minutes he had found it. As expected it wasn't very far away from the base station's frequency, and on it he could receive only very nearby cars, their signals mostly weak and broken-up as they passed behind buildings and obstructions, and coming in from every point of the compass. Now his picture was complete. He glowed with satisfaction at having solved the engineering puzzle. Now that he understood his enemy technically, the next step was to find its technical vulnerabilities.

Chapter Nineteen
A Rude Awakening

It was the weekend. Danny rose and had a leisurely soak in the bath before going down to help his mother with the breakfast.

She was standing over the gas cooker. "Morning, Son," she greeted him.

"Let me do that," he said right away, taking the wooden turner from her hand and continuing the task of moving the eggs around on the frying pan.

She sat down heavily at the kitchen table and wiped her hands on her apron. "Are you going out to Bangor today, or is she coming here?"

"No. Joyce has lessons all day today. She's too busy."

"I'd like to meet her. Your da says she's a lovely girl."

"That she is." He carefully lifted the three fried eggs one by one onto the plates containing the buttered toast. "I wish…"

"Yes, Son?"

"Oh, just sometimes I wish that she had a bit more time for me."

"So – what will you be doing today? Making more tapes for that radio station of yours?"

"No. Bernie does most of that now. And Joyce sends him stuff. All I do is the opening and closing announcements and one or two of the dedications. It's really their station now. Joyce and Bernie. I'm just the technician."

"The reason I asked – your da is free for a few hours and I thought it might be nice to get out as a family today. We haven't done anything together for a long time."

Danny didn't reply straight away. He shouted upstairs to his father that breakfast was ready. It gave him a moment to decide if he wanted to agree. As he put the plates down on the table he smiled at her and replied: "Where would you like to go, then?"

"Oh, it doesn't matter. Just out for a drive. You know I can't walk very far."

"What about a wee drive up Divis Mountain then? See the city from up high while there's still a bit of sunshine?"

The car was parked at a giddy angle in the last lay-by where the rough gravel road that ascended Divis Mountain's heather-and-rock strewn upper slopes faded to a rutted track fit only for vehicles with four-wheel-drive. Danny and his parents sat on a wooden bench that had been thoughtfully provided as a viewing point, Danny's new Ordnance Survey map unfolded on his knee. Before and beneath them the city nestled in a multi-coloured crescent around the mouth of the River Lagan, bright and clean-looking, windows glinting in the sun, apart from where a small cloud-shadow was slowly travelling across the panorama from east to west. The whole of Belfast Lough was visible in one glance, the entire scene, including even the Harland and Wolff shipyard with Sampson and Goliath, the mighty yellow cranes on Queen's Island that had helped build the Titanic, reduced to the scale of a child's train-set landscape that you might find on a table top.

Danny's mother looked from the map to the scene before them and then back to the map. "Can you tell where our house is?" she asked.

"Well, using Belfast Castle as a landmark..." he mumbled to himself, studying the map with deep concentration and then transferring his attention to the reality, "No, I think it's going to be too far away. It's one of those ones with the red tile roofs, just to the right of the castle, directly down from that factory with the two chimneys..." He pointed but quickly gave up. "No. I think you would need a telescope or something. It's too far away."

"All those houses," his father muttered, "all those people, all thinking how important they are, and from a few miles away you can't tell one from the other. You can't even see them. That's how important we really are. Like ants on a log in some little field in a swamp in a country that nobody has ever heard of. And did you know that there are more stars in the known universe than grains of sand in all the deserts of the world? I read that in a book by Patrick Moore. That's how important mankind is. We're bacteria living on a dust particle revolving around one grain of sand in one desert in one little corner of creation..."

"Careful, Da. You're getting a bit mystical. If you don't catch it early it could develop into full-blown Religion."

"No, it's okay. I've been vaccinated. Will we get the picnic out?"

"I'm not really hungry yet. I think I'll go for a walk. Would you like to come with me?"

"No, you go ahead. I'll stay with your mother."

His mother handed him the Kodak Instamatic. "Will you take a picture of us before you go, Danny?" she requested. He folded the map and stood up, pushing it carefully into his side-pocket. As he looked through the viewfinder to take the picture he noticed that his mother had taken his father's hand. He had never seen her do that before. And his father was not drawing away. For the first time since he was a very small boy they seemed to be acknowledging some kind of bond of affection.

The shutter clicked and he lowered the camera. They were still holding hands. He slipped his fingers through the wrist strap and with the camera swinging from his hand started up the path towards the plateau, not wanting to intrude.

"This is what it looks like," Danny explained, handing Big Jim two of the photographs he had taken on his walk. "Just a concrete building with a wire fence around it, and that steel lattice tower right beside it. Everything is locked up, and by the look of the locks they aren't used very often. I would guess it just gets a yearly inspection or something like that. There are high voltage cables coming up the side of the mountain to power it…" he handed him another photograph "and we could, of course, do something to put those out of action, but since it's so important I'm pretty sure it would have some kind of back-up power supply. Either storage batteries or a diesel generator. If we just go for the cables it might be back on the air in minutes or even seconds."

"And you say it's too powerful to jam with another transmitter?"

"It might work or it might not. It would depend on how powerful the other transmitter was, and how high up it was." Danny was enjoying the role of lecturer. He could see that he had Big Jim's total attention. "We wouldn't get that absolute certainty that you talked about. But don't worry. I've come up with something else. Something that I think is fool-proof." He paused for effect. "In the couple of weeks that I've been listening, there have been three occasions when the system went down without any help from me. The cause was very simple. There's a lock on the 'transmit' button on each of the microphones in the cars. If the operator accidentally pushes the lock to the 'on' position the unit continues to transmit until they realize what they've done and release the button. During that time – however long or short it is – the whole system is paralyzed. If a second car tries to talk while somebody's button's down all that people hear is a high-pitched whistle called a 'heterodyne'. So even a very low-powered transmitter on the car frequency can lock everything up."

"So is that all we need? A low-power transmitter on the right frequency?"

"Essentially, yes. But there's a snag. What they call 'button down' incidents are fairly common and they have a procedure to deal with them. I can't be absolutely certain but I suspect they use the police helicopter to triangulate and work out where the careless car is. They may have other procedures as well. If we just switch on a transmitter on the car frequency they're going to find it very quickly. Even if it's up a tree somewhere and we're miles away, they won't catch us but they'll find the transmitter and disable it."

Danny let Big Jim know by his smile that this wasn't the end of the trail. "But a couple of mornings ago I woke up with the answer. Here it is." With a flourish Danny produced a small aluminium box about the size of a packet of cigarettes from his jacket pocket. It had a switch on one of its larger faces and four very small telescopic aerials, one on each of its smaller faces, which, when they were extended, gave it the appearance of a spindly cross, or the skeleton of a small kite. The total span of the miniature aerials was about eighteen inches. "That big transmitter pours out a lot of power when it's working. Enough to light a neon tube if you just held it in your hand near the transmitting mast. That power can be harvested and converted back to direct current. And then it can be used to power a small transmitter on the car frequency. Do you get the picture?"

A smile began to spread across Big Jim's face. "The big transmitter powers the little transmitter – and the little transmitter causes the big transmitter to keep on transmitting."

"Exactly. It's a closed positive feedback loop. We put this somewhere near the transmitting mast, and once Uniform comes on, it can't go off again. It's locked in the 'on' condition, and if any of the cars tries to say anything, it comes out as a high-pitched whistle. The beauty of it is, the parasitic transmitter's power is so low it'll be almost undetectable a few hundred metres from the mast. Especially as they won't know it's a physical object they're looking for. It'll look more like a fault in the main receiver at the relay station. If it's concealed right beside the mast, its signal will be swamped by the signal from the main transmitter. The helicopter won't be able to pick it up unless its receiver is fantastically selective. Tracing the fault will be a radio engineer's nightmare. As soon as they switch off the big transmitter, the signal they're looking for disappears with it. As soon as they switch it on again the weaker signal is swamped by the stronger one and their receivers can't separate the two. And there's no battery to run down. In theory it'll go on doing that forever. I think it'll give us a few hours quite easily. I just wish I could see their faces when they find it!"

Big Jim broke into a laugh. "When Northern Ireland gets her freedom there'll be a song about you, Danny!"

Danny noticed that an attempt had been made to get the spray paint off the outside of Mrs Laverty's house. It was still legible but the orange colour was fainter and the letters had become blurred and spread out, as though dissolving in the steady rain that now trickled down the hood of his plastic mac. He knocked as he had done before and waited.

This time Mrs Laverty looked positively terrified and pulled him inside before he had time to say anything. She stared as he unzipped the front of his coat. "I heard something on the police radio…" he began, but was interrupted by a man's voice.

"Keep those hands where I can see them."

Startled, he looked up and realised that he was in a scene that belonged in a Hollywood gangster film. There was a man at the bottom of the stairs aiming a gun at Danny's chest. He froze as Mrs Laverty took the wet coat and hung it in the hallway.

"Take it easy, Liam," she said in a shaky voice, "I'm sure it's not him. This is Wee Hughie's friend, Danny."

The man advanced, keeping the gun level. Danny's attention had been totally fixed on the weapon, the appearance of the man holding it had barely registered, but now that they were pretty much looking into each other's eyes he saw that it was a fit-looking middle-aged man a few inches shorter than himself with an untidy grey beard. He didn't know him. "Frisk him," said the man.

Mrs Laverty felt Danny's pockets and the top part of his jacket. "He hasn't got anything, Liam. He's only a boy. He goes to St. Benedict's."

"I know who he is. Into the front room, Danny. Make us a cup of tea, Sadie."

Without lowering the gun he followed Danny into the small front lounge and indicated for him to sit down. When they were both seated, at last Liam lowered the gun, placing it carefully on the seat beside him. "You said you heard something on the police radio. What was it you heard?"

Danny took a moment to find his voice. When he did it came out at a higher pitch than usual and didn't seem to belong to him at all. "It was in code but it sounded like they were getting ready to drive somebody home from prison."

"That's right. We're expecting him any minute. Sorry if I frightened you with this," he nodded towards the weapon, which was an exact duplicate of the one that had killed Hughie, "we're expecting a hit man as well."

"From one of the Protestant paramilitaries?"

"No. From the IRA."

Danny gave the man a puzzled look. "But that's you, isn't it?"

"And you."

"I'm afraid I don't know what you're talking about. I'm completely lost."

"Don't give me that. I know all about you. You're Jim Harrison's blue-eyed boy. He reckons you're the most useful person in the whole Belfast organisation."

"But I'm not in the Belfast organisation. I'm not in the IRA at all. I'm just… I suppose you would call me a sympathiser. Or just a friend. I help out on the technical side. I'm not a member of anything."

"You help out on the technical side."

"Yes."

"Why?"

"Why?" Danny suddenly realised that this was a question he hadn't thought about at all. Liam picked up his hesitation.

"The crazy thing is, I believe you. I don't think you have any notion why you've got involved. You think this is some kind of game, don't you?" Danny didn't answer. "They ask you to jump, you jump. Don't you realise who these people are? Don't you realise that you're a member now as far as the police or anybody else is concerned, no matter what happens? The IRA doesn't issue membership cards like a trade union you know. Don't you understand that the RUC could lift you off the street and put you in gaol and throw away the key any time they want to?" Danny remained speechless. "Get out, Danny. Stop while you still can. This isn't your fight. You're not even from around here. If you stay in they'll destroy you, like they destroy everybody. Big Jim isn't even the worst of them. There's new young people rising up through the ranks in Dublin who'd shoot their own mothers to get Jim Harrison's job. There's a whole new generation of them coming along that's even worse than the present lot, and that's pretty bad. They'll use you and when they're finished with you, you'll be found floating in the Lagan with a bullet in the back of your head."

There was a long pause that was broken by Mrs Laverty's arrival with a tray of tea and a plate of biscuits. The event was sufficiently comical to break the tension. She put the tray on the small table between them and left.

"Why do you think there's an IRA hit man coming for Connor?" Danny asked, feeling light-headed, not wanting to think about the other things that Liam had said.

"Because they need him to get murdered. He's been great publicity for the movement. His face has been all over the TV and the newspapers, both north and south. If he doesn't get murdered they lose their martyr. That would never do, would it?"

117

Chapter Twenty
More Unpleasant News

Liam's words chilled Danny – gave him that feeling in the pit of his stomach that came before an exam, or when he had been told to report to Father Walsh in his office. It couldn't be true. He refused to allow himself to believe it. "You're bound to feel bitter…" As soon as he had said it he knew it was the wrong word but it was too late to take it back. "I mean about what happened to Wee Hughie. But I think you're wrong about Big Jim. He fought against the Fascists in Spain alongside my dad. He wants to make Northern Ireland better for everybody. Even the Protestants. He's an idealist. He offered Connor a safe house. He told me so…"

"You're the same as everybody else. You see what you want to see. I've been around Jim Harrison and his kind long enough to know the way their minds work. I was like you too, you know. Believed everything the movement told me. Thought we were building some kind of paradise on earth for the Irish people. It's all bollocks, Danny. But believe it if you want to. Not my problem. More fool you."

It suddenly occurred to Danny to wonder who exactly Liam Laverty was on the run from. "Won't they… come after you if you do this? I presume you intend to take Connor away."

"Bet your balls I do. I've got a car out there with his things packed in the boot. Nobody's going to find us where I'm going. Let them try all they want."

There was a pause. Danny picked up a cup and nervously added sugar. It helped his state of mind to have something to do with his hands. "What do you want me to tell Big Jim if he asks me?"

Liam took a moment to reply. He picked up the gun again and began to toy with it. "Better tell him you saw me. He'll find out anyway. Tell him we had a nice polite conversation, and that I took Connor away to a safe house. As far as you're concerned we took him up on his offer after all."

Danny nodded. He tasted his tea. "Maybe it would be best if I left now," he suggested.

"Think about what I said, Danny. It's too late for me, but isn't for you." He motioned towards the door with his gun. Danny put his tea back on the tray and left without another word.

The rain was a bit lighter now but it hadn't stopped entirely. He pulled up the hood of his mac and walked slowly away from the house, confused thoughts buzzing around in his head. Without conscious decision, he made his way to the window of Paddy O'Neill's paper shop. It was as though his body automatically sought the comfort of another, more innocent, life.

There was a display panel now with the heading "Kingston Radio" in big red letters, and alongside it a crude sketch of an aerial mast seemingly radiating lightning bolts, probably drawn by Paddy himself with a felt-tip pen. It had been there for the last couple of weeks, taking advantage of the interest that the radio station had generated and serving as a dedicated display space for the cards from listeners. But now there was a new element. As well as the signed pictures of Joyce that Paddy had placed either side of the heading there was a different black-and-white photograph of Joyce's smiling face accompanying an article cut from the Belfast Telegraph that Paddy had pinned to the board. The headline was "Belfast Hears Pirate Radio Station". Despite his anxious state of mind Danny felt a stab of excitement as he started to read:

For the past several weeks a pirate radio station calling itself "Kingston Radio" has been heard by Belfast residents on Sunday afternoons, broadcasting pop and folk music, and songs composed and sung by this young lady who simply calls herself "Joyce". Listeners are invited to write to Paddy O'Neill's, a newsagents shop on Lansdowne Road, Belfast, enclosing a fee to have their cards displayed in the shop window. The station accepts requests communicated in this way, and for five shillings you can have a signed photograph of the lovely Joyce, pictured here.

The Telegraph's investigative reporter, Will Calvin, managed to get an interview. "I'm almost fifteen," said Joyce, "and I've been playing the guitar and writing songs since I was 11. I want to be an actress or a professional singer when I grow up." Joyce has applied for a place as a boarder at the famous Hammond School in Chester, one of the world's finest theatre schools for children and young people, after which she intends to apply to RADA, the Royal Academy of Dramatic Art in London.

There was more, but at this point Danny stopped reading. Hammond School in Chester? He had never heard of it. Going away to be a boarder? How could she have kept it to herself?

With anger and hurt added to the mixture of emotions that Danny was already feeling, he hurried home and went straight to the telephone.

"Hello. Can I speak to Joyce, please?" His mother stuck her head around the door, but seeing him on the phone went back to the kitchen. "Joyce? I've just seen the Belfast Telegraph article. You didn't tell me you were going to England."

"Oh, don't be silly, Danny. I'm probably not. They get thousands of applications from all over the world. Europe, America, Japan… everywhere. You have to do an audition to get in, and next year will be the first year they take boarders. My chances are less than one in a thousand."

"Don't you be silly. Of course you'll get in. They're not stupid, are they?"

"That's very sweet of you, Danny, but honestly, I've got hardly any chance. It's just a fantasy – a pipe dream. I didn't want to upset you. I'm sorry. I suppose I should have told you, but there are lots of things in my life that I don't talk about. There are probably things in your life that you don't tell me about too." Danny's embarrassed silence proclaimed that she was right. "I've been absolutely honest with you from the beginning. We had a holiday fling like lots of people do. It was so good we both wanted more, and so we've met up a few times since. But I'm not proper girlfriend material. I made that clear. I'm the kind of girl other girls call nasty names. Boys even nastier, probably. That's who I am. Don't build it up into something that isn't real. I'll always have a place for you, but that's all it'll be. A place. Do you understand?"

There was a considerable pause. Danny's world was crumbling. "Anybody who calls you a nasty name will have me to contend with," he said in a hollow voice.

"Even if I do get in – there'll still be the summer holidays."

"Won't you be performing? Touring? Whatever trainee actors and actresses do?"

"I suppose that's possible. You know quite a lot about this, don't you?"

"I'll really miss you," he whispered.

"Honestly, Danny. It's wildly unlikely. But I will go to theatre school one day. I'm quite sure about that. Even if it isn't RADA it'll be somewhere. Don't wait for me. Don't think I'm going to change. Find a regular girlfriend. What you want is what ninety-nine per cent of girls want. I just happen to be that weird one per cent. Your bad luck, I'm afraid."

Danny's mother followed him into the front lounge and watched him switch on the TV set and lower himself into a chair in front of it. She looked at the pained expression on his face.

"You look like you haven't had a very good day." As she said it she sank into a nearby chair and joined him.

"It's been a strange sort of day," he admitted.

As the set heated, the black-and-white picture formed on the screen, rolled for a moment and then settled down and became stable. "…got away with a sum in excess of half a million pounds," the news reader's voice grew in strength along with the picture. "The slow response of the police was due to a technical problem with their mobile radio system, which took more than fourteen hours to put right. One person, an employee of the bank, received a gunshot wound to the hand in the course of the raid. There were no other injuries. A police spokesman said that closed-circuit television foot-

122

age from the scene showed three men wearing Balaclava helmets and carrying weapons, but the chances of identifying them from these pictures was slight. Police are anxious to interview anybody who saw the men entering or leaving the bank, or who were in the vicinity of the Ulster Bank in Royal Avenue between the hours of..." He stood up and turned the sound down.

"What about you, Ma? What kind of day have you had?"

Her reply barely registered. Danny was thinking about his invention, the parasitic transponder. More than fourteen hours! Pretty goddamn impressive! And half a million pounds. That must be some kind of record. But a gunshot wound to somebody's hand. Why did they need to use guns? They weren't in any danger. There was no realistic way the police could have been alerted. It was unnecessary. It shouldn't have happened. It put a damper on his pleasure at the successful operation. This should have been a crime against property, a political crime, not an excuse for violence against people. He imagined a shattered human hand and began to feel ill. That's the trouble, he thought to himself. You plan something to perfection, get all the engineering details just right, and then human beings come along and screw it up. Why do people always have to screw everything up?

Chapter Twenty-one
Partings & Police Raids

Danny woke up very early, even though it was Sunday and he didn't have to go to school. He didn't seem to be sleeping as well as he used to. Anxiety about the robbery? Sadness about the possibility of losing Joyce? Perhaps. Or perhaps it was just something to do with joining the adult world. Danny had never been very good at making a distinction between what was serious and what was only pretend. The bank robbery hadn't seemed real until he heard the newscast about the gun-play. Bernie had since told him that the injured bank clerk had been a girl. That somehow made it worse. Robbing a bank had been little different to passing 'Go' in Monopoly and collecting two hundred pounds. "Go directly to Gaol – do not pass Go, do not collect two hundred pounds." Maybe that was exactly what the future held for him.

The thought of two hundred pounds reminded him that he had quite a lot of money left over from what Big Jim had given him. He could buy Joyce something really nice for her birthday. It would relieve some of his misgivings if he didn't spend it on himself. What would she like? Something that she could take to Chester with her. Something she would look at or use every day. He wondered about a really good guitar. He knew that the one she played had been a present from her father when she was eleven. You don't buy a really good guitar for an eleven-year-old. How much would one cost? How would he know it was a really good one he was getting? He remembered the violin that Mrs Whittaker had left to his dad. Worth a fortune, he had said. That was what Joyce deserved. The best guitar in the whole world. Bernie would know. He knew about music.

He had a quick shower standing up in the bath and plodded down to the kitchen. There was nobody about. He saw that Bernie had pushed the packet containing the day's Kingston Radio tape through the letter box. He picked it up and returned to his bedroom to listen to it. Each new tape was still a thrill, containing as it usually did a new song or two from Joyce. This one was no exception. She introduced it herself, in her clear, perfectly modulated voice: "I think this is the first love song I've ever written. Or at least the nearest that I've ever come to writing one. It's for someone I know who needs reassurance."

The guitar intro was as flawless and captivating as ever. If she could do that on a cheap guitar, what could she do on the best guitar in the world? She began to sing. It was a slow ballad:

Thank you for the moments when you walked a while with me
Full of joy and understanding when we gave our love for free
And you never tried to make me what I didn't want to be.

In a world that's ever circling round a slowly dying sun
The past alone is constant and can never be undone.
Every living person changes every moment of the day
But the past is always present, it can never go away
And we'll always be together now, no matter where we stray.

All the people who have held me help to make me who I am
I remember every gentle touch, the passion and the calm.
We'll always have these moments that we've shared so tenderly
Though we may be separated by a mountain or a sea
We're a part of one another now – for all eternity.

Ever growing, ever learning, ever striving to be free
To create the man and woman that will soon be you and me.
There's a world beyond that's waiting, we're too young to settle down
It's our time to find our bearings, test the water, look around
But there's nothing that can take away the friendship that we've found.

There's no clause of limitation on the love I share with you
It will always be there waiting, ever eager, ever new.
The deepest love we'll ever find is love without demands
That doesn't ask for promises or bind with wedding bands
That can celebrate the freedom that the other one commands.

Love that asks for nothing but is given like a song
Love that doesn't wonder if it's right or if it's wrong
Love that doesn't stifle, doesn't limit, doesn't scold
Doesn't ask for grim assurances or suddenly run cold
Love that never judges, and resentment will not hold

Thank you for the moments when you walked a while with me
Full of joy and understanding when we gave our love for free
And you never tried to make me what I didn't want to be.
No you never tried to make me what I didn't want to be.

Through tearful eyes, Danny found the stop button and pressed it. What did the song mean? He wiped his eyes.

Well, he decided, she had definitely acknowledged that she was going to get into the Hammond School. It was all about parting, going our separate ways. But there was also that line about no clause of limitation on their love. No expiry date. Maybe she was saying that what they had was outside the usual pattern where you have a boyfriend or a girlfriend, then you start a new relationship with somebody else and split up, or the other person is unfaithful and you have a big row... Maybe this was something new. Without rules, without expectations. And without a time limit. Maybe they could go on being lovers every time they met for the rest of their lives, and do whatever they liked with whoever they liked in between? When you really came to think about it , it wasn't such a bad deal. Was that what she meant? He played the song again.

Yes, it couldn't be interpreted in any other way. Lovers forever but not exclusive lovers. That's what she was saying. Suddenly Danny didn't feel so bad anymore. It maybe wasn't exactly what he wanted – or what he assumed he must want because it was what everybody else wanted – but when you really thought about it, where was the down side? Without knowing why, Danny cried. He was glad that there was nobody there to see him. Afterwards he felt better, and as he made his way back to the kitchen for breakfast he was whistling the melody of *The Times They Are a-Changing*.

Danny followed his usual routine of switching on the transmitter, starting the tape, and then setting off with his transistor portable to listen to the show as he walked down to Paddy O'Neill's to pick up the new batch of postcards for the following week. Now that Bernie was preparing each tape solo, his input to the station had become very small, but the truth was that the technical management of the operation was what most appealed to him.

The afternoon was chilly and there were few people on the street. Most of the businesses were closed for Sunday and he could smell the smoke from a bonfire where somebody was burning rubbish in their back yard. A cat strolled by his side, making its tour of the little piles of bagged-up litter at the door of each shuttered shop.

As he approached Paddy O'Neill's he could tell instantly that something had changed. The centre display board in the front window, where the red heading and the two photographs of Joyce had recently been pinned, was now cleared and bare, as though Kingston Radio had never existed.

Danny switched off the transistor radio and slipped it into the shopping bag that he had taken with him for the cards. The bell above the door pinged as he entered the shop. He was the only customer. After a moment's delay Paddy emerged from the inner depths looking pale and angry. "I thought you told me what I was doing for you was legal," he snapped at Danny, who opened his mouth to speak but could think of nothing to say. "I had the fuckin' RUC around here last night. They wanted to know all about you and your goddamn radio station. They took away the cards and the photographs – everything. What in God's name have you been up to? You told me pirate radio wasn't a police matter. You said it was the Post Office that came after radio pirates. What the fuck exactly have you got me into?" Danny could think of no quick answer. He opened and shut his mouth like a fish out of water. "I was a fuckin' fool to listen to you. Come on, tell me. What's it all about?"

"I think…" said Danny at last, "that it might have something to do with that bank robbery last week. You remember the police radio went wrong? Maybe they think I had something to do with it because I've got the radio station…"

Paddy waited for further explanation. "So – why would they think that? Did you have something to do with it?"

"No, of course not. It'll be because I built a transmitter. Because I know about radio. They probably think I jammed the police radio signal... Did you tell them anything about me?"

"I'm no grass. Not that I know anything about you anyway. I don't even know your fuckin' second name, and I don't want to. I gave them a description – several descriptions, in fact – of school-boys nothing like you. I said it was a different schoolboy that comes in every week to pick up the cards and leave the photos. I said they all had the same school uniform and they all looked the same to me."

"Thanks. I really appreciate that."

"And so you fucking well should. Now get out of my shop and never come through that door again as long as you live."

Genuine fear was a new emotion to Danny. This wasn't the same as being called to Father Walsh's office. This was something complete-ly different. His own breathing seemed deafening. He arrived at Bernie's door with a dry throat and a floating sensation in his head, as though his body belonged to someone else. Bernie was smiling when he came to the door, but the smile soon vanished.

"I've got to see Jim Harrison." Danny whispered. "Now. Straight away."

"It's okay, Danny." Jim assured him, placing a paternal hand on his shoulder, "I know how scary it is the first time it happens. Sit down there and let me talk to you." They seemed to be in a modern hotel room this time. It smelled of air-freshener, the walls were painted a faint lilac and all the furniture and fittings were spotless but totally impersonal. There was a dim watercolour landscape over the mantel-piece and a coffee table with a vase of flowers. Jim went to a minibar and produced a bottle and two glasses. "I know you don't drink but this might be a good time for a little medicinal whiskey."

"No. Sorry. I'd rather not."

"As you like." Jim poured one for himself and sat down opposite his guest.

"We had a contact inside the RUC for a while, but not anymore. It's one hundred per cent Protestant, right down to the cleaners and the cooks. Very hard to penetrate. But I've studied their little ways and I can give you an educated guess as to what's going on. Are you sure you wouldn't like a sip of whiskey? You look like you could use one." Danny shook his head. "They haven't really got anything on you. Or if they have, they've come under political pressure to soft pedal. If they were going to lift you they would have done it straight away. My guess is, you won't hear another word about it. You see, every move is made on the basis of how it's going to play out in the media. That's the modern world. The game we all play. Now it probably hasn't escaped your attention that the position of IRA teenage hero is currently vacant." The thought sent a shiver down Danny's spine. "The last thing they want to do is hand us another propaganda victory. Can you imagine what the press would make of it? 'RUC Outsmarted by a Clever Teenager.' They look like fools already, they don't want to look like even bigger fools. That's probably what's really behind it. If they do suspect it was you they just want to give you a scare. Anything more and they're playing straight into our hands. More likely though, they have no idea who it was, but there's been an article in the Belfast Telegraph about a pirate radio station so there just might be a connection. They're fishing around. I would do exactly the same in their position." He took a leisurely sip and savoured it before swallowing.

"Now here's what you need to do. First of all, there's a chance – even if it's a remote one – that they'll search your home. Your radio station isn't of any interest to them. There's no need to hide it or to stop broadcasting."

"Really? I was going to tie a few bricks to the transmitter and throw it in the Lagan."

"No, no. Don't do that. If you don't want it we'll have it. Is Bernie able to operate it?"

"Yes, I think so, or if he isn't he could soon learn. Why do you ask?"

"It's an idea I've had at the back of my head for a while. You've heard of this new Civil Rights movement at Queens University?" Danny shook his head. "It's a peaceful movement aimed at righting a lot of political wrongs in Northern Ireland. Nothing to do with the Republican movement, but we're watching it closely. I thought it might be a nice gesture if we offered to set them up with a radio station. We would keep overall control, of course, but they could do the broadcasts. Like you and Bernie. We can't call it an IRA station because if we did the authorities would have to act. But call it a Civil Rights station and you've got the moral high ground in most people's estimation. The day may well come when the Republican movement needs a local radio station, and when it does we'll be all set up and ready."

"If you want it it's yours. I'd be too scared ever to switch it on again. You can have the police radio receiver as well. If they find that in my bedroom I'm probably sunk too."

"There are things you need to hide or get rid of, but not the medium wave stuff. If you have any sketches or circuit diagrams of that thing you built, any maps with the position of Uniform Relay marked, any logs of police radio activity – anything that links you to the bank business, destroy it. They already know you have the Kingston Radio stuff. All the boys at your school know about it, anybody who wants to can find that out, but they have nothing to link you to that police jammer. You did wipe it for fingerprints like I told you to?"

"Yes, with surgical spirit, very thoroughly."

"Then there's no way you can ever be linked to it. Only if somebody informs. And people know that that isn't good for their health. Relax, Danny. It's all right. You've done a great job. In fact…" He stood up and went to take something from a drawer at the back of the room. "I've had a word with Dublin. We've put you on the payroll. It's a special account, you'll need to write down the details."

"The payroll? I don't understand."

"Thanks in no small measure to your good self, the movement is now able to look after the living expenses of a few more of its friends. There aren't any strings attached. You just carry on, keeping your eyes and ears open and maybe doing us the occasional little favour. But in recognition of your contribution, the movement pays you something towards your living expenses. Currently £25 a week. That's about thirteen hundred a year."

Danny drew in a sharp breath. "I think that's more than some of my teachers earn."

"We've got to have some little perks for putting our freedom and sometimes even our lives on the line." He handed Danny a Bank of Ireland savings account book, which Danny opened and avidly examined. "I've back-dated it to the day of our first conversation." Big Jim smiled broadly and held out his hand. After a few moments' hesitation Danny took it. "Comrade Danny Gallagher, welcome to the Irish Republican Army."

Chapter Twenty-two
The Martin Guitar

Danny knocked on Bernie's door across the road and his mother answered. "Good morning, Mrs O'Shea. Are Bernie and Joyce in?"

"Hello, Danny. They're up in Bernie's room recording a song or something. I'll give them a call." She turned around. "Bernie! Danny's here!"

Listening harder, Danny could make out the sound of Joyce's guitar. The music stopped and they came down hand-in hand, Bernie carrying their two overcoats over his free arm. There was something very intimate about the scene that made Danny start, but he was careful not to let his reaction show. She released Bernie's hand and gave Danny a hug and a kiss full on the lips. Everything was fine now. He stroked her hair. "Hello, sweetheart. Still making tapes? There won't be any more radio programmes, you know."

"I know. Bernie's making a demo tape for me. Something I could use to get gigs. Maybe even send it to a record company. He says it's what everybody does."

"That's good of you, Bernie." Danny's voice sounded a bit hollow.

"Got to have a demo tape," Bernie assured him. "Can't do anything without a demo. Are you ready then?"

Danny gave her one final hug and released her. "All ready." He waited while the two of them put on their coats. Then Joyce took both their hands, which Danny found faintly worrying, and walking in the middle, led the two of them briskly down the road. "I'm really excited about this. You're ever so good to me, Danny." He let go of her hand and put his arm loosely around her waist instead, hoping that this signified a greater intimacy.

Black Flag Music was a surprisingly large but somewhat dark and drab shop that fronted on to a minor street off Winetavern Row. The two big windows were crowded with every kind of musical instrument – violins, drums, trumpets, saxophones, brass and wind instruments of every shape and size, accordions, a solitary set of bagpipes, and better represented than anything else, acoustic and electric guitars. The centrepiece of one window was a baby grand piano, of the other, a full-size DJ mixer desk with twin turntables. There were music stands, microphones, speakers and PA amplifiers tastefully integrated into the arrangement, and the background consisted mainly of tall shelf units loaded with sheet music. Posters of Elvis Presley, Ray Davies, Bob Dylan, Billy Fury, Manfred Mann, Dusty Springfield and Cliff Richard adorned the side walls, interspersed, no doubt for balance, with portraits of the eternal greats like Beethoven and Mozart. Joyce peered in like a child at the window of a sweet shop.

"This is definitely it," Danny said, unnecessarily. As they entered, the bell over the door pinged like the one in Paddy O'Neill's paper shop. The under-lit interior smelled faintly of furniture polish.

A tall thin man in Bermuda shorts and a non-matching floral-patterned shirt, with unkempt shoulder-length brown hair and a small beard, strolled slowly down behind the counter to meet them. Danny noticed that his eyes locked on Joyce and they exchanged a smile.

"Mornin' young lady. Young gents. What can I do for ye'all?" He had a strong overlay of American on top of his standard Belfast accent. It sounded cool. Danny was envious.

"Joyce has a birthday coming up and I want to buy her a really good guitar. I wanted it to be a surprise but Bernie here says you can't buy a guitar for somebody else – it's like buying shoes for somebody else. They have to try it for themselves."

"Bernie is right." Joyce and the man smiled at one another again. "Now, what kind of guitar are we talking here? Acoustic, electric, acoustic with built-in pickup, classical…?"

"I play contemporary folk, mostly slow ballads."

"Sounds good. Okay. Are we talking genuine top-of-the-range professional standard here, or just pretty good?"

"We want the real deal," Danny said.

"In that case, it has to be the Martin D28." He walked a bit towards the rear of the shop and produced a black guitar case, which he reverentially laid on the counter. His hand hovered above the clasp. "Now I'll tell you from the outset, I can't offer a discount on the D28, but I can show you other instruments that are very nearly as good and a lot cheaper."

"We're not looking for a cheap guitar," Danny said quietly, feeling very grown-up as he did so, "we're looking for a great guitar."

"Good. We understand each other." The man opened the case and lifted out the instrument like a priest performing a religious rite. Danny wouldn't have been able to tell it apart from any other guitar, but Joyce and Bernie drew closer and stared at it with fascination.

"Solid Sitka spruce top, Brazilian rosewood back and sides." The man turned it over to show the reddish body. "Genuine ebony fingerboard and bridge, build standard that has never been equalled by any other manufacturer. No other guitar has ever sounded like it either, right through the range, top notes to bottom notes. This is the one you judge other acoustic guitars by. It's played by Bob Dylan, Elvis Presley and Joan Baez, to name just three. It comes with a lifetime warranty. And you can expect it to last a lifetime if you look after it properly. This is the last guitar you'll ever need to buy, even if you get to Carnegie Hall." He handed it across to Joyce. "Give it a try."

She put the strap over her neck and checked the tuning. It was perfect. Next she tried a few chords, followed by increasingly complex melodies that she picked out effortlessly and flawlessly. Even Danny could tell that it sounded a lot better than her old one. Eventually she stopped and smiled at the shop assistant, who was visibly in awe. "That's the best guitar I've ever seen or heard. It's fantastic."

"May I ask you how old you are, Miss?"

"I'll be fifteen on Friday."

"Fifteen. I'm thirty-six, and I've been playing for the best part of twenty years, earning my living as a session musician for a lot of that time… and you're better than me."

Joyce was obviously delighted. "I've had a few lessons."

"You shouldn't be having lessons, you should be giving them." He seemed to regain his composure and returned to the immediate business. "I think you should play it a bit more to make sure it's comfortable. It's a full-bodied instrument and you're quite small. You may find that you're having to reach for the frets, know what I mean?"

"It's perfect, I wouldn't want to change anything about it, but it would be nice to play a bit more."

"Hang on a second – I'll get my old Gibson Dove and keep you company." He hurried off to the back of the shop and returned with a guitar which, apart from being somewhat battered and faded, and having a picture of a dove on the fingerboard inlay, didn't look that much different to the Martin. He sat on a high stool behind the counter and propped it carefully on his knee. As they jammed together they broke into song occasionally, sometimes individually, sometimes in a duet, and laughed when they couldn't remember the words or got something slightly wrong. They started with Phil Ochs' *Too Many Martyrs*, moved on to Leadbelly's *Where Did You Sleep Last Night?*, Tom Paxton's *The Last Thing on my Mind* and ended off with the outlandish guitar gymnastics of The Animals' *House of the Rising Sun*. All through the impromptu performance they maintained eye contact. To the layman, which was what Danny was, it seemed as though the pair had been making music together for years.

He beckoned Bernie to the front of the shop and spoke to him quietly. "She's doing it again. Flirting. She does it all the time. She's got that man in the palm of her hand – already."

Bernie looked embarrassed. "Yes… I've been meaning to talk to you about that. You see… we've been doing these recording sessions together…"

"It's okay. I guessed it. You don't have to say any more."

"I didn't… you know, lead her on…"

"Neither did I. What line did she give you? 'I like you, you're funny'?"

"No, she just sort of… started to unbutton my trousers."

"It's okay. I know what she's like. I just have to accept it, there's no alternative. We're pretty lucky really, aren't we? I mean to have a girl like that around?"

He nodded. "I think it's some kind of new hippy idea. In a few years probably all the girls will be like her."

Danny looked unconvinced. "You think so?"

He shrugged. "Maybe. We're still okay, then, aren't we? I mean, you and me. You aren't mad at me?"

"No, what's the use? If a girl unbuttons a boy's trousers it would be bad manners not to give her what she wants. And you know, when you come to think about it, what she's giving us isn't a scarce resource. It doesn't run out or anything. She's got loads to go round."

"Certainly seems that way."

"We're sort of blood brothers now, aren't we?"

"There was no blood involved."

"I'm speaking figuratively. I mean we're joined... sort of related now."

Bernie considered the notion. "Yes, I suppose so. Sort of related."

Danny held out his hand and Bernie took it. "Make love, not war. That's what the hippies say."

"Definitely a better way to spend your time." They smiled sheepishly at one another.

The two musicians had stopped playing now and were chatting. Danny and Bernie returned to hear the conversation. "Did you hear that, Danny?" Joyce asked him as he approached.

"No. Bernie and I were talking."

"Mo here has a gig on my birthday in a folk club on Meadow Street. He wants me to do a few numbers with him. I know I said I'd spend the day with you, but we could meet as soon as I can get over after school and we'd have time to go to bed, get some food, and then get to Mo's club for nine o'clock. You could come and listen."

The proposition was greeted with a shocked silence from Danny and Bernie. It was the 'time to go to bed' reference that had silenced them. Joyce had said it without a thought, the most natural thing in the world. Mo took it in his stride. "I guess school's pretty tiring," he said without changing his expression.

"Oh, yes, that's what I meant." She giggled.

Danny had recovered sufficiently to respond. "Joyce lives in Bangor. That's a long way to go home afterwards."

"No problem," Mo assured him. "I've got a car. I'll drop her off home afterwards."

Danny and Bernie looked at each other helplessly. Joyce's birthday evening was clearly fully mapped-out. "I hope you both have a great time," said Danny. "I'm sure you will." There could be little doubt about the outcome of Mo driving her home unaccompanied in his car. He took the wallet from his pocket and opened it to reveal a bulging wad of twenty-pound-notes.

Joyce seemed astounded. "Where did you get that kind of money?" she breathed.

Danny shrugged. "Oh, it wasn't any trouble. Just sold my soul, that's all."

She put the guitar gently back on the counter and put her arms around Danny's neck. "You did well to find a buyer."

She stretched up and kissed him enthusiastically and Danny found that all his misgivings had melted away. "Yeah. That's what I thought."

Joyce had put on a black dress with a low square-cut neckline for the occasion and wore a black CND medallion on a silver chain around her neck and a white Alice band to hold back her shining jet-black hair. She looked absolutely stunning, a teenage Joan Baez, and Danny knew that he wasn't the only one who thought so. There were wolf whistles and muted obscenities as she walked up to the platform.

"This is the young lady I told you folks about." Mo said, exaggerating his Southern States American drawl, "Her name's Joyce MacPherson and you'd best mind your tongues 'cause she's only just fifteen years old today. She's got a better voice than me, a better guitar, she plays it better, and she's not far off better lookin'."

This got a hearty laugh. She settled herself on the chair beside him and rested the guitar carefully on her knee. Danny had never seen her perform publicly before and watched with fascination. She was the very picture of confidence and composure.

"We'd like to do a song called *Dirty Old Town*, by Ewan Mac-Coll," Mo continued, "written about Salford in Lancashire, but it could easily have been Belfast. I say we'd like to do it because we've never sung it together before and I don't know what'll happen when we try. And, ladies and gentlemen, we will be performing entirely without a safety net." He gestured to Joyce and she did the guitar intro by herself. As Danny fully expected, it was perfect. Mo started to play as he came in to sing the first verse. They harmonised on the bridge and choruses and alternated solo voices for the verses. If it had been rehearsed for weeks, the performance could not have been more polished. The applause was deafening. As it died down, Danny heard a few people shout out: "Hey! You're Joyce off Kingston Radio! I know you!" "Hey! Joyce! Sing *My Lagan Love*!" "Give us *The Orange Maid of Sligo*!" "Sing that dirty one about the wee girl that wants to sleep with everybody!"

This last remark clearly upset Joyce. Unwisely perhaps, she tried to address the underlying attitude from which it sprang. "That's not what the song's about. It's about how people try to own one another and see sex as bad and hatred and violence as good. About jealousy and possessiveness... how we go along with rules that make people unhappy..."

"Yer' just a wee whore!"

At this Danny stood up. His face was red and he stared at the heckler. The room went silent. "I think you'd better take that back," Danny said beneath his breath. The man was in his twenties, big, unshaven and had the half closed eyes of a drunk.

Danny had no idea what he meant by the threat, but if he had possessed the physical ability he would not have shrunk from murder. To his relief several other men, older and tougher than himself, stood up also and advanced on the seated figure. One of them lifted him from his seat by the scruff of the neck and held his face two inches from his own. "You were just about to leave, matey, weren't you?" Still holding him by the shirt collar he turned the heckler around and frog-marched him to the door at the rear, propelling him into the street before the barman could get to him. With the door closed and the barman hovering ineffectually beside it, all the men who had stood up made their way calmly back to their seats and sat down. Only then did Danny look back at the platform. Joyce was as serene and composed as ever.

"Oh well," she said calmly, "I don't think he was enjoying the music anyway, and it's probably past his bedtime. I'll be happy to sing *My Lagan Love* for whoever it was who requested it."

And she did, impeccably.

"I had a really fantastic time tonight." She stretched up to kiss Mo on the cheek.

He took one hand off the steering wheel and tenderly stroked her back. "Me too. It was a privilege to share the session with you. One of the nicest things that's happened in my whole life."

"That's a sweet thing to say." She cuddled up to him as close as she could without interfering with his driving. "It's a beautiful night. Why don't you park up for a while. We don't have to go home straight away, you know."

He found a convenient spot slightly off the road and pulled over, switching off the engine and the lights. With the lights off they could just make out the silhouette of the Craigavad hills dotted with the lights of a few farmhouses, but more importantly, without the glare of the headlights to drown them out, a dazzling expanse of pin-sharp pastel-coloured stars appeared in the sky above them. She took Mo's hand and hugged it to her breast. He turned to look her in the eye and she gave him a heart-stopping smile. "Are you trying to seduce me?" he inquired politely.

"That's right. How am I doing?"

"Pretty well."

She took his face in her two hands and kissed him tenderly on the lips. He returned the kiss with growing enthusiasm. "You're not a closet Catholic or something, are you? I'm not sending you to hell or anything?"

"No Ma'am. My family is Jewish."

"Really? How did you end up in Ireland?"

He stroked her face as he spoke, letting his hands slip down from time to time to trace the delicate line of her shoulders. "We left The Netherlands before the Germans arrived. My grandfather was a very wise man. He got us out of there just before the war began. It was one of the first countries the Germans occupied. We lost six members of our family to the gas chambers, People who failed to see what was coming. But not my grandfather. He got us all out in time, and he picked this place."

"Why here?"

"He was the only man ever to come to Belfast to get away from religious persecution. His reasoning was that every society needs some group to hate, so you should go where the hate pattern is already well established. Anywhere that doesn't have a clear group to hate always chooses the Jews by default. He reckoned that's why we're called the 'chosen people'."

She giggled. "I know it's not something to laugh about, but it is funny."

"My people have learned to laugh about everything. Life, death, God, sex, politics, human stupidity, Auschwitz. If you don't laugh at it all you might go mad."

"Well, you've just been chosen again." She started unbuttoning his jacket. "Do these seats go back?"

Chapter Twenty-three
Meeting Sheelagh

Danny eyed the steel skeleton of the part-built Divis Tower enviously. When that was finished they would hopefully have a location for their aerial some two hundred feet above the heart of Catholic West Belfast, higher than any building for miles, but for the moment he would have to be satisfied with the roof of the block he was in, rising to about a third of that height. It was still a magnificent aerial site, and the signal over most of the city was rivalling the BBC Home Service, but the engineer within him longed to take the project on to its next technical milestone.

He moved away from the big French window that led to the balcony and looked instead through the adjacent one that gave him a free view of the road below. The scene resembled a helicopter news shot of a crowd gathering for a political march. Beneath the spider web of telephone lines and trollybus cables that were strung out along Divis Street, overflowing into Ardmoulin Street, Finn Square and all the other minor roads that ran off the main stretch, the static procession seemed to pulsate with barely contained energy. Flags and banners fluttered in the breeze and loudspeakers barked messages that were rendered distant and incoherent by the double glazing. The assembly was a mighty beast crouching down, awaiting the signal that would make it leap into action.

He turned from the window and gave his attention once again to the people around the table. Bernie, engrossed in adjusting the mixer panel ready for the opening music and announcements, wasn't interacting with any of the others, but the grey-haired Nationalist MP and his teenage daughter were talking earnestly, and the two young members of the Civil Rights Committee, typical male jean-and-T shirt Queens University students, were listening attentively and occasionally joining in. All appeared engrossed, and, Danny thought, unfriendly. From the moment that he had arrived and started assembling the electronic gear, both he and Bernie had been subtly excluded. Nobody had been overtly rude to them but nobody had initiated any conversations with them either, or done anything to imply that they were comrades engaged in a common enterprise. There was what Danny's mother would have called "an atmosphere", and Danny didn't know why.

The lounge area was small and overcrowded and Danny felt the need for fresh air. He opened the French window and wandered on to the balcony. "Shut the window behind you," Bernie shouted over to him. "The microphones are picking up the street noise." Danny did as he was instructed.

Leaning over the railings he could see the full length of Divis Street and the huge black-and-white banner at the head of the march bearing the stark phrase: "Civil Rights". People were still joining from the side streets and lining the pavements either side, behind temporary barriers that consisted of fabric tape hung between wooden poles on portable bases. Bored RUC men stood by at intervals, watching for any sign of trouble.

He looked at his watch. Less than five minutes to go. A lot of the marchers, he knew, would be carrying transistor radios for the express purpose of listening to the first official broadcast of the radio station he and Bernie had spent the morning setting up. it would broadcast as Radio Free Belfast, the voice of the Queens University Civil Rights Committee, a society within the student body with ambitions (and many would say potential) to grow into a fully-fledged mass movement for peaceful reform. Danny was pleased at the way things had developed. He could think of no finer role for his cherished transmitter than to become the voice of a peaceful Civil Rights organisation whose declared aim was to end religious discrimination, electoral malpractices and other injustices built into the social structure of Northern Ireland. For once he felt himself unambiguously on the side of the angels. Yet the angels in the immediate vicinity seemed distinctly reserved.

He produced his own battered transistor radio from the large pocket of his coat and switched it on. Although he had taken the precaution of wrapping cooking foil around the internal ferrite rod aerial, at this range there was mild distortion due to overload, but he could tell from experience that the harp music he was receiving was in fact perfectly 'clean'. He sat on one of the two metal chairs on the balcony, feeling the chill of the cold steel through his shirt, and settled down to listen to the new station's opening announcement.

Like ants down there, he thought to himself, running his eyes over the crowd. He vaguely remembered a biology lesson where they had talked about the theory that individual ants were pretty dumb but the colony as a whole behaved intelligently and could perform such tasks as planning for the future, waging war, exploiting other creatures and taking evasive action when threatened. With human beings, it occurred to him, the exact opposite was the case. Individuals acted intelligently, mass assemblies became mindless.

The harp music faded down, and through the window he saw Bernie raise and then slowly lower his arm. It was the MP's teenage daughter who spoke. He hadn't realised that she was to have the honour, such as it was, of being the first person to speak on Radio Free Belfast. He could see, though, that it was appropriate. It was her generation, which was also his, that would be the real beneficiaries of political reform in Northern Ireland.

Her voice was clear and confident. "This is Radio Free Belfast, the voice of the disenfranchised and exploited people of Northern Ireland, coming to you for the first time on two-hundred-and-two metres, medium wave. This radio station exists to keep the people of Belfast and of the whole world informed about the true situation regarding the oppression of the minority community in this city and this nation. Radio Free Belfast is a non-sectarian radio station free of any form of censorship or state, political or corporate control. The opinions you will hear expressed on Radio Free Belfast will be those of the people expressing them or of the organisations for which they speak. No editorial control of any kind will be exercised by the station itself. This is something new in the history of mass media. This is people's radio. We are committed to providing a voice for all the people of Northern Ireland, particularly the weak and marginalised, whose voice is never heard on any other radio station. Today, freedom of speech has finally reached Northern Ireland. Use it well."

It was stirring stuff. Danny allowed himself a moment of pride.

As she finished, the harp music swelled again, and Danny saw the girl's father pat her on the back. She rose from her chair, as did Bernie, and they exchanged a few words. Then one of the two university types took Bernie's place and donned the headphones. Danny knew what this meant. Control of Radio Free Belfast, at least for the moment, had been handed over to the Civil Rights Committee of Queens University.

Bernie approached the French window accompanied by the girl. This was the first small act of friendship that Danny had witnessed that morning. He opened the window to let them come through.

"That was great," he told the girl, taking her hand, "you're a real pro." She nodded but seemed to withdraw her hand rather abruptly.

"This is Sheelagh," Bernie introduced her. "Her da is the Nationalist MP for West Belfast."

"Yeah. I know. My name's Danny, by the way." It occurred to him that as he had spent the entire morning in the flat he might have expected people to know this, but he didn't say anything.

She picked up the implied criticism. "I'm sorry. We're not used to having people from... your organisation around."

Sheelagh was much the same age as himself and wore a loose v-neck red jumper over what looked like a white school blouse. Her hair was blonde, he suspected dyed, since her eyebrows were a much darker brown, and he had to concede that she was quite pretty when she smiled.

"Well don't be shy. We're all on the same side, aren't we?"

"My dad's party is against violence," she said hesitantly.

"Against violence? Well, of course, isn't everybody?"

She seemed to find his answer puzzling. "But... you're from the IRA," she reminded him, clearly embarrassed at having to mention it.

"So what? The border campaign was years ago. We're not engaged in any military activity now. Anyway, I'm just a technician. A back-room-boy. I wouldn't know one end of a gun from the other."

She was silent for a few seconds. "That's just accidental. If there was a new campaign the IRA wouldn't hesitate to use the gun. It's an army, for Christ's sake."

Danny was more sympathetic to her sentiments than he dared to reveal, but he knew the stock answers. "The RUC have guns. The Protestant paramilitaries have guns. Can you imagine what it would be like if all the guns were on the Protestant side? The IRA carries guns for the protection of the Catholic people of Northern Ireland. Not for any other reason."

"You sound like Jim Harrison."

"Jim Harrison is a good man. Have you met him?"

"Jesus no. Have you?"

Danny hesitated. "I'm sorry, I can't answer that question."

"That's not a very friendly attitude."

"It's nothing to do with friendliness. We can't talk about the organisation or who we know or who we don't know. I have to trust you not to talk about meeting Bernie or me either. Surely you can see why?"

"Yes, I suppose so. You're all boys playing games. That side of things doesn't interest me at all."

"It doesn't interest me either. But there are good reasons for it. And there are genuine injustices out there, genuine issues. I don't think that the English have a right to be in Ireland or to rule any part of it, any more than you do. The cause is just. Your da is a Nationalist. His party stands for exactly the same thing."

"Nationalists believe in the ballot box. Peaceful development towards a political settlement that'll give us a united Ireland. Not bloody revolution – or a communist dictatorship."

Danny shook his head. "You've got so many prejudices. So many wrong ideas…"

"Maybe we should stay clear of politics," Bernie suggested with a genial smile.

Danny smiled too. "I'd like to talk to you properly, though. Get to know you a bit."

"Are you asking me out?"

"Time I left, I think," Bernie suggested, edging towards the French window.

"No," said Sheelagh with considerable firmness, "time *I* left." She opened the window and went back inside, followed by Danny, who wanted to continue the conversation but noticed that the new technician in Bernie's chair was signalling that the microphone was about to become live. He closed the French window quietly.

Sheelagh's father started to speak. "Assembling in Divis Street at this moment is the biggest peaceful non-sectarian march that has ever taken place in Northern Ireland. Our single banner bears the words: 'Civil Rights', a cause that unites every progressive party, trade union, student body, church body and fair-minded individual in this city. As I speak to you, those carrying the banner at the head of the march are starting to move off in the direction of the Falls Road, and behind them in orderly rows more than five thousand people are..."

His speech was interrupted by what sounded like two loud backfires from a nearby motor vehicle. He stopped speaking and there was dead silence in the room. The technician signalled that the microphone was no longer live. "What in God's name was that?" the middle-aged politician asked in a hushed tone.

Chapter Twenty-four
The Guardian Angel

The total silence of the little room was broken by Bernie flinging open the French window and shouting: "Somebody's been shot down there!"

Sheelagh's father signalled for the technician to make the microphone live again and remained at his seat, silent and stony-faced. Everyone else crowded onto the balcony and gazed down at the scene below. People were scattering in every direction, pushing each other aside in their desperation to get away. Even the police who had been standing at intervals along the roadside barrier were no longer to be seen, the barrier itself having been ripped to fragments and cast aside. Within seconds the street had totally cleared, leaving discarded flags and banners scattered around, including the big black-and-white one bearing the words: "Civil Rights", now laid horizontally in the road where the head of the procession had been moments before. After assessing the scene for a few seconds Sheelagh ran back into the flat to explain the situation to her father. At once they heard his calm, measured announcement: "There has been a shooting incident on Divis Street, but it is now over. The Civil Rights march has been postponed. There is no longer any danger except the risk of people being crushed or trampled in their haste to get away. It is vital that you leave Divis Street in a calm, orderly fashion. I repeat, the shooting incident is now over. Proceed to your homes calmly and stay tuned to this wavelength to hear further details of the incident, which I repeat is now over..." He continued in the same vein, reassuring people that there was no danger, begging them not to injure one another in their panic to leave the area. Danny was delighted to see his transmitter employed to such a laudable end.

As the street emptied completely he realised that what had looked like an abandoned pile of clothes almost directly beneath the balcony was moving and giving rise to a growing dark stain on the roadway. It was a fallen marcher, and he was losing blood terrifyingly fast. "Christ!" he shouted. "It's a man. The blood's gushing out of him and there's nobody near him. Give me something made of cloth – a sheet, or anything – quickly!" Without waiting for help he dashed inside and ran from room to room, throwing open doors until he found a bed and ripped the white cotton sheet violently from its tidy nest. He gathered it into a crude bundle and headed for the corridor as fast as he could run, Bernie at his heels. "Take the stairs, Danny!" Bernie shouted. "It'll be quicker!"

Danny was already in the stairwell, leaping down the steps three at a time, his precious sheet fluttering behind him like a huge flag of surrender, almost tripping Bernie as they took the corners between the flights. In a few seconds they were in the street, running up to the fallen man.

The man was lying on his back and his eyes were closed. The puddle of blood had extended to about a foot in each direction around the upper half of his body and Danny had to kneel in it to rip off the man's coat and thin nylon shirt. Buttons flew in every direction like demented tiddlywinks. The wound was on the right side of the man's torso, close to his nipple, its exact location unclear due to the pulsing fountain of dark venous blood.

Danny ripped a large section from the sheet, hardly believing the reserves of strength he was discovering in his far from athletic frame, and rapidly folded the material into a large pad which he held tightly against the wound. "Tear some strips, Bernie," he barked out his instruction like a sergeant major, "I need to tie this on very tight." Bernie did as he was told.

Only when he had completed his improvised dressing did it occur to Danny to worry about their safety. "You can go now," he told Bernie. "Make sure they've called for the ambulance. I think there's a telephone in that flat. We may be in somebody's rifle sights here."

"It's okay, Danny. If there's any shooting I can return the fire." He undid the single button and pulled back his jacket to reveal a hand gun of the type that was now quite familiar to Danny, this time in a leather shoulder holster.

"For God's sake don't wave that around. The RUC will open fire on us if they see it."

"It's all right, I won't. Just letting you know it's there if it's needed." Bernie re-buttoned his jacket and looked down at the casualty, whose eyes flickered open. The man was middle aged, slightly balding, and as well as the smell of blood he radiated a strong odour of stale tobacco. Danny found it hard to resist the urge to tell him that smoking was bad for his health. His breathing sounded slow and laboured and was accompanied by gurgling. He looked straight into Danny's eyes and spoke in a rasping, barely audible voice. "Who are you?" he asked.

Danny smiled and the tension of the situation seemed to drain away. "I'm your guardian angel. Don't worry, you're going to be fine." As if to confirm his words they heard the swelling sound of an approaching ambulance siren.

The vehicle came in from the Falls Road end, travelling at a speed that matched the urgency of the situation, and two paramedics were with them almost before it had stopped.

The men were calm and efficient, repeated Danny's assurance to the casualty that he was going to be okay, and set about inserting a cannula in his arm for administering emergency saline. Danny's crude dressing was quickly replaced with something a lot more efficient. Within a couple of minutes the man had been stretchered into the ambulance and the paramedics were climbing into the back beside him, but they were still working on their patient and didn't move off straight away. "You did a great job," one of them assured Danny. "Can I take your name please?"

"No, sorry, no names."

"Okay. But well done. I mean it."

"Just basic first aid. But I admit I was a bit worried that I might be walking into the sights of somebody's rifle."

"I don't think it's a rifle wound," the second ambulance man said as they made their final checks on the man's condition. "It's a jagged tear and there's no exit wound. More likely a small calibre weapon with a plain bore. Some kind of hand gun. Wouldn't be accurate beyond twenty or thirty yards. They'd have a job hitting you out here in the open. Just a random shot into the crowd I would think. Okay, we're off now. God bless the two of you."

With that they slammed shut the rear doors and performed a rapid 'U' turn, before heading back towards the Falls Road with siren wailing and blue lights flashing.

Suddenly everything was perfectly calm. Danny looked down at his hands, shirt and jeans. He was covered in blood, and he noticed for the first time that he was trembling all over. He could hear the distinctive siren of a police car now and knew that it was time to leave.

As the two of them turned toward the block of flats a familiar large black car with tinted glass windows came to an abrupt halt between them and the entrance. The two side doors were flung open, revealing Big Jim's driver Rory and his ever faithful companion Finbar, both of them sporting fashionable sunglasses. "Come on comrades. We'll take you home. Can't have you leaving a trail of blood straight to the door of that MP's flat."

On the journey, with Danny in the front passenger seat and Bernie in the back, they didn't talk to one another at all. The delayed reaction jumbled up Danny's thoughts. He knew this was the kind of event his father had dealt with many times and taken in his stride, but he had never before had somebody else's blood, or his own for that matter, all over his hands and clothing, and had never had so close and intimate a brush with human mortality. He just wanted to sit down alone in a warm darkened room with a cup of tea and sort out his head.

Bernie didn't want his parents to see the relatively modest traces of blood on his hands and clothing, so he asked if he could clean up in Danny's house and maybe borrow a school shirt and a pair of jeans and return them later. It was the first words they had exchanged since getting into Big Jim's staff car.

As soon as they arrived Danny took him upstairs, pausing only to shout to his mother in the kitchen that he was home and that he and Bernie were going upstairs. She acknowledged his arrival but, as he had expected, made no attempt to come out to meet the two boys. He took Bernie straight to the upstairs bathroom, where they started to strip off their clothes.

"It's best to soak bloodstains in cold water first," Bernie explained, opening the cold tap of the bathtub. Danny nodded and threw his soiled jeans into the water, which instantly turned a streaky and gruesome red in the best Hammer horror film tradition. He removed his shirt and threw that in too. Soon the two of them were in their underpants with even their shoes and socks consigned to the rising, cold bathwater. Only Bernie's gun-belt had been singled-out to remain dry, hanging from the hook on the back of the bathroom door. "You have a shower first," Danny said, handing him the soap from the wash-hand-basin. "I'll wait for you."

"You haven't said very much," Bernie said, studying his friend's face.

"What is there to say? It was a nightmare."

"It could have a good outcome, you know. Jim would like the Civil Rights people to accept IRA protection for their marches. They wouldn't before, but maybe they will now."

"What's so good about that?"

"Jim reckons the Civil Rights movement'll be the next big thing. Very important politically. He says we need to get inside it, shift the political colour from Nationalist to Republican as much as we can. Otherwise we may get left behind. That's why he wanted us to give them the radio station."

Danny finished the other's thought. "And why they wouldn't take the protection." He looked at his younger friend, naked now apart from his underpants, a ridiculous schoolboy who carried an automatic pistol and spouted political theory he didn't understand. Of course he was little different himself, right down to the underpants, but at least he had no gun. Just bloodstained hands. He turned on the tap in the hand-basin and tried to clean some of the blood away. Thoughts of Lady Macbeth flitted across his mind.

"You were out on the balcony when those shots were fired," he said in a flat monotone. "Did you see where they came from?"

"No. Of course not. I would have said."

"They sounded very close. The French window was shut, we couldn't hear a thing from the road, yet those two shots were deafening."

"They're pretty noisy, these cheap Russian automatics that everybody's using now."

Danny said nothing but turned to stare at Bernie's gun-belt on top of the dressing gown on the bathroom door. There was a long pause.

"What are you trying to suggest? That I fired those shots? Are you nuts? What kind of person do you think I am?" Danny turned back to his friend but did not reply. Bernie began to sound angry and defensive. "That's not how the IRA works. We don't shoot innocent Irishmen and pretend it was somebody else. We're not savages. The Volunteers are honourable men."

"Honourable men. You've not studied much Shakespeare then, have you?"

"I don't know what you're talking about."

"It was convenient the way Rory and Finbar were right there to pick us up, the minute they were needed, wasn't it?"

"You're nuts, Danny. I don't know what kind of propaganda you've been listening to."

"It'll be okay if I take a look at that gun of yours then, won't it?"

There was an uncomfortable silence.

"What's going on here, Danny? What's happening to you and me? We're friends. Mates. We trust one another. I wouldn't lie to you about something like that."

"Wouldn't you? Even if you were acting under orders?"

"What have I ever kept back from you? Even when I slept with Joyce."

The mention of Joyce seemed to strengthen Danny's resolve. He went over to the door and carefully removed the gun from its holster. Bernie's look of anger turned to one of anxiety. "Go on then," he said with exaggerated indifference. "Look at it if you want to."

Danny smelled the barrel. "It's been fired," he said without apparent emotion. "It stinks of cordite."

"Of course it's been fired. Gun practice is on Saturdays and yesterday was Saturday."

Bernie slipped the magazine out of the handle. To his surprise it was completely empty. He felt a momentary flash of relief, followed

154

by anger. "You said you were going to cover me – with an empty gun?"

"An empty gun still has a deterrent effect. People don't open fire if they think it's going to be returned. It's mostly a game of bluff, you know. Anyway, like the ambulance man said, a handgun is only accurate at very close range. I'd never have been able to hit somebody firing from one of those flats."

He replaced the gun in the holster. "Sorry about doubting you, Bernie. This business has shaken me up pretty badly."

"It's okay, Danny. No hard feelings. Perfectly all right."

For a few moments they stood, foolishly looking at one another in their underpants. It was Danny who broke the silence. "Bernie, there's something I've been meaning to ask you." he hesitated. "I'm not saying that I do, but just as a theoretical question… If I wanted to get out – I mean completely out – would there be a way to do it?" Bernie said nothing but his silence answered Danny's question.

After a few moments he turned and left Bernie to have his shower while he made his way to the bedroom to look for clean clothes. As he left the room it occurred to him that it was perfectly possible that there were only two bullets in the magazine to begin with, but he decided to say nothing about it.

Chapter Twenty-five
Engineering Assignment

"Un-named Guardian Angel Helps Injured Man as Civil Rights March Ends in Gunshots". There was Danny's face as he leaned over the injured man, photographed using a telephoto lens from many yards away, but clear and unmistakable.

"I don't understand you," Sheelagh announced, folding up the much-fingered copy of the *Irish News* and slipping it back into her shoulder bag. "You're supposed to be IRA and yet you go down to the street and risk your life to save some complete stranger who's been shot."

"That's why the IRA exists. If Catholic men and women weren't under threat of death from the other side we wouldn't need a Republican Army. I was just doing my duty. Nothing more, nothing less."

"You're a weird kind of Volunteer. You say you don't have a gun, and I know for a fact that girlfriend of yours sings Orange songs. I've heard Kingston Radio, you know, and I've seen her picture. I'm not a fool."

"You're right," Danny shrugged. "She's a Protestant. What of it?"

"What of it? She's a Protestant and you're in the IRA? Don't you think that's a bit crazy?"

"Protestants aren't the enemy. Religious persecution is the enemy. Injustice… poverty… ignorance. Those are the enemies. This isn't a religious war."

"There's where we're different. I don't see it as a war at all."

"Maybe war is the wrong word. Campaign. Cause. You know what I mean. We're working for a new nation of all Ireland where everybody has a good life, a good standard of living, decent housing, freedom, security and self respect…"

"My da says all those things."

"Yes, and he's right. Those are the things we all want. We're on exactly the same side."

There was a pause. Sheelagh buttoned up her coat. "It's cold out here." The domed glass Palm House of the Belfast Botanic Gardens was still beautiful in winter, but the lawns and dormant flowerbeds that surrounded it were bleak and forbidding in the chill breeze that swept through the park and ruffled Sheelagh's dyed blonde hair. Danny could feel the coldness of the concrete bench through his trousers and his school jacket.

It was a moment before Sheelagh spoke again. "She's very pretty, isn't she?"

"They don't come any prettier."

"And she's a great singer."

"Great. Writes her own songs too. She won't be here much longer though. She's applied to some kind of boarding school for singers and actresses in England. She has an audition in a couple of weeks, but everybody knows she'll get in. I probably won't see her again until next summer when she goes."

"Will you miss her?"

Danny gave her a sideways glance. "What do you think?" He wondered if he should risk a similar personal question. "Have you got a boyfriend?"

"Sometimes."

"That's a funny answer."

"No, it's the truth. There's someone I see now and again... but I don't think it's going anywhere. I seem to be doing all the work. I don't think he's... very committed. I don't know why I bother, really..."

"I don't think this boyfriend/girlfriend thing is ever really perfect. It's the same for me. I try much too hard as well. To please her, I mean. I don't think she feels anything like as much for me as I do for her. You know, I don't think I've admitted that before. Even to myself. I think she likes me... has a good enough time with me. But I don't think she loves me. Not like people are supposed to love one another... sorry, I shouldn't be telling you this really."

"Why not?"

"It seems a bit disloyal, I suppose. A bit unkind. And she isn't unkind to me. Far from it. It's just that... I don't think I'm very important to her. Not really. She's strong and self sufficient. I need her but she doesn't need me. I don't think she needs anybody..."

"I'm certain she needs somebody. Everybody does. It's human nature."

Danny thought about this. "Joyce has this theory – a sort of hippy idea – that we could have lots and lots of people that we love, groups instead of couples. Not depend completely on one partner... do you know what I mean?" Sheelagh nodded but did not comment. Danny detected disapproval. "I'm not sure what I think about it. It kind of makes sense, I suppose. And it does seem to work for Joyce. But I find it a little bit scary to be honest. Kind of new and unfamiliar."

"I think she's probably... an unusual sort of person."

"She's certainly that."

They caught each other's eye and smiled. Sheelagh's hand crept towards Danny's and their fingers touched, self-consciously at first, then with more assurance. He took her hand and held it tenderly. After a few moments he gave in to an urge to put his arm around her and stroke her back, share the warmth of their bodies. She didn't resist. It wasn't the same as having Joyce in his arms but it was exciting, pleasurable, satisfying. In a few moments perhaps he would venture a kiss. And it didn't mean that he loved Joyce any less. She wouldn't hesitate for a second in this situation, why should he?

He didn't even have to tell her any lies. In fact he knew that she would be pleased with him. This was what it was going to be like in the new world that Joyce had been talking about. It really did make sense.

"Welcome, Danny!" Big Jim held out his hand and Danny took it. "Sit down. It's a shame you won't have a drop of good Irish whiskey when we've got something to celebrate."

Danny sank into the plush sofa and waited for Jim to pour his own drink. "Good Irish whiskey hasn't done my family any favours," Danny explained.

"Fair enough." Jim sat down. "I'm sorry I wasn't in town to congratulate you as soon as it happened. I was in Dublin for a big meeting of the top brass. But we got a phone call – heard all about it before it was on the news. You did a great job. A fantastic job. They're calling you The Guardian Angel down in Dublin now. The Republican movement can't claim responsibility, of course, because that would identify you as a member, but everybody who matters knows it was one of our men. The best bit of press we've had for years."

"I didn't do it for the press. I did it for the man."

"I know that, Danny. I know that. And he's going to pull through as well. You're right, that's the most important thing of all." Jim took a sip from his glass and savoured it as he had done before.

"There's stuff I need to talk to you about." He put his glass down on the coffee table and looked at Danny, clearly thinking about how best to explain. "The border campaign a few years ago was a failure as everybody knows – in fact it was totally daft. It was a continuation of the war we'd had in 1916, when we drove the English out of Southern Ireland. Irish men in uniform firing on the British Army and the British police force. It worked back then because England had nobody to send over – they were all away getting blown apart in the trenches in Northern France and Belgium. So the British had little choice but to negotiate. But we tried to fight that same war fifty years later, and that was insane. Ireland is never going to win a conventional shooting war against the British Army. Those days were long gone then, and they're even more remote now. If we're going to get anywhere, it's got to be a different kind of campaign entirely. That's what we've been talking about in Dublin." He took another sip from his glass.

"In a way, your friend Connor Laverty was right. This is the beginning of the Second Irish War of Independence. But this war is going to be fought on the TV screens and in the committee rooms of the British Government in Westminster. Perception is everything, I told you that before, and the truth is that the ordinary English man in the street doesn't give a damn about Northern Ireland – probably wouldn't be able to point it out on a map. There's no stomach amongst ordinary British men and women to maintain a colony in the north-east corner of Ireland, especially if that colony is bleeding them dry and turning America and the world against them. If we make it unpleasant for them, make it expensive, provoke over-reaction, attack British interests in the six counties, and maybe even on the British mainland if that doesn't work, they're going to get fed up with this little corner of empire pretty goddamn fast. They'll be ready to come to the table in a year or two if we play our cards right. That was the decision that was made in Dublin over the weekend."

Danny thought about Jim Harrison's words. "When you say attack British interests in Northern Ireland, what do you mean exactly?"

"Sabotage. Explosions."

Danny considered this. "But not violence against human beings?"

"No, definitely not. That makes bad press. We'll be issuing a warning every time if it's a bomb. You have my word."

"I have your word? Where do I fit into all this?"

"You're right at the heart of it. We've got loads of the old guard in the movement, people who've been in it since the year dot and know how to shoot a gun but not much else. Preferably a forty-year-old gun, not anything too modern. Then we've got the new brigade, the university types. Ever since the eleven-plus came along we've had Catholics coming out of university and into the movement with degrees and professions and god-knows-what on paper. But those degrees are all in things like politics and law and philosophy and sociology. They can spout theory till the cows come home but they don't know how to make things or do things. Some of them can do okay in a press interview and put ideas across, but they don't know anything about the nitty-gritty, the technical side of television or modern communications, or bombs or timers, or how to sabotage a factory or close down an airport. They don't know how the technical world works. They're not engineers. You're about the only one of those we've got. You're the linchpin of the whole operation. If you play your cards right you can have my job in five years time and maybe a ministry in the government of the new United Ireland a year or two after that. I'm not exaggerating, I'm telling you the truth."

"I'm not an engineer, Jim. I'm a schoolboy. I'm sixteen years old."

"We can make you an engineer. We can put you through college, open all kinds of doors for you. But you've already got the skills we really need. You know how to find things out, design things, make things, solve technical problems. And maybe most important of all – the movement trusts you. We've got faith in you. We know you're someone who delivers. That's what really counts."

There was quite a long silence. "So," Danny asked at last, "what is it that you want me to do?"

Chapter Twenty-six
Open Relationships

Danny's parents didn't generally listen in on his telephone conversations, but this time, after explaining the significance of the call and discussing it over dinner, he had invited them to stand beside him in the hallway, and he held the receiver at an angle that he thought would allow them to hear.

"Hello Mr McPherson. It's Danny in Belfast. I know Joyce has a lesson this evening, but I'm just phoning to ask how she did in the audition."

"Oh, she's here all right, Danny. She was too excited to go to the lesson. I thought she would have phoned you herself by now..." There was a pause and Danny could hear Joyce's voice faintly in the background, "...Okay. I'll tell him. Well, Danny, she had applied to both the Drama Department and the Music Department and they've both offered her a place. As far as we know it's the first time in the whole history of the school that it's happened. She has to decide which offer to accept. And they even said she could have a bursary if there was any problem with the fees. They can't wait to get hold of her. We haven't recovered from the shock yet. Isn't it wonderful? Would you ever have expected it?"

Danny felt tears welling up and for a moment was unable to speak. He handed the phone to his father. "Kieran here. Danny's in shock too I think. Congratulations, Mr McPherson. The family must be very proud."

"We're still reeling, Dr Gallagher. We knew she had talent but we didn't think it was anything on that scale. When you live in a little place like this you assume your daughter's a big fish in a small pond, but now it looks like maybe she's just a big fish full stop."

"I'm sure she has a brilliant career ahead of her. We'll all be proud that we've known her in years to come. Will you give her our congratulations and best wishes for the future?"

"Of course I will. Here she is herself."

He tried to hand the phone back to his son but Danny turned away and walked slowly up the stairs.

There was a gentle tapping at Danny's door. He got up and opened it. It was his mother.

"Are you sitting in the dark?" She switched on the light and made her way across slowly to the only chair. Her breathing was fast and laboured.

"What is it, Ma? You didn't need to come up the stairs, I would have come down."

"I can walk a lot better these days." She waited for him to return and sit on the bed beside her, and a little longer for her breathing to settle down. "It's only England, you know. It's not Australia. And she'll be back every holiday. You should have spoken to her. She'll be upset."

"No, Ma. She won't be upset. That's the thing. She doesn't get upset about me. It's only me that gets upset about her."

His mother took a deep breath and paused to collect her thoughts.

"I never told you about this, but when Kieran went off to Spain we had a big row. We'd only been going out together a few weeks and I couldn't understand why he wanted to go. And I was afraid he mightn't be coming back at all. And I knew there would be girls out there, and I knew what soldiers are like. And I was right, as it turned out. About the girls, I mean."

"Mrs Whittaker?"

"Yes. I wouldn't talk to him for ages after he got back. I felt that he'd chosen between Spain and me, and between her and me. But I was wrong. She had her own man too, and he took her back. I don't know whether she ever told him about Kieran. But for them, Spain didn't change anything. So I decided I shouldn't let it change anything for me either. And I took him back. And we agreed that the past was the past and we didn't have to let it destroy us. A bit like you and Joyce. She isn't the faithful type, is she?"

"You're not kidding."

"But Danny, the thing is, I never thought I'd hear myself say this, but it doesn't really matter. It's what you and Joyce have with one another that matters. Not what she has with other people. It can only hurt you if you let it. You don't have to let it. It took me a long, long time to understand that. It nearly destroyed me, but in the end, it didn't. Even when he found her again here in Belfast and opened up the old wound. It didn't mean anything. Kieran has a big heart. There was room in it for both of us."

Danny looked at her strangely. "You're sounding just like Joyce. Big hearts, loving everybody. I've got a swinger for a mother."

She smiled. "The truth is, there's nothing new under the sun. No real relationship is ever like it is in the story books. The only rule that matters is, try not to hurt one another."

For the second time that evening, there was a knock at Danny's bedroom door. He looked up from the physics exercise he was working on and said: "Come in." This time it wasn't his mother.

"Joyce?" He stared at her. "What are you doing here?"

"That's not much of a welcome."

He almost leaped from the chair and ran over to where she was standing, took her in her arms, smothered her in kisses, held her so tightly he could feel her heart against his ribs. "Don't you have to go to school in the morning?" he whispered in her ear.

"Yes. In theory. It doesn't matter all that much any more. I won't be going back to that school after Christmas." He relaxed his hold to make it easier for her to speak. "Why wouldn't you talk to me on the phone? Were you very upset?"

"Of course I was. You know I don't want you to go. Well, I want you to go to the Hammond School and RADA and all that and have a great career, but I want to be part of it. I don't want to lose you. I don't want to be stuck here, with you over there. You're the most important thing in my life and you're going away."

"I've told you, Danny, this isn't the end of anything. We'll have to see a bit less of each other for a while, but nothing's going to change between us. Why should it? We've been through all this before." She wiped a tear from Danny's eye that he hadn't realised was there. "Now. Have you found anybody to keep your bed warm while I'm away?" Danny hesitated. "You have, haven't you? Come on. Tell all." She led him gently over to the bed in question, where they sat down.

"Well, there's this girl named Sheelagh. The daughter of the nationalist MP Terry Flannigan. She lives in one of the Divis flats."

"Yes… and?"

"And nothing. Yet, anyway. We've kissed, that's all."

"Good for you! Tell her I'll write you a reference if she likes."

In spite of the state of his emotions Danny smiled. "I don't think that'll be necessary but I'll keep it in mind."

"I suppose it was this guardian angel thing that did it?"

"Well, I suppose it must have made some difference. It was right outside where she lives. But she isn't like you. She's quite timid… vulnerable. I'll probably screw it up with her."

"Not if she has any sense. Just be yourself, don't rush her. Let her get to know what you're really like."

"Do you think you know what I'm really like?"

"I hope so. You're the sort of person who spends all his money on a new guitar for somebody who's set on going away to England and leaving him alone and unloved. It was wonderful for the audition, by the way. The Head of Music had a go on it himself, said it was the best guitar he'd ever played."

"I bet you made eyes at him."

"Certainly not. The drama teacher looked a bit of all right though."

"Poor man. Be careful you don't get him kicked out of the school and arrested for statutory rape."

"What do you take me for? I'm just a poor innocent little school-girl. Anyway, do you fancy violating some statutes?"

"Why not." He placed Nelkon and Parker's *Advanced Level Physics* face down on top of his exercise book. Joyce's suggestion unquestionably took precedence over homework.

Mrs O'Shea answered the door to Danny, who declined her offer of a cup of tea and made his way up to Bernie's room at the top of the stairs. It was smaller than his own and a lot less tidy, dominated by Bernie's large homemade music console with its tape and record decks, and there were records and reels of tape scattered around on all the available surfaces, interspersed with general bric-a-brac and lots of the cowboy and war books that Bernie liked to read. Bernie was perched on the edge of the bed beside a strong-looking wooden box. He greeted Danny, asked him to lock the door, and cleared a space for him on the opposite side of the box.

"Is that it, then?"

"Certainly is."

Danny opened the hinged lid very gently and lifted out one of the nine-inch-long brown rods with which the box was neatly filled. He held it between his fingers and twirled it around. There was lettering down its side that read: "Danger – High Explosive". He replaced it carefully and closed the lid.

"This is crazy, Bernie. I don't know anything about this stuff. Can't the IRA find some real experts? They must be out there somewhere."

"The Soviets would be happy to send experts. Probably Cuba and China and a few other places too. But Jim doesn't want to do it that way. Our political wing is called '*Sinn Féin*'. Do you know what that means?"

"I nearly failed Irish. Something about 'ourselves'?"

"'Ourselves Alone'. That's the way they want it. No outside help. No favours owed to anybody. Jim says if we accept outside help we could end up a puppet state of the Soviets or somewhere else. He says we don't need it either. He's got great faith in you, Danny. I used to think that maybe he'd gotten you mixed up with your father, that he was giving you too much credit, but now I'm beginning to think he might actually be right. You've got a lot more talent than you realise. When you take on a job it gets done."

"Well, I wish I felt the same. Let's face it, there's no margin for error here. One mistake with this stuff and its all over. I don't even know where to look for information. The Belfast Central Library?"

"Why not? You've got to start somewhere."

"Let's hope they've got an 'Urban Guerrilla Warfare' section. They certainly should have, in this city."

Chapter Twenty-seven
Partings & Pyrotechnics

By the time Joyce's actual day to leave came along, Danny had resigned himself to its inevitability and was able to go to the quayside in a reasonably positive frame of mind to see her off and wish her good luck. Both her parents were going with her to help her settle in to the accommodation at the school. The trickle of rain kept all the others who had come to see people off inside the shelter of the corrugated iron departure area, with its seats and slot machine refreshment area, but a small group, including a *Belfast Telegraph* photographer and a few of Joyce's girlfriends from school, had assembled on the pot-holed roadway outside expressly to mark the occasion of her departure. Danny and Bernie joined them, along with Mo Posner, Joyce's singing friend from the music shop, now dressed in standard jeans and a long-sleeved black sweater beneath his transparent plastic mac, and looking particularly crestfallen, confirming to Danny that they had become more than just singing partners. There were two other men that Danny hadn't seen before.

After a very brief parting ceremony and the exchange of a restrained kiss with Danny in front of her parents, Joyce's car made its way to the boarding ramp, and the photographer and the girls hurried off, leaving the remainder of the group to wave after the car as it vanished into the gaping jaw of the enormous and bland 'roll-on-roll-off' ferry. There was none of the cheery chaos of *The Manxman* about this vessel, it was a thing of pure utility. Several minutes passed but the family group had not reappeared on the deck by the time the vessel's grey bulk started to move away from the jetty, and the little group could only watch dejectedly as it began to cross the equally grey waters of Belfast Lough on its way to the Irish Sea.

The two male well-wishers whom Danny didn't know were closer to Mo's age than his own and looked well dressed and respectable. Danny smiled at the one nearest, who seemed to be of a nervous and jumpy disposition. "How do you know the McPhersons?" he asked, trying to sound as casual and unthreatening as he could.

"Me? Oh, I'm Joyce's English teacher."

"Oh, Mr Rake. I think she's mentioned you."

"What? Has she? Really?"

It's okay, Danny felt like adding, she didn't give me any details of what you get up to in the textbook cupboard. "Sweet" was the description she had used of this gentle live-alone social misfit. Danny felt slightly sorry for him, he was the kind of man that Joyce would take great pleasure in playing with. Eat for her breakfast might be closer to the mark. He identified with him, somebody else lacking in confidence, who would have had a hard time finding a girlfriend under the usual rules of the game, and would again now. He hoped the misnamed Mr Rake realised what a lucky man he had been. "Yes. She says you have a very good student-teacher relationship." His eyes flickered nervously. It was tempting to go on teasing him, but Danny resisted, and turned his attention instead to the other stranger.

The second man, the one farthest away from Danny, looked a lot more confident, almost world-weary, with deep-set eyes, thick black eyebrows and slightly greasy-looking but neatly parted and trimmed black hair. Danny found it hard to imagine him with Joyce. He wondered what it was about the man that appealed to her. He stood unusually still, with his grey suit, white shirt and finely patterned blue tie visible beneath his unbuttoned full-length black raincoat. Bernie noticed Danny studying the man and drew closer. "Plain clothes police. I'd bet my life on it," he hissed under his breath.

Danny shrugged. "Do you think he knows something?"

"Doubt it. I reckon Joyce hasn't been choosing her friends too carefully. Or he might even be here for ye'r man." He motioned towards Mr Rake.

The group split up and Mo accompanied Danny back towards Mo's waiting car. Bernie had declined the lift, having further business in the city centre. "She'll go far," Mo announced dreamily, "I wish I'd got her to sign my guitar now."

"We'll see her again," Danny assured him. "Blood brother," he added incongruously. In his mind he was remembering another quayside parting, with Joyce in her yellow summer dress, fixing him with that heart-stopping smile, then the polite little curtsy…

"Why did you want me to come out here?" Sheelagh asked, joining Danny on the low dry-stone wall that separated the stubbled cornfield from the rough track leading up to the dilapidated single storey whitewashed cottage. They had been walking for about half an hour since getting off at the country bus stop and it was about a quarter of a mile ahead of them now, large holes visible in its thatched roof where the chimney stack had partially collapsed, a broken shutter hanging from one of the windows and a green streak of lichen discolouring a large section of the wall where rainwater had been flowing down unchecked for years.

"I thought you might be interested. It's a little bit of excitement that the boys and I have planned." He looked down at his watch. "In about four more minutes."

She smiled. "Some kind of surprise?"

"Exactly. Some kind of surprise."

"But there's nobody here, Danny."

"That's right. Just you... and me."

There was a pause. "Is this some kind of silly excuse to get me on my own in the middle of nowhere?"

"No. I don't need an excuse to do that, do I?"

"Of course not. If you want a kiss, just ask."

"Really? Okay then. I'm asking."

She embraced him and they kissed tenderly. In the middle of the kiss a powerful nearby explosion almost knocked them off the wall. "Hey! You're quite a kisser!" Danny told her with a smile.

"Danny! What's going on? That was freaky!"

"Relax. It's just a fireworks display. Like Guy Fawkes night." He loosened his embrace and they turned to look at the cottage again. There were flames leaping from the roof, which no longer had any thatch, and a huge plume of black smoke was snaking its way into the sky, but the basic stone structure was relatively unchanged. Even the remaining part of the half-collapsed chimney stack was still in place.

Danny stood up and helped Sheelagh on to her feet. "That's a bit queer."

"You're telling me it is! You've just blown up some poor bugger's house."

"It's okay. We had permission. The owner's a sympathiser and it was due for demolition anyway. But the queer thing is – it hasn't suffered all that much damage."

Sheelagh was puzzled. "Well, you haven't exactly done it much good either."

"Agreed, but I would have expected more. The walls are still there, and with the state they're in you could almost push them over with your hands. There's something wrong. We're missing something. Four sticks of gelignite should be enough to split ten feet of solid rock in half. That was a bit pathetic."

"This is really scary, Danny. What exactly are you doing? What's going on?"

"I'm learning my new trade, Sheelagh. Experimenting. You're going to get very used to the sound of bombs going off in Belfast in the next few months. But don't worry, nobody's going to get hurt. There's going to be warnings and people will be evacuated. It should be pretty exciting. 'Interesting times', the ancient Chinese used to call it."

They stood watching the remains of the little cottage burn. Danny embraced her again and she responded by leaning towards him and giving him a kiss on the cheek. "I know you're a good person," she whispered. "You won't let any innocent people get hurt."

Bernie was perched on the end of his bed, leafing through one of his garish *Star-Spangled War Stories* comics, while Danny sat on the wooden chair by the bedside table studying the flimsy 28-page pamphlet that he had managed to order from the Belfast Central Library. Its less than catchy title was: *Safe storage, handling, and use of commercial explosives in metal mines, nonmetallic mines, and quarries: Revision of Information circular 7380 (Information circular / United States Bureau of Mines, 1958)*.

"How can you read that kind of stuff?" Bernie asked him absently.

"How can you?" Danny countered, laying his pamphlet face down and hunting around amid the debris on the bed and table for a ballpoint pen and a school exercise book. "It's very helpful, actually.

Exactly what we need. I can see now why we've been getting such half-hearted results with what should be high explosives. Not the best available, mind you, that would be the new plastic explosives, but quite good stuff nevertheless. We've been making a very simple and basic mistake."

"You mean, you've been making a very simple and basic mistake."

"Yes, all right, I have." Bernie put down his comic and looked over Danny's shoulder as he made a sketch.

"The thing is," Danny explained, taking an obvious pleasure in passing on technical information, "to get any force out of an explosion, the explosive has to be contained. It has to be in a restricted space." He drew a picture of several sticks of gelignite getting blown away from one another by what looked like a spiked ball in the middle of the page. "We've been putting four or five sticks together with a detonator in the middle. The detonator goes off and starts the explosion. Now the explosion is really a very rapid chemical reaction that produces a big volume of gas, but as soon as it begins the sticks of gelignite themselves are blown apart and separated. The gas is being produced within a bigger space, where it has more room to expand, so the effective pressure is much smaller. The sticks themselves are blown apart too before the chemicals have time to complete the reaction, so it's only a partial detonation." He drew a second picture, this time of four sticks inside what looked like a sealed box. "Put them into something that holds them together, just for a tiny fraction of a second, and the resultant pressure will be hundreds of times higher. The components of the reaction will stay in close proximity long enough to react fully with one another, and all the gases will be created in one small space so they'll move outwards with a much bigger shockwave. Explosions need time to happen. That's what I didn't understand before. Only one or two thousandths of a second maybe, but if you don't give them that time, you end up with a much smaller bang. Does that make sense?"

"Probably, but not to me if I'm honest. Are you saying we've got to put the sticks inside a box?"

"Exactly. Some kind of tightly-sealed metal container."

"Isn't that what they call a pipe-bomb?"

Danny was impressed. "Yes. I think you're right. I've heard of those too. Why didn't it occur to me before? What we need is a tightly-sealed piece of steel pipe. Something like a big rainwater pipe or sewer pipe, with a cap at each end."

"That's going to be a bit heavy, isn't it?"

"It doesn't have to be a long pipe. Just big enough to contain the gelignite, the detonator, the timer and the battery. Or I suppose you could have just the gelignite in the pipe and everything else outside, with the wires going in through a small hole. I don't think a small hole would make much difference…"

"You want to start testing all over again, then, do you?"

"I'm afraid so. But one or two tests ought to be enough."

"I'll talk to the boys. See if there are any more farm buildings we can blow up."

Danny and Bernie watched the small fenced-off electricity substation from the back seat of Rory's parked staff car. Finbar occupied the passenger seat next to Rory. The housing estate that the installation served, one of the still uncompleted medium-rise ones on the north-western extreme of the city, was spread out across their field of view beyond a narrow strip of wasteland where earth-movers were parked and piles of bagged-up cement and building materials peeked from beneath makeshift shelters and tarpaulins. None of them spoke, but the two in the back kept an eye on the watch that Danny had unstrapped from his wrist, and braced themselves.

Exactly on cue, a mighty white flash obliterated their view of the substation, followed almost immediately by a stomach-wrenching noise resembling a very nearby clap of thunder. The car lurched on its springs as a smoking pile of twisted metal took the place of the substation that had been there a moment before. The pylon that had stood by its side slowly and gracefully bowed downwards amid a shower of white sparks, like a gigantic welding tool. As it settled to the ground and buckled, small stones began to rain down on the car roof and Rory cursed loudly.

In the back, Danny and Bernie cheered.

"Don't listen to Rory," Finbar assured them, removing his sunglasses for the first time since they had known him. "You've done a bloody brilliant job. Big Jim'll be over the moon."

174

Chapter Twenty-eight
Gun Politics

Danny locked his bedroom door and pulled the heavy improvised curtain across the door and the back half of the room before starting the session. Speaking into a microphone was something that he had always found embarrassing, and the curtain helped to make his voice almost inaudible from the corridor, as well as reducing the "live" acoustic of the room. He made himself comfortable in the wooden chair by the long bench and glanced down at his notes before pressing "record".

"Hello Joyce. Thanks very much for your last tape. I don't know where you find the time to record them, with all the stuff you seem to be doing over there. They mean everything to me and... well, I just can't thank you enough really. It's great to know that you're still thinking about me... and just to hear your voice.

"Your two latest songs are fantastic – even for you. I love the melodies and the guitar work... and the words, of course. I think they sound maybe a bit more commercial than some of your other stuff – the kind of thing I could imagine Johnny Cash or Peter, Paul and Mary or somebody singing. And congratulations on the summer tour with The Diggers. I knew there would be a summer tour. I knew you wouldn't be back in Belfast for a while. But maybe I can go over there and be your groupie?

"Have you heard a record called *Society's Child* by an American girl named Janis Ian? It was on the radio but I wasn't fast enough to tape it. You'll hear it where you are before long. She's even younger than you. It's about race prejudice in America. About a white girl with a coloured boyfriend. They said a radio station in Atlanta was burned down for playing it. Now that's what I call making a hit! You've got to hear it – it's absolutely fantastic.

"You need to send your songs off to some record companies. What happened to the tape Bernie made for you? Oh, he sends his love by the way. He's always talking about you. Mo as well. I've been to hear him sing a couple of times since you left. Oh, and people at the folk club were asking for you. Mo explained to them that you move in higher circles these days. Mo sends his love too. I don't think you're too short of love over there though, somehow or other. I'm sure you've made a whole load of new conquests since you went to England. I hope you're having a great time and that everybody's treating you well and being nice to you.

"Well, I read that *Warm Fuzzy Story* you told me about, and you're right, it explains things very well. I feel okay about that side of things now. And I'm getting along all right with Sheelagh. Sex is quite a big deal with her. We've only done it a few times, very hush-hush, in locked rooms, and she's not very comfortable about it. I have to wear rubbers because she won't go on the pill. It's not her fault, she's a well brought-up convent girl and pretty well everything's a sin. You don't know how lucky you are, not being a Catholic.

"I think you got out of Belfast just in time. Things have got very nasty over here since you left. A lot of big shops and businesses in the city centre have been bombed, and now the trouble has spread to ordinary streets, and a couple of Catholic families have been burned out of their homes. There's been shootings at public meetings again too, and of course on Civil Rights marches again. You've probably heard it on the English news. Nowhere in Belfast is safe any more. We've had snipers shooting at people going to church, and a Catholic school petrol-bombed, and all kinds of things... it's like everything's coming to a head after years and years of quietly smouldering and festering... all we can hope for is that it gets settled for once and for all, and quickly, and the air gets cleared. Everybody says England is about to send the troops in. God knows what it'll be like then. I'm glad you're out of it."

Danny pressed the "stop" button. It gave him a wretched, hollow feeling in his stomach not to be able to tell her anything – to have to lie to her, almost. While things had been quiet he had been able to avoid politics, now it was the only thing anybody talked about in Belfast. It couldn't be avoided any more. If she condemned the IRA and said they were monsters, he would have to agree with her not to arouse her suspicions. Maybe deep down he *did* agree with her. He didn't really know what he thought any more. Whether the violence they had sparked off was worth the potential gains, or whether the Nationalists were right, and everything could be done equally well through the ballot box if people were a bit more patient. Things seemed to get more complicated every day. Less black-and-white. He had tried to talk about it with Sheelagh, but her mind was already made up. She would never go along with the idea of a campaign of bombing – even bombing of property. She wasn't capable of listening to the other side or really thinking about it. He ended up in a corner each time, defending what looked like an entrenched position, even though he wanted to question it and examine it, afraid to let any doubt or weakness show. This huge area of his life, this twilight world that he had somehow wandered into and the worries he was having about it, couldn't be shared with either of them. Other people seemed to be able to make up their minds clearly about such things, adopt a position and stick to it, but Danny felt only an aching need to analyze, to satisfy his engineer's soul that he had understood the problem correctly and was going about its solution in the right way. More than anything else he felt totally alone, and pushed along by a great tide of events over which he had no control.

"It's for you, Danny." His father handed over the receiver and returned to his wife and his dinner in the kitchen.

"Hello Dan." Nobody had ever called him Dan before, now it was Sheelagh's pet name for him. It didn't seem to belong to him at all. "Are you free tomorrow?"

"I've got a bit of homework but I can take time off. Why? Have you got plans for the two of us?"

"My da's addressing a constituency meeting about security. About the people getting burned out. I thought you might be interested."

"What time is the meeting?" He tried to sound enthusiastic but in reality it was very familiar material, he knew the Nationalists would never accept IRA protection, and he knew he wouldn't have the courage to speak in public himself, even if Terry Flannigan said something he completely disagreed with. But it would be a chance to meet up with Sheelagh again and he could do with a bit of tender female company.

177

"Just after lunch. Starting at two o'clock in St. Jude's Hall. We could meet there."

"Did you know that St. Jude is the patron saint of lost causes?"

"Save it for the meeting, Dan."

"Okay, lovely. I'll see you there."

Sheelagh insisted on leading Danny by the hand to the very front row, where many of the seats were empty, most people having a natural impulse to avoid conspicuousness. They sat one empty seat away from a reporter and photographer whom Danny assumed would be from the *Irish News*, Belfast's main Catholic local newspaper. Sheelagh's father, who acknowledged her with a smile, was already standing behind a table in the middle of the platform and loosely holding a microphone, flanked by two seated younger men. Danny recognised one of them as the student to whom they had handed over control of Radio Free Belfast. A crowd close to the hall's capacity had come to hear what Terry had to say.

"*Go mbeannaí Dia is Muire duit*," he began, establishing his credentials with the familiar Irish greeting, "May God and Mary bless you". The low rumbling of conversation became still.

"In case you don't know who I am, my name is Terry Flannigan, and I am proud and honoured to represent the people of this constituency at Stormont. I've asked you to come here today because our community has come under a terrifying threat of violence and victimisation by criminals using religion and politics as an excuse to threaten the lives and property of their fellow Irishmen. These evil men are trying to drive innocent families from their homes with guns and petrol bombs. It's no longer safe for our children to walk to school or our women to go shopping or our men folk to go to work in the city that we live in. It's the job of the RUC to provide protection and law enforcement equally and impartially for every Belfast citizen. They are well paid for that job and everybody here knows that they aren't doing it. Three West Belfast families, the McGuinness family of Melbourne Street and the Connery and Boyce families of Dunluce Street have had their houses burned down by criminal mobs and their lives threatened by murder squads on account of their religious and political views. Nothing was done by the

RUC to protect those families, even though the death threats were reported over a period of three weeks prior to the attacks.

"The first thing I want to say to you is: congratulations on your restraint and tolerance in the face of attack and provocation on this scale. You have refused to give up your civilised values and resort to revenge and recrimination. You haven't lowered yourselves to the level of these evil and cowardly thugs, who send screaming mobs with bricks and petrol bombs to drive helpless families from their homes at dead of night. I am inspired by your strength and your refusal to be goaded into answering violence and injustice with the same, and allowing this intolerable situation to deteriorate into full-blown civil war.

"I've asked you to come here today to consider what our response ought to be, as decent Christian men and women faced with persecution and violence, and denied the protection of an impartial police force as guaranteed to us by the constitution of this country and our British overlords.

"Now, I know as well as you do that there is one organisation that we could turn to that would be happy to provide the kind of protection that these thugs actually understand, to meet fire with fire, so to speak, but I want to explain to you why I don't believe that to be our best course of action, and I want to tell you about the other alternatives that are open to us…"

This was as much of his speech as Terry Flannigan managed to deliver. Two deafening gunshots silenced him. Blood spurted outwards, first from Flannigan's stomach, then from somewhere near the small of his back as he twisted around and crumpled downwards. For half a second the audience seemed paralysed, then all gasped as one person. Women screamed. An indecipherable torrent of outrage erupted everywhere. People jumped to their feet, overturning chairs and knocking each other to the floor, surging mindlessly towards the side door through which the gunman had made his getaway.

A three-man St. John's Ambulance crew was by the side of the MP almost as soon as his toppling body reached the floor. Danny's amateur first aid services were not needed. He stood up with Sheelagh, cradling her in his arms. Her scream reminded him of the sound made by a dog that he had once seen struck by a car on the

Malone Road. He tried to look behind him, hoping to glimpse the gunman, but all that he could see was the confused mass of people still lurching in the general direction of the side door.

He hugged her until the scream became muffled and slowly abated as she ran out of breath. Then she began to struggle to get free and no doubt run to her father's side. Gently but firmly he held her back. "There's nothing you can do," he told her. "The ambulance men are with him. Let them do their job." Her horror spent, she seemed to become limp in his embrace. He held her gently and stroked her back while she shivered uncontrollably, and the hall, now in total chaos, emptied around them.

Chapter Twenty-nine
Sheelagh Decides

"I'm really uneasy about this," Danny pleaded.

"It wasn't your da that got shot."

She sat stiffly upright by his side, eyes hidden beneath the blindfold, body jogging up and down with the motion of the car. Finbar sat next to Rory in the front. They had been silent for almost the whole of the journey.

"It's a big move. A big decision. If I'd really sat down and thought about it I mightn't have joined at all. Once you're in, nothing's ever the same again."

"Give over, Dan. It's my decision. I know what I'm doing."

"Do you, though? Are you sure you do, Sheelagh?"

"I thought you'd be pleased. You people were right all along. I can see it now. We do need protection. We need it big time. Those bastards have to know that the next time they shoot some innocent Catholic there's a chance they'll get as good as they give right back again. And I'll be happy to be the one giving it to them."

Danny was quiet while he considered her words. "If you'd never met me, you wouldn't be doing this, would you?"

"How do I know? What's that got to do with anything? If my da hadn't got shot I wouldn't be doing it. That's for sure."

He gave up his attempt to change her mind. He wasn't even sure if that was what he was trying to do. He just wanted to get her to think about it – think about it properly. That was all he really wanted.

The car drew to a halt beside the vandalised wreck of a Hillman Husky in the courtyard of the oldest block of flats on the Newton Breda estate. Crude sexual and political graffiti adorned the lower walls, and off-white sheets hung from an improvised clothesline along the middle balcony. The courtyard echoed to the harsh cries of boys playing football and smelled of a recent bonfire that had been extinguished by the rain. This is the IRA's real constituency, Danny thought to himself, even more than the Divis Flats where Sheelagh lived, let alone the posh lower slopes of the Cave Hill where he lived himself. It was quite an act of faith that any imaginable political change was going to make this place more bearable.

In the lift, Sheelagh screwed up her nose at the pungent odour of urine. "It's not a great location," Rory explained, "not this time anyway. Big Jim can't stay too long in any one place. Sometimes it's a mansion, sometimes it's a slum. Comes with the job."

They were delivered as usual into Big Jim's presence before Sheelagh was allowed to remove the blindfold. Danny was no longer required to wear one. She blinked nervously at Big Jim, who beamed down at her and held out a huge right hand in greeting.

"Welcome Sheelagh. Welcome Danny. What's the latest on your father?"

"Hello, Mr Harrison." She fixed him with a fascinated stare, like someone who had just shaken hands with a superhero from a Dell comic. "He's... as well as can be expected. That's what they're saying. The stomach wound isn't too bad, they patched that up with a bit of surgery, but there's a chance that his spine has been damaged by the other one. There's a chance that... that he won't walk again."

"Jim. Jim's the name, not 'Mr' anything. That's a terrible thing! Terrible! I hope the bastard that did it gets what's coming to him good and quickly. He would if I knew who he was, that's for sure. Would you like a wee drink to settle you down?"

"Thank you, I don't drink, Mr Harrison. Neither does Dan."

"No. Very wise. Sit down then, the two of you."

They found seats in the cluttered little lounge while Jim poured himself his customary whiskey.

"The first thing I want to say to you," he began as he sat down, "is that we won't be giving you a gun and sending you out to shoot Protestants. If that's the way you think it works you can forget it."

"I know it's not like that. I'll be happy to do whatever you want me to. Whatever you think's going to help."

"At the moment, we're trying to keep up the economic pressure on England. Attacks on large businesses, police stations and army barracks, infrastructure like bridges and power stations. That kind of thing. If you join us you'll be used as a bomb courier – like a delivery girl. It's dangerous and not very glamorous. But a teenage girl is an ideal person for the job from our point of view. Who could be less threatening?"

"Fine. That's what I'll do then."

"I admire your guts, but I don't want you to rush into this. There are serious risks. Not just of getting caught but even of getting injured in an explosion yourself, or getting shot at if somebody sees what you're doing. This most certainly isn't a game."

"Dan said that kind of thing too. But I've thought about it and it really is what I want to do. Anything that takes the power away from the people who shot my da, and burned those people out of their houses. I can look after myself. I'll be okay."

Jim put down his drink and looked her straight in the eye for several seconds. She did not flinch. He held out his hand again and she took it eagerly. "Welcome to the Irish Republican Army." They shook hands for the second time.

"A lot of the basic stuff I don't need to tell you, because you're Danny's girlfriend and he can explain it to you just as well as I can, and answer all your questions. I'll just say that the most important rule of all is to keep your mouth shut. You don't talk about anything to do with the Volunteers to anybody. Not even your own mother or the priest in Confession. Is that bit absolutely clear?"

"Yes. Absolutely."

"Okay. Danny, will you tell Sheelagh here a bit about the hardware? I'll get the one we use for training." He stood up and went to a cupboard from which he pulled a large and heavy-looking rucksack.

"Right." Danny took on his teacher role. "A bomb is the simplest piece of engineering you can imagine. It's like a flashlight – there's basically a battery, a pair of wires and a detonator. When you connect the battery to the detonator by means of the wires it goes off like a penny banger. That little explosion triggers the big one. So you don't want that to happen prematurely. One of the battery wires is permanently connected to the detonator, but it won't go off until the other one is connected too. The second wire passes through two switches. The switch that arms the bomb, and the switch controlled by the timer. A couple of hours before you want it to go off, you set the timer and then arm the bomb by closing the arming switch."

He reached into the rucksack that Jim had put down at his feet and one by one lifted out the objects it contained, naming them and placing them on the table in front of Sheelagh.

"The detonator... the arming switch... the battery... the timer. It's a standard clockwork timer that's used in things like tumble dryers and washing machines. It's no more complicated than the alarm clock at the side of your bed, and no more expensive. You can buy it as a standard spare part at any electrical wholesaler. You wind it up and set the clock, then you move the two extra hands into position with this knob." He reached across and demonstrated. "The red one is the 'on' hand. When the hour hand reaches the same position as the 'on' hand a switch is closed and the detonator fires."

"And that's all there is to it?"

"Very nearly. The explosives have to be packed inside a confined space so that they reach their full power output. We put them inside one of these..." He lifted the heaviest object from the rucksack, a section of steel pipe about a foot long with threaded ends. "This is a thing called a 'straight connector'. It's designed for joining two sewer pipes together. But we use the threads to cap off the two ends with these..." He handed the pipe across to Sheelagh and produced two internally-threaded steel caps resembling large steel coffee-jar lids. Taking the pipe back, he screwed one on to each end to form a closed container. "Now it's a sealed steel chamber. It holds the gelignite sticks together long enough for the detonation reaction to take place. Then it blows apart with a force that you wouldn't believe. I didn't believe it myself the first time I saw it. It'll take the entire front wall out of a two-storey house, or make a six foot crater in a solid concrete patio. Anybody within about a hundred yards is likely to get cut to pieces by the fragments. Buildings and streets have to be properly evacuated. The RUC know that now."

As he handed it over to her for examination he noticed that her jaw was quivering slightly. He felt an impulse to stroke her or comfort her in some way, but resisted. She held the tube in both hands and pumped it into the air like a dumbbell. "It's very heavy."

"Even heavier when the explosives and the other things are inside it."

"So the timer and the battery and everything goes inside?"

"It does now. The first few we made had just the explosives and the detonator inside and a hole for the two wires, with everything else outside. But a smart-Alec RUC man cut the wires on one of them, and of course that rendered it safe. We don't want to make that mistake again, so now we put everything inside and seal the two end threads with a super-strong glue called Araldite. Once the bomb is armed and sealed, there's pretty well nothing on earth that can stop it from going off at the planned time. We haven't had a single failure or a single successful disarming of one of those."

"I see."

He wondered if she really did see the full significance of what he was telling her. "But it's potentially a very lethal piece of gear. Once it's sealed there's no turning back. Are you absolutely sure you want to get involved?"

"No, I'll just stay here and make the tea. Of course I want to get involved! Don't you listen to anything I say?"

Danny could see that her prickliness was a cover-up for almost paralysing fear. He touched her hand and she drew it away. "She's all yours, Jim," he said quietly.

"You're a brave kid," Jim assured her. "May God take care of you."

"So this is your room. It's very neat. I thought boys were always untidy."

"Bernie's room is a tip. Not mine. I couldn't live that way."

"And all this electrical stuff. I suppose that's all got to do with the pirate radio transmitter?"

"Not specially. Just radio in general. I've been building radio sets since I was about ten."

"You're very clever."

"You can believe that if you want to, but I'm afraid it's not true. My dad is very clever. I'm just good at making things and solving technical problems. Nothing much else."

"You're always running yourself down."

"My dad says that too. I'm modest because I've got a lot to be modest about."

"That's funny! Did you make it up?"

"I'm afraid not. I think it was Winston Churchill."

"You read a lot too. Not many people would know that."

"I can tell you the formula for calculating the 'Q' factor of a tuned circuit. Even fewer people know that."

"You are funny. You are nice." She put her arms around him and drew him close for a kiss. He held her the way that she liked to be held – very gently around the waist. It was easy to overdo things with Sheelagh.

"Have you got any pictures of that girl in England?"

"Well, yes, of course. I've known her for more than a year now. Why do you ask?"

"Did you hide them because I was coming?"

"No, of course not... well, maybe one or two. Why do you want to talk about her?"

"I can't help it. She's prettier than me, isn't she?"

"I don't make comparisons. You're both wonderful in your separate ways."

"You might at least deny it!"

He silenced her with another kiss. When they separated again she moved on to a different topic.

"Something I want to ask you. Why were you so negative about me joining the IRA? I thought you would have been pleased."

"I don't think I understood what I was doing when I got involved myself. I thought it would be a lot simpler than it's turned out. Sort of neat and tidy. Like a chess game. You make this move and that move and as a result your side wins and Northern Ireland gets her freedom. Blow up empty buildings, nobody gets hurt, England has to pay the bill. The English voters get tired of it and tell their politicians to get out of Northern Ireland. All very clean and logical. But what really happens is that you stir up all that fierce tribal hatred that's just below the surface here – the stuff that gets people maimed and killed and afraid to leave their houses. And I don't see much evidence that England gives a damn. I'm beginning to think now that at the end of it all there'll just be a whole lot more dead and injured people, and this will still be the same rotten old society it's always been. I'm not convinced that the campaign is going to do any good. And even if it does, maybe the price is going to be far too high."

"And that's why you didn't want me to join?"

He shrugged. "Not really. The real reason is that I'm scared you might end up like your father. Or worse. I *do* want you to stay home and make the tea. And stay alive. That matters more to me than anything else."

She held him very close and buried her head in his shoulder. It seemed almost more intimate than kissing. "Have you got a rubber?" she whispered.

"Of course. Do you want me to get it?"

"Why not. It'll calm the two of us down."

"You're right. I'll get it."

Chapter Thirty
Bomb Courier

With a pounding heart and a light feeling in her head, Sheelagh pedalled slowly, the unaccustomed weight in the right pannier giving the bicycle a list to that side and making it difficult to steer. Inconspicuously dressed, she willed herself to be invisible as she cruised down the narrow gap between the pavement and the long line of cars that had unaccountably stopped along North Street, just ahead of the junction with Royal Avenue.

Drawing nearer to the source of the delay, she saw that there was also a line of queued-up pedestrians on the pavement, and that the cause of both holdups was the presence of four military jeeps which were parked nose to tail across the road, forming a narrow funnel through which vehicles were being allowed to pass one at a time after a perfunctory search by members of the little group of rifle-bearing soldiers manning the road block. This was something new – in the last few weeks there had been a few temporary RUC checkpoints set up outside shopping centres and public buildings, where pedestrians' pockets and bags were checked, but it had the feel of a half-hearted operation, intended as window dressing to make the public think that something was being done. Sheelagh had not seen soldiers involved before, or anything as obviously serious as this. She watched them frisk irate middle-aged women with shopping baskets and sullen dockyard workers with lunch boxes on their way to the evening shift at Donegal Quay, while children pulled at their parents clothing and complained that they wanted to go to the shops.

With a couple of hundred yards still to go to the back end of the queue, she applied the brakes and drew to a gentle halt. Obviously, there would have to be a change of plan. She glanced anxiously at her wristwatch to see exactly how many minutes she had in which to come up with a new one. Why hadn't anybody told her what to do in this situation? Why hadn't they given her any instructions about how to abort the operation if it became necessary?

Sweating now, she stood motionless for a few moments, still holding the handlebars but with her feet on the ground, trying to come up with a viable Plan B. She could take the bicycle and dump it and its deadly pannier in the River Lagan – that might kill a few fish but humans would be at no serious risk. Yes, that would have to do. She lifted the front of the bike and started to turn it around.

"Hey! You there! Young lady!" It was a distinctly English accent and it was coming from close behind her. "Where do you think you're going, then?"

She lowered the front wheel back on to the road and looked around. There was a young British soldier in helmet and full combat gear approaching rapidly. "I'm turning back. I don't have time to go through all that." She could hear a quiver in her voice and hoped that the soldier hadn't picked it up. He leered down at her, his thoughts clearly ranging over more than just his military duties.

"Ain't ye? That's too bad, because we've got lots of time and our orders are to search everybody on this part of North Street. Not just the ones what want to be searched. So I suggest you park that bike over there," he pointed to the wall of a nearby shop, "and let me have a look in that shoulder bag of yours."

"My shoulder bag?" Sheelagh had completely forgotten that she was wearing it. She meekly wheeled the bicycle onto the pavement, leaned it carefully against the wall, and returned, offering the soldier her bag, and breathing a little easier. He took it from her roughly and rifled through it with enthusiasm, tossing her rolled-up plastic mac onto the pavement, ignoring her colourful cloth purse with its brass clasp, and fixing his attention instead on a bunch of old crumpled election pamphlets right at the bottom.

"What've we got here then?" He opened one of the leaflets and read it slowly, his lips flickering with the shadows of words. A smile spread across his face.

"Just old pamphlets. My father was a candidate in the Council elections a few months ago…"

"This here is subversive literature, Miss. Going to have to take you in for questioning."

"Subversive literature? What are you talking about? They're election pamphlets. My father is a Stormont MP. He's also on the local Council. Those are…"

"I've just told you what those are. Now shut up while I make a call." He unhitched a field two-way radio from his shoulder strap and spoke into it. "Kilo-seven-two to Kilo-one. I'm on North Street, just opposite Church Street. I've apprehended a female with anti-government literature on her person. Request female officer to collect her and take her to the Interrogation Centre. Over."

The machine barked back, its voice too distorted to make any sense to Sheelagh. "You stay put, Miss. Somebody'll be here to talk to you in a few minutes."

"But this is ridiculous. Those aren't anti-government literature. My da is in the government. The Stormont one. He's a Nationalist MP. It's a perfectly normal, respectable political party."

"Is that so? Well…" he held the pamphlet up to read it again, "it says here: 'We look forward to the day when this country will sever all ties with the United Kingdom and become part of a new republic of all Ireland'. That's called 'Republicanism', that is. As in 'Irish Republican Army'. I ain't thick, you know."

"We have nothing to do with the Irish Republican Army. We're an ordinary constitutional political party…"

"Sweetheart, I ain't interested in arguing the toss with you. I've got a job to do an' I'm doing it. Now stand over by your bike and wait. I ain't asking, I'm telling."

For what seemed an eternity Sheelagh waited by the bicycle while the soldier seemed to lose interest and started to watch the queue growing ever longer further down the road by the improvised road block.

He received another unintelligible message on his radio and replied. More minutes ticked by.

Sheelagh wiped the sweat from her forehead and looked at her watch. "I need to go home. I need to go to the bathroom." She tried to move off but the soldier grabbed her wrist. "You just ain't listening, are you, sweetheart?" He twisted her arm behind her and lifted it just enough to hurt. "Now you'd better learn to do what you're told or you'll be in worse trouble than you are already."

Still holding on to her he reached for the switch on his radio with his free hand and spoke into the microphone without taking it off its strap. "Kilo-seven-two to Kilo-twenty. You there Nige?" The device squawked again. "I'm just opposite Church Street. Got this little Irish bitch here with IRA pamphlets in her bag. Doesn't know how to behave. Can you nip over and give me a hand? Kilo-one's sending somebody to take her in. Over." A further squawk which seemed to end in a laugh. "She's a cheeky little bit of blonde gaol-bait. Just your type. You'll love her." Another amused squawk. "Yeah. Fuck you too. Out." He switched off the machine and loosened his grip on Sheelagh's arm. "Must be your lucky day. You're going to meet my pal Nige. He's got a soft spot for kids like you. Well, soft but sometimes it goes a bit hard." He laughed loudly at his own joke. In the distance Sheelagh saw one of the soldiers leave the group at the road block and start to walk slowly in their direction. He was tall and walked with his head back and a swagger that suggested arrogance and cruelty. Sheelagh's thoughts raced. She looked at her watch again.

"You can stop doing that, sweetheart. You ain't going nowhere. Not for the moment anyway. Relax. A few questions, and maybe we'll check if there's a gun hidden up your lovely little pink pussy. You'd like that, wouldn't you? Then you can go. I'd do it right here, only my sergeant won't let me." Again he found his own joke highly amusing.

The second soldier walked right up to them without hurrying and looked her in the eye. His lips curled into an unpleasant grin. "Need a bit of help to keep her from running off, do you, Ed? Don't blame you, kid. I'd want to get away from that smelly bugger too." She realised that the first soldier's hand was now on her breast and pulled it aside.

"Oops. Sorry, Miss. My hand slipped. Maybe you can help me to keep this dangerous prisoner under control, Nige."

"Oh yeah. I can help Ed. I'm good at that." He reached towards her and she pressed back into Ed's chest.

"Maybe I was wrong, Ed. Maybe she likes you after all. Is that right? You fancy Ed here, do you? Pretty weird taste, I'd call that."

Sheelagh spoke in a voice that had risen in register and become mixed with tears. Her tone was now one of desperation. "Please listen to me. You're in terrible danger. We all are. Jesus, there's almost no time left. You have to believe me. We've got to get away from here, right now. In God's name, we've got to start running. Please! I beg you! In God's name!"

The two men looked at one another and laughed. Ed was the first to find his voice. "In danger, are we? Is that so? What's that? Some kind of threat? You got a stick of dynamite up your jacksy, maybe?"

Sheelagh's words sounded so ridiculous, even to herself, that she could barely get them out. "My bicycle... My bicycle is... going to explode!"

"Your bicycle is going to explode? Did you hear that, Nige? Her bicycle is going to explode! Bugger me, that's the funniest thing I've heard since I came to Ireland!" Nigel and Ed looked at one another and doubled-up with laughter.

In a desperate attempt to take advantage of their loss of concentration, Sheelagh kicked Ed as hard as she could on the shin and managed to escape his grip. But before she could take more than a single stride the powerful right arm of the still laughing Nigel was around her waist, dragging her backwards as she pummelled his ribs with her elbows.

Then there was nothingness.

Chapter Thirty-one
Condolences

Two dark-suited men wearing black Balaclava helmets strolled slowly along the top corridor of the block of flats until they came to a door where a large wreath of white lilies hung from an improvised hook. There was a faint murmur of conversation coming from inside, which stopped when one of the two men wrapped smartly on the door. It was opened by a middle-aged woman wearing a sombre grey business suit, who gasped when she saw the two men. "Holy Jesus, what is it that youse two wants?"

The taller of the two masked men spoke. "Please don't be alarmed, Mrs Flannigan. We've come to offer our deepest sympathy at your great loss. We have a Mass Card from the men and women of the Republican movement." He handed her a white envelope. "We also have some people downstairs who would like to come up and offer their respects to yourself and your husband, if it's a convenient moment."

"People? What people? Who are they?"

"I'm afraid I'm not at liberty to say, Mrs Flannigan. And we have to insist that you and your husband meet with them in private."

She looked puzzled and uneasy. "We're on our own. Is that what you're asking?"

"It is. Will I ask them to come up?"

She swallowed hard. "Suit yourselves. I'll tell Terry they're coming, will I?"

"If you wouldn't mind."

The two men turned and started back down the corridor at the same unhurried pace. Mrs Flannigan closed the door and called to her husband. "Guests, Terry. Men in Balaclavas."

"Don't those bastards have any human feelings? Don't they know when to give it a rest?"

"I thought maybe we should see them and get it over with. They've given us a Mass Card." She opened the envelope while she walked towards her husband in the lounge. As well as the card there was a folded sheet of white paper. She opened it carefully. It was a receipt from the undertaker for the advance payment in full of the cost of Sheelagh's coming funeral. It included the price of the coffin, the cemetery plot, the limousines and a horse-drawn hearse. It was clear that they had gone for the top of the range in every instance. Mrs Flannigan started to cry.

Some minutes later, after she had composed herself, she and Terry opened the door to seven males of varying ages, all of them in dark suits, four wearing Balaclava helmets and flanking the other three, who were Jim Sullivan, Bernie O'Shea and Danny Gallagher. The escorts remained outside, allowing the others to enter and face Sheelagh's parents in embarrassed silence.

Terry looked up from his wheelchair with an expression that combined blazing hatred and suicidal depression. He was the first to speak. "I can hardly believe that you people have the nerve to come here like this, after what you've done to this family."

"You have the right to be angry," Big Jim said very quietly, "and it's possible that my judgement wasn't sound in allowing your daughter to take part in the operation that ended in tragedy. I accept responsibility for that error of judgement, if that's what it was. But your daughter practically begged me to allow her to do anything that was within her power to help free Northern Ireland from British domination. And to be perfectly frank, I don't feel that I have the right to turn away any Irish person who wants to play their part in the struggle for the liberation of this country. Your daughter was a patriot and a heroine, and I respected her decision then, as I do now. That's the kind of person that she was, the kind of inspiring young person that makes the struggle for Irish nationhood worthwhile."

"You're talking about decisions freely made by adults who understand all the facts. My daughter was sixteen years old – she wasn't old enough to join any army. She wasn't old enough to vote, or to buy a glass of Guinness in a pub. And you think she was old enough to lay down her life for some daft pipe dream of a United Ireland brought about by the bomb and the gun?"

"Yes, Mr Flannigan, I made that decision, and I've welcomed other young people into the movement as well. I'm known for it. Two of them are standing beside me right now. I believe in the young

– I trust them more than I trust any other generation, my own included. I'm inspired by their idealism, and their energy, and their loyalty and dedication to the movement. But I am only a man, only a human being, and my judgement may have been wrong. And I've come here tonight to talk to the two of you, and to admit that I may have been wrong, and to apologise and ask for your forgiveness if I was."

Terry Flannigan, for the first time in his life, seemed almost lost for words. "You have the brass neck to come around to my home..."

His wife put her hand on his arm. "Terry. Mr Harrison has come around to apologise and to say that he may have made an error of judgement. I think it takes a pretty brave man to do that. Nothing's going to bring Sheelagh back. Wouldn't it be more fitting for us to kneel down and say a few prayers for her soul, and our own?"

There was a pause. Terry Flannigan turned to Danny. "And you. What have you got to say for yourself? Do you think I'm so daft I can't see who put her up to it? Sheelagh wouldn't have touched the IRA with a ten foot pole before she met you. Do you think I'm bloody stupid that I couldn't see what you were doing to her?"

Jim answered for Danny. "There I have to put you straight, Mr Flannigan. Danny didn't want Sheelagh to go into the IRA. He did everything in his power to stop her, offered every argument against it under the sun. I swear to that on my mother's grave. I tried to get her to reconsider as well, but obviously I didn't succeed. You may not believe any of that, but it's the God's honest truth nevertheless. The only person who thought it was a good idea for Sheelagh to join the Volunteers was Sheelagh. That's the truth of it, so help me God."

"I believe you, Mr Harrison," Sheelagh's mother said in a calm tone. "None of you needed to come here tonight. It was the right thing to do, but it wasn't the easy thing to do. I think you deserve credit for that." She turned to Terry. "Mr Harrison has said that he may have got it wrong. He's said that he's sorry if that was what happened. What more can the man say? What more can anybody say? Ask these people to sit down, Terry. I'm going to put the kettle on."

"I'm sorry, it's very kind of you, Mrs Flannigan, but we can't stay. We're putting the two of you in danger by being here at all. If it's all right with you we'll just conclude our business and go. We have a favour to ask of you."

Terry looked up in disbelief. "A favour?"

"We would like your permission to fire a volley over your daughter's coffin. The boys have asked me especially if they could have that honour. They want to give her the proper respect due to a fallen comrade. It means a lot to them."

"You want to fire a volley over my daughter's coffin? And what in God's name do you think the world's going to make of that? Don't you know perfectly well I've been working day and night to try to stop the people I represent from turning to the gun? And you want me to advertise to the whole world that my daughter got herself killed on some kind of botched IRA bombing mission? That my own daughter was in the Volunteers?"

"Nobody knows the exact circumstances in which Sheelagh lost her life, including us. All anybody knows is that she was caught up in a bombing incident for which no side has claimed responsibility. You can deny that she was ever in the Volunteers. Say that it was some kind of political move on our part, trying to claim her as a martyr. Say you don't know anything about it. We'll neither confirm nor deny – not until Northern Ireland gets her freedom. Then your daughter's bravery will be acknowledged with the highest award for gallantry available in the new Republic of all Ireland. You have my personal guarantee about that. Your daughter will have her place in history. She'll be remembered by the Irish people long after the two of us have been forgotten, and rightfully so. May God grant her the highest place in heaven, where she can pray for us all, and ask the Almighty to forgive us for our sins and our honest mistakes and all our lapses of judgement. Will the two of you say amen to that, and tell me that you don't harbour any hatred in your hearts for myself or the other members of the Irish Republican movement?"

On the way back, Danny travelled in the lead car with Big Jim. The growing shades of dusk covered up the way the blood had drained from his face. "God, I didn't think I could feel any worse, but I felt terrible in front of those two."

"As you rise up in the movement you'll realise that that kind of thing comes with the job. It's the hardest part of all."

"I don't want to rise up. I know it can't be done, but to tell you the truth what I really want is to get out of the movement entirely."

"You're bound to feel like that right now, Danny. I can't count the number of times I've felt that way myself. So I'm giving you a direct order. I'm telling you to take indefinite leave until you've finished your time at school, or until we maybe need you again for something. You've done a great job for us. You've given us the Police car jammer, the radio station, the bomb design, and even the training course so that anybody can assemble them. You've done more than enough for the time being. The school holidays are nearly here. Take a good solid break from all this. Go over to England and pay Joyce a visit. Become a sixteen-year-old again. That's the best thing you can do for yourself and us right now. And it's an order."

Danny was quiet for several minutes, imagining a summer with Joyce, trying to blot out the guilt he felt, that somehow the times he had spent with Sheelagh had never had the same magic as the times he had spent with Joyce, piled on top of the far deeper guilt that, intentionally or not, he had started Sheelagh down the path that had led to her death. From now on he had to live with the knowledge that he had designed and probably even assembled the bomb that had killed her. It was he who had made the decision that the risk of a premature detonation didn't outweigh the desirability of making the bombs impossible to disarm once they had been sealed. Without really thinking about it he had weighed up the life of Sheelagh and every other bomb courier, and decided that it was less important than the possibility of a bomb being successfully disarmed by the RUC or the army. He had been casually playing God, or much more accurately, the Devil. Big Jim had apologised to her parents for his lapse of judgement – why hadn't he? How could Jim go on, having to make decisions like that day after day and live with the consequences?

"I have another battle to fight now," Jim said quietly, "inside the Republican movement itself. There are a lot of people who think that what Sheelagh did by accident is what the movement should be doing by design. Targeting the forces of British imperialism directly. The institutions and personnel by which England retains her domination of Northern Ireland, the RUC and the British Army. There's a big split developing in the Republican movement. If things get really bad we could end up with two IRAs gunning for one another, while the English sit back and laugh. It would set the cause back twenty years. That's where my work's going to have to be concentrated for a while to come. Holding the IRA together and keeping our guns trained on the right target."

Chapter Thirty-two
The Diggers

Carrying a large rucksack, Danny entered the rear of the hall and found himself a table to perch against. He pushed the rucksack underneath. The seats all seemed to be taken and the opening set had begun.

Joyce, looking as jaw-droppingly beautiful as ever in a low-cut short white dress with silver embroidery, sat with the Martin guitar on her knee between two slightly older standing men whom Danny recognised from the cover of Bernie's "Diggers" EP. The third member of The Diggers, the pale-skinned and delicate-looking blonde singer Nina, waited to one side, presumably sitting out this particular song. Remembering the names from the cover notes, Danny was sure that the heavily-muscled tin-whistle player with the tanned, weathered skin and the wiry brown hair would be Morgan. Danny had him down as a Welsh rugby player as soon as he saw him. The tall lean fiddler with the neat beard and Jesus shoulder-length sandy-gold hair held in a white hair-band would have to be Robin. There was something instantly charismatic about him, partly the handsome regular features, partly the openness and warmth of his whole demeanor, like an American evangelist beaming goodwill to his congregation. Joyce seemed tiny between the two men, her body almost hidden behind the guitar, but her voice filled the room with a sweet crystal clarity that held the audience enchanted. She was singing the old Scottish ballad *Over the Water to Charlie*.

When the song ended, with the chilling assertion that she had borne and lost an unspecified number of sons and would willingly bear them all again and lose them all for Charlie, the applause was, as Danny had expected, thunderous. When it died down Joyce made an announcement. "My best friend Danny from Belfast has just arrived. Is there a seat for him anywhere?" There was a shuffling towards the front and someone answered: "We've got an empty one here." Embarrassed, Danny made his way towards the proffered chair. "And hands off him, girls." Joyce added. "He's mine. At least for tonight." This got almost as much applause as the song.

In the darkened prop-room behind the stage, Danny stopped kissing Joyce and slackened his embrace to be able to speak. "What did you say that for? It was awful. I was embarrassed as hell."

"They loved it. And all the men were jealous."

"You're the most confident person I've ever met. Doesn't anything throw you?"

"I like men who are nice to me. I like sex. What's the point of pretending otherwise?"

"You're scary. I don't think the world's ready for you yet."

"Forget about the world. Are you ready for me? For a summer together?"

"What do you think?"

"Have you got anywhere to stay tonight?"

"No."

"Well, you have now. Come and meet the rest of the group."

She slung the guitar case over her shoulder and Danny did the same with his rucksack. He followed her through to where a battered light-coloured Ford minibus was waiting in the semi-darkness of the back alley, with four people on board and a number of amplifiers and musical instruments stashed neatly behind the rear-most seats. Three of the occupants were the performers that Danny had seen on stage, the other woman he didn't know. They sat as though partnered-up, Nina in the front seat with Robin the driver, the second slightly older woman, whom he didn't know, with Morgan in the two seats behind them. Joyce and Danny climbed into the back, stashed Joyce's guitar and found a vacant seat for Danny's rucksack.

Joyce made the introductions. "The two in the front are Robin Green and Nina Clarke. The other two are Morgan Williams and Eileen Cole. They're all sort of one big family."

The four turned around as best they could and smiled. "So this is the lucky man who came in late," Morgan greeted him, in a Welsh accent that was as broad as Joyce and Danny's Northern Ireland. "Welcome to the family. Joyce has told us great things about you."

"Joyce exaggerates a lot."

"Well she thinks a lot of you, so some of it must be true. We're planning to drive to Wales tonight. It's about a hundred miles. I hope you don't mind."

"No. Of course not. It's very kind of you to offer to put me up."

"Well, I hope we can do more than just put you up."

Danny didn't know what Morgan meant by this, but he nodded his thanks. "Are you all musicians?"

"Oh, I wouldn't make a claim as big as that." Morgan continued to answer for the group. "Some would dispute that any of us are, except your friend Joyce here. But we all make some kind of noise, under the right circumstances and conditions. Eileen here tries to play the Welsh harp, but it's a bit impractical for touring. Mainly, she's our roadie and business manager. You'll soon get to know us. We do everything together." Again, Danny was unsure of the full import of Morgan's phrase.

Joyce leaned over and rested her head on his shoulder. "They're really great people. I'm ever so lucky to have found them." He embraced her and kissed the top of her head.

"Why don't you all try to have a nap while I drive," Robin suggested, starting the engine as he spoke, "and we can get to know each other properly tomorrow."

Danny's first impression of the farmhouse was vague and dulled by his tiredness. It seemed remote, accessible only by a long unmade road, and smelled faintly of animal dung outside and wood fires within. There were three mattresses containing random cushions, throws and covers arranged around the fireplace on the floor of the living room, which was lighted by a single dim light-bulb in the centre of the ceiling. Danny got the impression of a lot of books lining the walls, with a few cabinets and cupboards and the usual bric-a-brac of a much-used living space.

"This farm belongs to my mother," Morgan explained, "but she doesn't do very much with it now. When my dad died she started renting out most of the land and went to live near my younger brother and his wife in the town. Her health isn't too good and she can't cope with it any more. We can pretty well do what we like with it."

Danny acknowledged, wondering what kind of thing they might have in mind.

"We're off to bed now. I'll show you where the bathroom is. If you want to make tea or eat anything the kitchen is through there," he pointed. "Make yourselves at home. Will the two of you be okay here in the lounge for tonight?"

"Of course. This is great." After a few more instructions the others left them alone.

Danny and Joyce took a shower together, which inevitably led to sex on one of the big mattresses. They were both quite sleepy and in a tender and gentle mood, and it was over very quickly. Afterwards, in total contentment, they fell asleep in each other's arms beneath the cover of a single sheet.

In the morning Robin wore a light blue kaftan that made him look even more like a Westernised Jesus when he gave Danny his guided tour of the farm. Joyce, who was in a particularly affectionate mood and wearing a bikini top and a sarong wrapped around her waist, tagged along, holding both their hands and dividing her attention equally between the two. The weather was exceptionally fine, with no wind and a cloudless sky, the early morning mist softening the shades of the distant hills to a delicate purple and melting their hazy shapes into the sky.

They walked along the course of a stream, up the wooded hill behind the farm, as Robin tried to explain the basics to Danny. "The land here isn't very good. The topsoil is thin, with heavy clay and rocks underneath it. Most people just use it for grazing, or grow grass for winter fodder. You'd be surprised what a valuable crop grass is. But if you plough it to put in wheat or barley or anything like that the topsoil disappears and you have to add a lot of organic material to get any yield. Plenty of arable further down the valley but up here it isn't economic. Morgan's experimenting with some new techniques, though, trying to grow stuff without any soil at all in the conventional sense. Can you see the big glasshouse behind the farm?"

"Yes."

"Hydroponics. Crops like beans and tomatoes grown in a liquid medium that comes from the septic tank. Takes a lot of control and management, but potentially a big step forward. What he's going for in the long term is self sufficiency."

"Growing all your own food?"

"More than that. Generating our own electricity, Producing our own methane for cooking and heating. Maybe spinning our own wool and weaving our own cloth eventually. It's a long term project. A life's work."

"That sounds brilliant. But why does he want to do it"

Robin found a convenient log and sat down, inviting the others to join him. "Did you listen to the words of the final song we did? And my little introduction?"

"I was pretty tired by then," Danny apologised, "not really running on all cylinders. Been travelling all day..."

"That's okay. It was probably written by a man named Gerrard Winstanley or one of his friends, in the time of Oliver Cromwell. The middle of the seventeenth century. I'll sing a bit of it for you again."

Robin began by beating out the rhythm on the log, then launched into the verse in his deep clear baritone. Joyce added harmony on the chorus.

You noble Diggers all, stand up now, stand up now,
You noble Diggers all, stand up now;
The waste land to maintain, seeing Cavaliers by name
Your digging do disdain, and persons all defame.
Stand up now, Diggers all, stand up now.

Your houses they pull down, stand up now, stand up now,
Your houses they pull down, stand up now;
Your houses they pull down to fright poor men in town,
But the Gentry must come down, and the poor shall wear
the crown.
Stand up now, Diggers all, stand up now.

With spades and hoes and plows, stand up now, stand up
now,
With spades and hoes and plows, stand up now;
Your freedom to uphold, seeing Cavaliers are bold

To kill you if they could, and rights from you withhold.
Stand up now, Diggers all, stand up now.

The club is all their law, stand up now, stand up now,
The club is all their law, stand up now;
The club is all their law, to keep poor men in awe;
But they no vision saw to maintain such a law.
Stand up now, Diggers all, stand up now.

To conquer them by love, come in now, come in now,
To conquer them by love, come in now;
To conquer them by love, as it does you behove,
For He is King above, no Power is like to Love.
Glory here, Diggers all, stand up now!

Robin interrupted the singing at this point to explain the background to the song. "You've got to try to imagine what it was like back then. The aftermath of a bitter civil war. People have been displaced, lost their houses, their land, their families. Those things are the same after every war, but this one was different. This time the people had risen up and executed their king, the old order was supposed to have been overturned. People had great expectations. No more poverty, no more bond slavery, power in the hands of the people instead of the ruling class. But guess what? The people remained poor, the land owners kept their land and their power – nothing really changed."

"We did a story like that at school," Danny put in, "called *Animal Farm*. About how revolution never changes anything. How the new crowd become exactly the same as the old crowd."

"Orwell was no fool. Yes, conventional revolutions shift the power from one group of oppressors to another. Nothing more. Real revolution, the kind that changes things, has to come from the bottom up. It has to ignore the power structure, replace it bit by bit, make it irrelevant. That was what Winstanley tried to do. He gathered together a ragged band of dispossessed people at a place called St. George's Hill in Surrey. The hill was what was called 'common land'. That meant that anybody was allowed to use it to graze their cattle, or for

206

a few other purposes, but they weren't allowed to grow crops on it or to live on it. Winstanley's group called themselves The Diggers. They broke the rules. They dug up the common land, ploughed it and planted crops. They believed that no man had a right to own land exclusively, that the earth was the common treasury for all mankind."

"Did they get away with it?"

"What do you think? The St. George's Hill commune lasted about eighteen months. The ruling class went ballistic. The law was used against them, Cromwell's New Model Army that was supposed to be the people's army was used against them, the villagers nearby were fed propaganda about them and told to drive them out – the whole might of the church, the state and the judiciary was enlisted against them, and Winstanley wouldn't allow them to defend themselves except with words and appeals to reason. His political writing is some of the finest and most passionate in the language. He was the first genuine socialist theorist ever, unless you count Jesus Christ. He believed that to avoid a new ruling class emerging, we have to stop using money at all. Property always means exploitation. Possessions are harmless, but as soon as you start using an abstract token to represent goods and labour it's inevitable that some people will accumulate more and more of these tokens, and others will have very few. It's the very existence of the tokens, the money itself and the economic system it spawns, that makes capitalism inevitable. You can't control it, you can only replace it. That's Winstanley's idea in a nutshell."

"Doesn't he explain things nicely?" Joyce said, kissing him on the cheek.

Danny nodded. "He's quite something. Like taking a walk with Jesus and Mary Magdalene."

Robin considered the analogy. "Jesus? No, he was a great moral reformer, but not radical enough on the economic front. Mary might have been more imaginative, I don't know, I never came across any of her comments on her pal's ideas."

They looked down at the patchwork of green fields, the stream running through them, the white dots of sheep and the misty hills fading into the sky in the far distance. "It's a lot to grasp," Danny said at last, "It's like changing human nature itself. Changing the whole world."

"Exactly. It might take a hundred years. All we can really hope to do is set up one or two groups living by Winstanley's principles and let the world see how good they are. What a great way it is to organise human society. Win over hearts and minds. Invite others to follow. That was what he tried to do himself, and there were other groups all over England that modelled themselves on his for a while, but they were all destroyed – nothing was left but his ideas and his writings – and they can't be destroyed. They're going to be around and they're going to inspire people like us until the end of time – until the human race is ready for them. He wasn't just ahead of his own time, he was ahead of our time as well. Three hundred years later, we're still only getting started on the dream. But now we have science to help us. The media to help us explain our ideas. Engineers like you to help us get the practical details right. Folk singers like Joyce here to help us to grab the world's attention. She's way out of our class, we know that, she's headed for a great solo career – and just imagine what she can do as an ambassador for Winstanley's ideas."

At this Joyce hugged him and kissed him full on the lips. "Isn't he sweet? He thinks I can have a solo career."

He held on to her gently and stroked her hair like Danny had so often done before. "You can have anything you like," he told her. "The world's at your feet. You know that." She kissed him again, more languidly this time, returning his embrace.

Danny ignored their intimacy. He had adapted to the kind of person Joyce was, her enthusiastic demonstrations of affection for others no longer worried him. His place on the list wasn't threatened. "Where did you come across all this stuff?" he asked Robin.

"I did Politics, Philosophy and Economics at Oxford. With that background the only career options open to me were Tory MP or anarchist. I chose the second one."

"We've written a couple of extra verses to Winstanley's song," Joyce said. "Would you like to hear them?"

Danny nodded and Robin tapped out the rhythm on the log once again.

The centuries go by, stand up now, stand up now,
The centuries go by, stand up now.
The centuries go by, but the vision will not die,
As to change men's hearts we try, reason our ally,
Stand up now, Diggers all, stand up now.

On a new St. George's Hill, stand up now, stand up now,
On a new St. George's Hill, stand up now.
On a new St. George's Hill, built with scientific skill,
Your words inspire us still, your dreams we'll yet fulfil.
Stand up now, Diggers all, stand up now.

Your vision long delayed, stand up now, stand up now,
Your vision long delayed, stand up now.
Your vision long delayed, all the plans that you have laid,
Will be manifold repaid, let the greedy be afraid,
Stand up now, Diggers all, stand up now.

Chapter Thirty-three
Commune Life

"But how could the world produce complicated, sophisticated things – things like cars, and aircraft, and... television sets?"

Danny had been pestering Robin with questions about his strange new social vision since they returned from their walk. Morgan was nowhere to be seen, presumably doing something outside. Joyce and Nina were rehearsing songs in one of the bedrooms and Eileen was stuffing envelopes with pictures of the group in answer to fan mail. Joyce's picture was separate, more recent than the one they had used on Kingston Radio, and a bit more restrained in terms of dress.

"That's no real problem. Worker-controlled factories are nothing new. Individual groups would specialise in particular parts of the production process, just as they do now. You would have a group producing tyres, another producing engine blocks, another electronic circuit boards, pumps, electric motors, whatever. The difference would be that they would have no incentive to waste resources or to respond to marketing requirements or sales figures. Cars would be designed to last fifty or a hundred years, and to run on fuels that were plentiful, or even renewable, like alcohol from plant material. People wouldn't be forced to work in one job or even one industry forever. They could move around, change their careers, follow their interests in whatever way they wanted to. Work would be meaningful, rational, fulfilling. You would waken up in the morning keen to do it. That's the kind of world I have in mind."

"But if it was a free acquisition economy as you call it, wouldn't it be possible for people to take what they wanted without contributing anything? What checks would you have that people were pulling their weight?"

"None, essentially. Freeloaders would be a possibility, but there would be strong social pressure against them, and they would only have access to the same possessions as everyone else anyway. Not like the freeloaders we have now, who hoard enough resources to end world poverty tomorrow, and ride around in chauffeur-driven cars and have houses in New York, London, Hawaii and the South of France. There would be no opportunities for big-scale parasitism."

Danny considered Robin's rebuttal. "You seem to have most of the angles covered," he admitted. "I'm not too hot on theory, but I think I might be able to help on the practical side." He pulled his chair over to the small desk behind the mattresses and found himself a blank sheet of foolscap and a felt-tip pen. "This is the hill behind the house," he explained, drawing a crude sloping line, "and this is the river that runs down it. You've been talking about generating your own electricity. Well, there's your power source. I've done a few very crude calculations in my head. The amount of energy you can extract depends on the total mass of water and the total height it falls in unit time. The mass isn't great, but you've got height on your side. I won't bore you with the details, but if my estimates are anything near right, assuming only about a fifteen per cent overall efficiency, that little river is going to give you a continuous output of about two kilowatts of electricity, far more than you need for cooking and light. Not enough if you were to heat with it as well, but you don't do that anyway, do you?"

"No, we just cut some wood and burn it. What would we need to do then, to get all this free electricity?"

Danny added a picture of a dam and a pipeline to his drawing. He sketched in a small lake above the dam. At the bottom of the pipe he drew a square and labelled it 'turbine'."

"The most efficient way would be to pipe the water for part of its descent and put it through a small turbine at the bottom. It could be an irrigation pump used in reverse. It would have to be one that used the turbine principle, of course, not a centrifugal pump. We could generate direct current – I would suggest at 24 volts, then you could use heavy-duty lead-acid accumulators to store it. Lorry batteries. A lorry voltage regulator would control the rate of charge for you. All readily available technology. Your transmission lines would be at 24 volts and you would use an inverter to step it up to 240 volts AC for things like the TV and the washing machine. The lighting could use the original 24 volts. Your bulbs would last a lot longer."

212

"So there's no real problem doing that?" Robin was clearly impressed.

"None whatsoever. I could do it for you in a summer. If you're serious about it, though, I would suggest you include a reservoir." He pointed to the sketch. "A small artificial lake about half way up the hill. It would even out the effects of wet and dry periods. Give you a constant head of water."

"How big would it need to be?"

"The bigger the better. One hundred, two hundred yards across ideally." As Danny spoke he added approximate dimensions to the lake in his drawing. "You could use it for other things at the same time. What about fish-farming? There must be some fast-growing fresh-water species you could stock it with."

Robin whistled in amazement. "This is fantastic! I thought my ideas were way out. Morgan was very doubtful about using the stream. You think big, and you think practical. I like it. Of course I can see problems. Cutting down trees, for one thing. That's a no-no at the moment. And we can't interfere with the river if it affects other farms lower down the valley. Everybody relies on it for irrigation."

"It wouldn't interfere with the water supply in a bad way, it would improve it. Give them more water during dry periods. We can't create or destroy water. Even if we put it through our turbine twice, which is the next idea I want to talk about, it all goes back into the river eventually and continues down the valley. No problem."

As Robin watched, Danny added more details to his sketch. A wind mill appeared, pumping water from the bottom of the pipeline back to the reservoir. Glasshouses sprang up to either side of the artificial lake, with pipes carrying water for the plants. Then Danny inserted a crude drawing of the farmhouse and Morgan's experimental hydroponics house. "We should have enough surplus power to provide a bit of winter heating for the indoor crops – and electronic controls for feeding and ventilation. We need to think about insulation too – maybe multiple glazing, or high efficiency plastics..."

"You really are one of us," Robin assured him, putting a hand on his shoulder. "We're not the only people thinking about alternative technology either. There are people working on things like clean water for Indian villages, solar power, wave power, recycling waste, new building materials, new forms of architecture – all kinds of things. And we can tap into it. I think I know how Winstanley would have reacted to all this and I'm going to try to do the same. Carry straight society along with us. Avoid confrontation. Make it easy for people to support us. Keep as many people as we can on side. There are colleges and Universities teaching this stuff now. People doing M.Sc. and Ph.D. dissertations in energy efficiency and alternative ways to generate electricity – all that kind of thing. University people have influence. We can offer them a field station. A laboratory for studying new approaches to living. A conference centre. A publishing house and library for this new field of knowledge. In ten years this could be a world centre for alternative technology and alternative lifestyles, right here in Wales. There's nothing to stop us. Will you help us? Will you join us?"

Danny stopped drawing on his sheet of paper. He didn't answer.

"It's okay. You don't have to answer right away. I should talk it over with the others first anyway. But I know what they'll say." Still Danny did not reply. "You will think about it, won't you?"

Danny's expression had grown serious. "Yes," he said quietly, "I'll think about it. Of course. I need to go to the bathroom just now."

There was a gentle tapping at the bathroom door. Danny realised that he had been there for rather a long time. With some embarrassment he stood up and undid the latch. It was Eileen, "Sorry," he began, "I wasn't really doing anything..."

"I know. I guessed," she joined him and closed the door behind her. "Robin said you seemed to be a bit upset. Do you want to tell me what it is?" She perched on the side of the bath. Danny didn't reply straight away so she continued, "I often come here too when I need a moment to myself. We aren't supposed to have any private space, you know, everything is supposed to be owned in common. But sometimes you just need a little somewhere – for a minute or two. I do anyway."

She waited. Danny felt compelled to say something. "It's nothing to do with anybody here," he said at last. "It's... something really foolish I did when I was younger. And now it can't be undone. And

214

because of it, I'm not sure that I can join you here. I want to, that's for sure, but I think I may have spoiled it. Made it impossible."

"It can't be that bad, surely? Tell me what it is. I won't tell the others if you don't want me to, I promise."

He shook his head. "Even Joyce doesn't know. And she would probably never speak to me again if she did."

There was a pause. "We've all done bad things, Danny. Every one of us. Will I tell you my secret? It really is a secret."

"You can if you want to, but I can't tell you mine in return. It's something I just can't ever do. It involves other people... and it's really bad. I'm not exaggerating."

"That's okay. It was just a thought. Maybe when we get to know each other a bit better... I just feel you might be somebody I could talk to. Somebody who isn't part of all this. Not yet anyway. I thought before you came here you were going to be exactly the same as Joyce, but you're not, are you?"

"I think I could hardly be more different. I don't know why she bothers with me. I'm sorry, Eileen. I would like to open up to somebody too – more than anything else in the world. But I don't know if I'm ever going to be able to."

She touched his hand for a moment before leaving.

By bedtime, after they had eaten and everyone had talked a lot more about politics and engineering and especially music, Danny had overcome his mood of self pity and was feeling exhilarated again about Robin's plans for the building of a better world.

Eileen and Morgan lounged together on one of the big mattresses by the side of the dying log-fire, while the other four shared the one opposite. The conversations slowly died down and became mixed with the strumming of guitars and humming of folk melodies. Danny loved the atmosphere. This must surely be what a hippy commune is supposed to be like. One element seemed to be missing though. "I see you people aren't into drugs," he said quietly to Robin.

"It's our free decision not to put any chemicals into our bodies except for medical purposes. None of us drinks caffeine either. We find we don't need stuff like that, and we feel better without it. We just get high on ideas, and our relationships with one another. And we always have to be aware that we're on show. If we get seen as part of a silly teenage drugs culture we can be dismissed. We hand them a stick to beat us with."

"My mum did herself a lot of damage that way," Danny said. "I wish she'd had the sense you people have."

The strumming died out and the murmur of conversation became softer, with people just talking to the ones next to them. Danny wondered when they would leave for the two bedrooms. He assumed the sleeping arrangements would be the same as the night before, but instead everyone took turns to use the shower and the bathroom and then arrived back in different variations of nightwear. Morgan wore a pair of conventional brown pyjamas, Robin a baggy pair of under-pants and the three women appeared in nightdresses of different lengths and degrees of transparency, Joyce's being, predictably, the least substantial.

Everybody seemed accustomed to this arrangement so Danny went last, showered, and changed into underpants and one of the loose T-shirts that he normally wore in bed. Joyce was now cuddled-up to Robin, and it seemed intrusive to approach them, but on noticing his return she beckoned him over and held his hand, while continuing a very quiet conversation with Robin. She was more or less on top of him so was effectively whispering into his ear. Nina, whom Danny assumed to be Robin's normal partner, lay nearby taking no part in what was going on. "It's okay," she said quietly to Danny, "we're cool about who sleeps with who. We're all one family."

Danny nodded. He was beginning to experience a degree of panic. This was a very unfamiliar situation, with totally unknown rules. The tongue-in-cheek slogan attributed to hippydom, "Make love, not war" crossed his mind, and he wondered how literally it was meant to apply.

He tried not to stare at Joyce, whose expressions of affection to Robin were becoming more and more extreme. She was clearly aware of his presence, and as they enjoyed a lingering kiss, took his hand and held it in an obvious gesture of inclusion. As she and Robin headed towards the inevitable, Danny began to find his own erotic involvement growing sharply as well. This was the ultimate blue movie. Releasing his hand for only a moment, Joyce disposed of her nightdress and eased Robin out of his underpants in one graceful movement.

Danny had never seen another man's erection before. Neither had he seen what came next. It was vigorous but gentle and beautiful, and Joyce kept a firm grip on his hand all the way through. During the actual few seconds when her little body went rigid with pleasure and she let out the involuntary sob of ecstasy that he had heard so often before, she squeezed his hand with all her strength and released it only as she became limp in Robin's arms. Then, to add total perfection to the most erotic experience of Danny's life, she leaned over and kissed him, with Robin still inside her.

Just as on his first meeting with Joyce, Danny teetered on the brink of losing control of his sexual arousal. Help, however, was at hand. Nina was suddenly on top of him, just as aroused as he was himself, tearing at his clothing and pulling her own up over her head and out of the way. Their union lasted only seconds, and he was uncertain if he had held out long enough to give her a climax, but she ended the tempestuous encounter by whispering: "Thank you" in Danny's ear and kissing him very tenderly on the lips before he could reply. Nobody had ever thanked Danny for sex before. It was without question the high point of his entire life to date. He knew that this night would fuel his fantasies and wet dreams for decades to come. A great wave of tenderness and contentment swept through his body. At that moment he loved everybody in the whole world, but most of all the other three members of the heap of sated humanity in which he lay.

It occurred to Danny that there were two more Diggers who had been somewhat left out. Joyce, clearly having the same thought, said: "Why don't you come over here, Morgan?"

Unconsciously, she had phrased it badly. "You do and you needn't come back again," they heard Eileen tell him coldly.

Chapter Thirty-four
Planning Paradise

There was a moment of total silence. Robin was the first to speak. "Eileen? Are you upset?"

"Yes. I'm tired of going along with things that are hurting me. We never agreed to all this stuff. We never talked about it. I'm sick of being pushed too far and too fast... I thought it would be different when her own boyfriend arrived, but it isn't. I need time. I can't cope with this. I'm tired of being made to feel wrong, and uncool, and... oh, just wrong. I know what I'm supposed to feel and what I'm supposed to think, but I don't. I can't go on with this act. It isn't me. I can't help my feelings. Nobody's listening to me..."

"Eileen, sweetheart, why didn't you say?" Morgan sounded genuinely surprised. "I never meant to do anything to hurt you..."

"It's not you. It's her. It's everybody. I feel everybody's disapproval – and she can do no wrong. She even makes me feel inferior as a musician. Old, and ugly, and prudish..."

Robin cut in. "No, I'm sorry, Eileen, you can't do that. You can't start blaming people. We have a problem as a group, not you, not Joyce, not me, all of us. It's a group problem. I didn't know about it before. We've got to solve it as a group, and we will."

"I know what's going to happen. You're all just going to take her side, aren't you?"

"We're not going to do that, Eileen," Robin assured her. "We're going to talk about it calmly, as a group. We're all going to have our say. I'll go first, if that's all right. I'm delighted to have both Joyce and Danny in the group. They're lovely people and they can help us in all kinds of ways. I find Joyce extremely attractive. I like everything about her. I'm willing to do whatever's necessary to keep the group together, just as it is now, and I'm sorry if I've hurt Eileen or Nina or anybody else. That wasn't my intention. I didn't know how Eileen felt. Nothing had been said. I want everybody to feel as good about this group and everybody in it as I do. There's nothing I won't do to make it work. That's all I have to say. Would you like to have your say next, Nina?"

"She's a pretty young girl with a beautiful body. Of course the men fancy her. There'd be something wrong with them if they didn't. But I don't feel sidelined or rejected. I don't feel that Robin or anybody else likes me any less because Joyce is around."

Eileen still sounded bitter. "Of course they fancy her. It's not them, it's her. She gives it to them on a plate."

At this Joyce could contain herself no longer. "Well, thanks very much! What am I supposed to do, then? Charge for it? The men here are all lovely. They're all my sweet boyfriends, and I'm happy to have sex with any of them at any time. That's the truth, it's how I feel and I'm not going to lie about it. I'm not competing with anybody else, I'm not trying to steal Morgan away from you or anybody from anybody, I'm just being myself. Having a good time. Not hurting anybody, or so I thought. You should have said something to me before. Why didn't you?"

"Are you trying to tell me you never suspected anything? Even that time I opened the bathroom door and you had your legs around his waist, shagging his brains out?"

"Oh yes, she likes that position," Danny put in, regretting it as soon as he had spoken.

"I can smell your perfume off him all the time. I can never forget about you, even when we're alone together."

"Look, I should probably keep out of this," Danny was hesitant, "but I just want to say, I do know what you're talking about. At the beginning, a couple of years ago when we first got together, I used to hate the thought of her with anybody else. I couldn't have coped either if it was in my face all the time like it is here. But gradually, I changed. I began to realise that nothing she did with other people made her like me any less. Eventually I started to feel fine about it. Really fine. All I care about now is that she's safe, that she doesn't get hurt by anybody, physically or emotionally. Just now was the most extreme test, and I was still okay. It was a huge thrill to see her having such a great time with Robin. I'm crazy about Joyce, stupidly, ridiculously in love with her, but I know she fancies other people, and she was so obviously happy and loving it – what was there to be upset about? I found myself loving it too, getting really high on her pleasure, feeling really good about it. You'll get to feel that way too, but you're right, it might take a little bit of time. It did with me."

Eileen seemed to be considering his words. After a while she spoke. "I do agree with all this non-possessive stuff in principle. I know I shouldn't feel the way I do... and maybe you're right, maybe I can change..."

"Of course you can," Danny assured her.

"I'm beginning to wish I hadn't said anything now. I feel silly..."

"It's not silly," Robin said. "Feelings are feelings. They're not silly or clever. They're feelings. We've got to be able to talk about them openly or we're completely sunk. You did exactly the right thing."

There was another pause. "Can I have a hug, Eileen?" Joyce asked.

"Of course. I'm sorry for the things I said. I'm sorry for being jealous. I know that's all it is really."

Joyce skipped over to the other mattress and hugged Eileen. At last the tension was broken. Danny could see that the two of them were smiling. "I'll try to give you a bit more time," Joyce promised, "take things slower. How about I'm allowed sex with each man once in every twenty-four hour period, and if we use the bathroom we have to lock the door?"

Giggles were heard from around the room. "She'll never be able to stick to it," Robin said in a solemn voice, "that would be like joining a convent for Joyce."

"Are you saying I'm a nymphomaniac?"

"Absolutely. It's one of your finest qualities. That and your guitar technique." There was more muffled laughter.

"I know how you people see me," Joyce said more seriously, speaking slowly, almost to herself, "what you think about me. You think I've had everything too easy. Nothing but praise all my life, no rejections. The truth is, I need a lot of approval. That's why I need to be a performer, I need the applause, the admiration. I'm scared that one day people will stop saying that I'm pretty and talented and all the lovely things they say about me now. I don't know how I'd cope if all that wasn't there. It's a need, maybe not a very healthy one. I don't want to be in competition with other women but I think I always have been. I've never had really close female friends. Even at school, when I was very little, all my friends were boys. I don't know how to relate to my own sex without being seen as some kind of rival, some kind of threat.

"I had a baby sister who died in hospital a few hours after she was born, and I've always had this fantasy that if she'd lived she would have been my special closest female friend, that my relationship with her would have made up for all the bad ones with all the other girls.

"With boys I've nearly always felt positive things: attraction, affection, admiration; but with girls all I usually feel is disapproval, distrust – hatred even. I know it shouldn't be like that and I don't want it to be. It would be really good if the two women here could help me to change that... I think I'm just asking the two of you to be my friends, if you can."

Nina was beside her and joining in the hug almost before she had finished talking. "I *am* your friend," she said with total sincerity. "I've never disapproved of you. I think you're great. I wish I could be just like you. It's because you're so happy and well-adjusted and so at ease with your sexuality that you can love so much, and achieve so much. You're my role model, and I want you for my little sister. Is that okay?"

Joyce laughed. "Of course it's okay, Sis."

There was a longish pause. "Has anybody got a bit of tissue?" Joyce whispered.

The days went by.

Danny found himself adapting very happily to the life of the group. Everyone tried to treat Eileen more gently, with Joyce asking permission every time she wanted a hug or a kiss or maybe more from Morgan, but it rapidly developed into a joke, Eileen pretending that she was keeping accounts and would charge Joyce an escort fee for Morgan's time. Danny spent most of his intimate time with Joyce rather than the other women, but neither of them escaped his attention entirely. Life for Danny was very, very good.

When Nina wasn't busy rehearsing for their imminent major gig at The Cambridge Folk Festival, or helping around the house, she drove Danny to the nearest large town, with its library and town hall, and he worked in the Reference section while she shopped or visited friends. Now that he was 17 he could learn to drive himself in principle, but at the moment he had other priorities. He started work on a formal planning proposal for damming the river and installing a small scale hydroelectric plant. He made sure that he worded it correctly, got all his sums right and used Ordnance Survey maps to produce accurate drawings. Morgan had a contact at the Electrical Engineering Department of the University of Wales at Bangor, who wrote Danny a very encouraging letter about the value of this kind of practical project, recommending that the local Planning Department look favourably on his outline proposals. Danny was confident that he would get permission. The time was right for this kind of experimentation, the local Council would want to appear modern and progressive. Then it would just be a matter of renting a chain saw and a small earth-mover and ordering up the piping and the steel reinforcement for the concrete. He was itching to make a start.

In preparing his application for Planning Permission, Danny came across what he was pretty sure was Eileen's secret. On a walk with her, down the long lane to do an errand, certain that they weren't going to be overheard, he faced her with it.

"I think I know what you started to tell me in the bathroom the other day. You're our landlady, aren't you? I had to go through the papers relating to the farm at the Town Hall. Morgan's mother transferred this place to you by Deed of Gift about ten months ago. The others don't know, do they?"

"No. You're right. You know now." She seemed relieved that she could talk about it.

"Why did she do it?"

She paused, searching for the right words. "Morgan and I aren't like you people. Not middle class, well educated, professional types since way back. I'm just a local farmer's daughter. We were a perfectly ordinary couple, known each other since primary school, planning to tie the knot. Then Morgan went to Agricultural College and Robin came to the Students' Union to give a concert with Nina, and a talk."

"A talk about Winstanley?"

"Who else? Morgan was hooked straight away. Head over heels, like he'd fallen in love. He offered Robin the use of the farm to try out his ideas. He wanted me to come along with them too, of course. And they became 'The Diggers', and made that record together, and came to live on the farm. And the idea of marriage was dropped. Robin didn't believe in marriage, so Morgan didn't any more either.

"Morgan's mother wasn't happy about any of it. The farm's nothing great, but it's the only real asset that Morgan's family has. She was afraid he would sign it over to Robin after she died. He's the eldest son, he would inherit it automatically. And it was always assumed he would get it, Rhys isn't interested in it anyway. So she decided to sign it over to me while she was still alive. She trusts me more than her son. She thinks the stuff that's going on with Robin will break down sooner or later, and Morgan and I will end up living on the farm without them like a respectable Welsh married couple. She's waiting for it all to go wrong, and the two of us to get our common sense back. I'm her spy in Robin's camp. That's my secret. I'm scared how they'll react when they find out."

"What about you? Do you think Morgan's mother might be right?"

"That's a hard question. When Robin's about, his magic sort of rubs off. I get carried along with it all. But when he isn't here, like right now, I start wondering. I think he's sincere, he means what he says, but I'm not sure whether it's for me or not. And I'm not sure if it can really work. Don't you ever think that maybe it's all a mad dream that's going to fall apart when reality cuts in?"

Danny shrugged. "What do I know? It's even newer to me than it is to you. I like it though. It feels good. I mean, the whole world is going through a huge change."

"You're starting to sound like Robin now."

"But I agree with him about that. It's obvious, isn't it? Cuba's had a socialist revolution and Ireland's headed the same way. The French students are on the streets, building up to something really big. Israel's got the kibbutz movement – socialist communes turning deserts into farmland. America's got the Flower Children marching against the Vietnam War. Martin Luther King's people are putting an end to race discrimination. The whole of South East Asia is going to be socialist soon. Everything's changing, all the old stuff's coming to an end."

"You certainly think big. You and Robin both. I just think about my own life. That's all I've got. One life. One future."

"But it does affect you. It affects women far more than men. All over the world women are demanding equality, standing up for their rights. It's like the whole patriarchal thing that powers the world is getting replaced. Whatever happens, we're not going to reproduce the world our parents lived in. There's a great unstoppable wave of something good out there. Don't you want to be part of it?" She hesitated, but did not speak. "I do. We're right at the moment when the whole world changes forever. It's exciting. I haven't got it all thought out like Robin has, but I want to be part of it. I want to help. It's not so much a theory as a feeling. It's in the songs of people like Dylan and Baez and Seeger and Ochs and Paxton. It's everywhere. I wouldn't have discovered it without Joyce, but now that I have, there's no turning back."

She took his hand and surprised him with a kiss on the cheek.

Chapter Thirty-five
Eileen's Story

"Why can't I come along and do one song. Nobody's going to mind. What's the problem?"

Morgan spoke almost too calmly, like somebody humouring a child. "I told you, Eileen. We've already submitted our set list. This isn't Floor Singers Night at the local pub – this is The Cambridge Folk Festival. We're on the main stage, the timing's very tight. The record company's sending people to do live recordings as well. It's all been agreed months ago. You were the one who wrote the letters and made the deal. Why didn't you bring it up back then? You know perfectly well we can't change it now."

"Only because you don't want to. We could ask. I could make a phone call."

"Okay. Fine. Make a phone call. See what they have to say."

"Why are you being so nasty about this? Why don't you want to support me? I bet it would be a bit different if Joyce wanted to do an extra song."

"That's not fair. It has absolutely nothing to do with Joyce. She's on the programme – we're 'The Diggers and Joyce McPherson', not just 'The Diggers'. Now you want to come in as another extra singer. It's going to look amateurish. Like we don't know what we're doing. I just don't think it's going to work, that's all."

Robin intervened. "I think Eileen has a point. She does all the donkey work for us and all she's asking is to be allowed to sing one song. With your harp, I take it?"

"Yes. Of course. With my harp."

"Okay. It's no big deal. We don't have to carry our amps and speakers this time, the stage is all set up. We would have room for Eileen's harp. Why don't we phone them and ask? I'll do it if you like."

Robin got up and made his way to the desk at the back. He lifted the receiver and started to dial. Morgan lowered his voice so that

Robin would be able to hear the phone. "Have you got something rehearsed, then?"

"Oh, I see. That's what's really behind all this. You don't think I'm good enough to share a stage with The Almighty Diggers, do you? You've kept me out right from the beginning and you intend to go on doing it."

"I didn't say that. Anyway it was you who didn't want to join us on stage, you who said you weren't ready. Now you say you are ready. So what's changed? I said I was happy for you to be in the group right from the beginning, remember?"

"You weren't exactly keen on the idea, and I think you still aren't."

They heard Robin speaking quietly at the phone. Almost at once he returned. "They say it can't be done. Not on the main stage. The schedule's too tight. But they can find you a slot on one of the smaller stages if you're interested."

"I thought they would say that," Morgan put in.

"Forget it. Just forget it. I'd rather stay here. I can get on with the paperwork."

Robin sat down and gave Eileen his full attention. "I don't want to leave you feeling like this. We need to talk it through properly. If you want to start doing songs with The Diggers that's fine, we've already said it is. But it isn't possible for it to start right now. Not with something as big as The Cambridge. We've got to rehearse with you and work out how you're going to fit in. And we will, just as soon as we get back. We don't have the time now, we're leaving in the morning. You know that."

"Tell you what," Danny suggested, "why don't I stay too? I could help Eileen with the paperwork and get to know her a bit better. It would be nice to spend a bit of time with her, if that's okay with you, Eileen?"

She smiled. "Really? You would want to do that? Stay here with me, with Joyce in Cambridge?"

"It would only be for a few nights. You wouldn't mind, Joyce, would you?"

They stood side by side and waved goodbye. When the van had disappeared around the first bend in the lane Danny turned to Eileen and smiled. "Is everything okay now? Are you happy with the way it's panned out?"

"Yes. I was a bit childish, wasn't I?"

"No, you just said what you wanted. Nothing wrong with that. They weren't able to give it to you this time, but it can all be sorted out for the future. You do feel okay about it, don't you?"

"Yes. Of course. Fine." There was a coldness in the way she said it that contradicted the sentiment.

They walked back together towards the cottage. Danny was already beginning to suspect that he had made a bad decision. His spending time with Eileen was not a source of stress or tension, but it meant that Morgan would be spending a lot of unsupervised time with Joyce, and that most certainly was. He realised that he was inept in this sort of area, he simply hadn't thought it through. That was probably why Eileen had decided she wanted to go along at the last minute, it had nothing to do with singing or playing the harp. In fact, he now realised, he had made things worse. If he had tagged along with the group as he had originally intended he would have been at least slightly in the way when Joyce and Morgan wanted time together, although he didn't honestly think his presence would make very much difference. But Eileen might think otherwise. As it was now, it was obvious that Morgan was assured of a lot of Joyce's tender ministrations. When he thought about it he felt a flicker of jealousy himself.

"It'll be a great chance for us to get to know each other," he said in the most positive tone that he could muster, realising that it sounded a bit feeble.

She didn't reply until they were indoors again. She sat on one of the mattresses and put a cushion against the wall so that she could sit up. Danny sat by her side. She seemed to be deep in thought for a few moments. Then she spoke. "I think I'm a hard person to get to know. I'm not sure that I know myself too well really. I seem to change the way I feel about things – and people – from minute to minute. Sometimes I really want this thing with Robin to work. Sometimes I want myself and Morgan to be back the way we were before we ever laid eyes on Robin, or heard the name Winstanley. Sometimes I just want to get away from it all, spend a bit of time on my own, have a break. I don't know what I want really."

"I've gone through the stage you're going through now. All I wanted two years ago was to marry Joyce, get a job – maybe on a radio station somewhere – have children, watch her career develop, do what I could to help. Get away from my mother and the atmosphere in that house. Have my own family and my own perfectly conventional life with the girl I was crazy about.

"But that would never have been enough for Joyce, and now I can see why. You need something more than just animal contentment – your life needs to have some kind of direction. Some kind of purpose beyond yourself. Something you can believe in, pour your energy into, get excited about. Some kind of vision."

"I seem to be able to get on okay without a vision like that."

"I suppose it's religion for a lot of people, but my dad showed me how ridiculous that was. So I got drawn into what you might call social visions. New ways to live, socialism, communes, national and personal liberation. Whatever you want to call it. Making human existence better and more enjoyable for everybody. Using my talents, such as they are, in the service of some kind of beautiful social dream."

"So you dream about the world? All my dreams are just about me."

"I'm no good at the actual dream. I let other people do that. My contribution has to be practical. That's what I'm good at. When I design something, when I make something, it works. That's all I've got to offer but it has some value and I do offer it. It's necessary. We aren't going to get anywhere without it. I'm the guy shovelling the coal in the engine room. Robin and people like him are at the helm. That's fine by me."

"God, I wish I had it all worked out as clearly as that. You haven't met my family, and Morgan's mother. Her especially. She thinks we're all totally bonkers. When I tried to explain Robin's ideas to her the first thing she said was, 'If he wants to be a farmer and make no money he's chosen the right country and the right farm'. She won't take it seriously at all. I try to defend it when I'm with her, but a lot of what she says actually makes good sense. Unless somebody pours money into this vision of his, unless somebody supports us entirely, there's no way we're going to survive. You say you're a practical person, can't you see that?"

"I can, and I've talked to Robin about it, and I think there may be answers, but just for now, what I would like to hear from you is what you want for yourself and for all of us in the long term. What's your dream, Eileen? Tell it to me."

"My dream? My dream was incredibly boring and ordinary. I wanted to have a big happy family, lots of children, trips to the seaside, big Christmas dinners, birthdays, watching them grow up and go to University and get married, relatives dropping in, and then grandchildren all around me in my old age. What you called 'animal contentment'."

"You said it *was* your dream. Isn't it your dream now?"

"It's gone. I've lost it."

"But you've said it may not work out here, and even Robin would have to admit that. You might end up with just you and Morgan and the farm. Exactly the way you were before."

She shook her head. "Another secret I haven't told you. It's just a grubby little one. I suppose most secrets are."

"Do you want to tell me?"

She lowered her voice. "I can't have children any more. I had an abortion when I was Joyce's age and it went wrong. Nobody knows that. Just me and my mother. I think what I really wanted from the setup here was a family. Children. They wouldn't be my own but I would be as much a mother to them as anybody else in the group. I could be the resident child minder. That's the role I would want. Something like that. I haven't thought it out very clearly."

Danny caressed her hand. He realised now why Joyce was such a problem for Eileen. How she must see her. The things she must represent. "This may sound a bit flippant, but have you thought about adoption?"

She smiled. "That's Plan B."

It took Danny a minute or so to realise that the phone was ringing. Eileen didn't waken at all. He gently disentangled himself from her arms and lifted her head off his shoulder and on to the pillow. She sighed and readjusted her position but her eyes remained closed. He couldn't resist the urge to kiss her on the cheek, and did it very gently.

The phone was persistent. There was no clock to glance at but he was certain it was long after midnight. Could Robin's van have been involved in an accident? Nobody phones at this time of night with good news. A terrible thought crossed his mind. Joyce could be injured, in pain, bleeding... He ran naked to the desk and grabbed the handset. Despite his anxiety he tried to talk quietly so as not to disturb Eileen. "Hello. Danny here. Who's that?"

Eileen was awake now. "Danny? Who is it?"

He covered the mouthpiece. "Just a minute, Eileen... Yes. Who's there?" As he listened he could feel the blood drain from his face.

"This is Kitty Mulhern – your mother's new maid. I've got a message for you. You need to come home straight away. Your da's been taken into hospital with a stroke."

Chapter Thirty-six
Bad News

In the few short weeks Danny had been away, Belfast had become even more of a battlefield. Sentry posts surrounded by sandbags on the corners of ordinary residential streets, rifle-bearing soldiers in full battle gear wandering incongruously amongst the weekend shoppers, burned-out shells of newly-bombed High Street businesses that had been open and trading at the time he left. Slogans of hatred daubed on every gable end in the poorer districts. Long queues of vehicles and people waiting to be searched at army checkpoints. It was totally unreal, a version if Belfast that he had up to then assumed to be an invention of the British journalists.

Danny used his key to open the front door and deposited his rucksack in the hall. "Ma! Are you there?" He hurried into the kitchen, where Kitty Mulhern, an overweight and rather sullen woman of indeterminate age whom his mother had employed to help out shortly before he left for England, was apparently making a snack for herself on one of the work surfaces.

"Hello Danny. You got over here very fast." She sounded detached. There was nothing in her voice to suggest the drama that was taking place in the Gallagher family. "Your da's in the Royal. Your ma's with him at the moment. Would you like a bite to eat or a wee cup of tea before you go over?"

"No. Just tell me which ward."

"Neurology. 4F. She wrote it down for you." She slowly retrieved a piece of paper from her handbag and handed it to Danny. "You know how to get there, don't you? Any bus along Falls Road. A 10 or an 81'll take you all the way. It's only a twenty minute run, if the bus isn't stopped by the army."

Danny knew that she meant well but her total lack of involvement angered him. "How is he? Has he come round?"

"He's able to speak now, but not very clearly, I think. You'll see when you get there." She turned back to the chopping board where she was dissecting a tomato. Danny left without another word.

He could feel his heart pounding as he walked down the stark corridor. It had never occurred to him that his father's health might break down before his mother's. It made no kind of sense. It simply wasn't fair. The man had lived what seemed to Danny the life of a saint. Practically every waking moment he had devoted to helping his fellow creatures, barely giving a thought to his own needs, always living up to the highest ideals of his profession; while she had self-indulgently destroyed herself with drink and become nothing but a burden to her ever kindly and patient husband. Even his sarcasm had been reserved for others; to the best of Danny's recollection his father had never uttered a harsh word to his spouse. And this was his reward. Had Danny harboured the faintest suspicion that the world might be in the hands of an all-loving god, this would have cured him of the delusion.

Danny always found hospitals forbidding places. All smelled of industrial disinfectant, were too brightly lit and magnified every footfall with reverberations from their tiled walls and hard linoleum floors. This one was no exception. The note said that his father was in a side ward to the right, and Danny had no trouble finding it. He entered soundlessly and marvelled at the baffling array of stainless steel instruments, bristling with knobs and dials and festooned with wires and tubes, to which his father seemed to be connected. His mother was in a wheelchair, her back to the door. Beyond her on the bed his father's head was heavily bandaged, his face pale and motion-less. Danny noticed straight away that his features were still symmet-rical. There was no sign of the classic loss of muscle tone down one side. What should he make of that? Frontal lobe damage, perhaps? On seeing Danny his expression changed for an instant, causing his mother to look around. She was thin and jaundiced with sunken eyes. At a glance she looked more ill than her husband.

"Danny. Thanks for coming. That was very quick. Your father's been asking for you."

He moved a chair to sit beside her and laid his hand on her lap. "Da, I just heard yesterday. They say you can talk. How are you feeling? What do you..." The meaningless sentence faded out. Dan-ny was babbling. He didn't care what question his father answered.

He just wanted to hear him speak. When he did, it was an alien voice that Danny heard – low-pitched, slow and laboured. He would never have identified it as belonging to his father. But the words were quite clearly articulated. That was a relief. It suggested that Kieran Gallagher's fine intellect mightn't have suffered too much destruction.

"Hello Danny. Good to see you. How is Joyce?"

"Terrific. Great. How bad is it, Da? What have they told you?"

A shadow of a smile passed across his father's face. "Well son, they won't let me see the angiogram. That isn't such a good sign. But then of course doctors make rotten patients. The very worst."

"You don't seem too bad. Your speech is fine. Just a little bit slow. But perfectly okay."

"Well, son, I've lived in this head of mine for quite a few years – and I'm sorry to have to report that a lot of the stuff that used to be in here isn't here any more. It's a lot less crowded than it used to be."

Both of them understood the import of what was being said. His father knew that his legendary sharpness was gone. It was the cruellest blow that nature could have dealt. He would probably have preferred outright death. "I think I'm going to be nearly as stupid as your Uncle John from here on in."

"Don't say that, Da. How can you possibly know?"

"Trust me, son. I know. There's a fog in here in this old head of mine. A fog like we used to get on the bog in Ballyrowan in the autumn. I can only see a little way through it. The landscape's… fading away. I suppose it's still there somewhere, beyond the fog, but I can't see it or get to it any more. In a strange sort of way, it's quite restful. Is your ma still there?"

"Yes, of course she is. Can't you see her?"

"Yes, of course I can. Silly. Silly thing to say. Some things are… just in here. Some things out there."

His father paused and Danny realised that he was squeezing his mother's hand. There was something terrifying about watching a brilliant mind come apart. It was the most unnerving thing Danny had ever experienced.

"The violin," his father said suddenly, louder and more clearly than before. "Have I mentioned about the violin?"

"No, Da. You haven't."

"It's very important. It's the most important thing that we have… to deal with. You're going to have to deal with it. Mrs Whittaker's violin. Will you do that for me?"

"Do what, Da?"

"Give it to Joyce's school maybe? What do you think?"

"You're talking about the violin that Mr Whittaker gave you when his wife died? You want to give it away, is that right?"

"Of course. No use to us. Got to go where it'll be appreciated. It's worth a lot of money, but that doesn't matter. The point is, it's a beautiful instrument. It has to go where people appreciate beautiful instruments. Young people. That's what she would have wanted."

"You're right, Da. The money isn't what matters. I understand that now. The money isn't real, but the violin is." Danny wasn't sure if he was making sense but he was beginning to choke up with tears. He wished that his mother wasn't there to see it.

"That's right. Exactly. The violin is real. Something that can never be replaced if it's lost. Something that really matters. Joyce's school. What do you think?"

Danny tried to pull his thoughts together. "Well, I think they concentrate mainly on popular music and the musical theatre. You really want a school for young classical musicians. There's this new place set up recently by Yehudi Menuhin in Cobham in Surrey. Very near a place called St. George's Hill… but you wouldn't know about that. I think that's where it should go… I think… that would be exactly what Mrs Whittaker would want."

"Good. You do it, son. You give it to them. That's where it ought to go."

Danny was able to help his mother in and out of the taxi each day when they visited the hospital. She struggled to walk or perform any physical task, which was nothing new, but now she seemed to be allowing herself to sink into depression as well. She cried in the evenings, and droned on incessantly about how wonderful her life with Kieran had been and how sorry she was that she hadn't been a better wife to him. A lot of what she claimed to remember Danny knew to be total nonsense, but he dutifully said "Yes, Ma" in the right places and let her "remember" whatever she wished.

236

With each successive visit his father had less to say. His level of consciousness was dropping, his confusion worsening. For Danny it was sickening to watch. His mother seemed not to realise the direction things were taking. The consultant called it aphasia, but he didn't seem to know why it was getting worse. The third time they visited he told them that they had taken another angiogram and that further surgery was needed to release pressure in his father's skull. It was obvious from the way the consultant talked that he didn't hold out very much hope. Danny simply sat and watched his father for the whole of the visit, while his mother babbled on about how wonderful life with Kieran had been and was going to be again. The whole scene resembled a Theatre of the Absurd production, one of his parents stubbornly denying reality, the other disconnected from it for ever. Danny urged her to set out for home early, before the afternoon rush hour, and she did. He had very little doubt that this would be the last time he would see his father alive.

That evening he had the telephone call that he had been expecting for some time.

"Danny? It's Joyce. I only just heard about your father. How is he?"

"Pretty bad. Very bad, actually."

"Oh Danny! I'm so sorry. He's a lovely man. I'm really fond of him. He is going to be all right, isn't he?"

"I don't think so." Silence from Joyce. "You don't have to say anything. There isn't anything to say, really, is there? People live, then they die."

"I know, but... I suppose it's something I don't want to think about. All the lives he must have saved, and now he's going to lose his own..."

"Nobody ever pretended that it was a just world. We're silly if we expect it to be. Anyway, he's not gone yet. Still hanging on – just about. How was Cambridge?"

"Cambridge was wonderful. Fantastic. We got a standing ovation at the end of every set."

"I bet you mean that you did."

"Everybody. They loved the whole group. It should be easy to get gigs after this. Big ones. Serious ones."

"That's lovely to hear. And when you got back, was Eileen all right?"

Joyce didn't reply at once. "She had a row with Morgan. It was pretty nasty."

"About who he'd been sleeping with?"

"More or less. I'm sorry for Morgan. She's sneaky. She says one thing to your face and another behind your back. You can't trust her. I'm not sure I can live with her myself. In fact… oh dear, this is a long story and a pretty miserable one. Do you want me to go on?"

"Go on. Tell me the worst."

"Well, in the middle of the row, she dropped a bit of a bombshell. She said it was her farm and she could throw us all out any time she wanted to. Morgan thought she'd gone nuts, but then he phoned and checked with his mother and it seems it's true. His mother has given Eileen the farm. I don't know if she can chuck Morgan out, he's lived there all his life and so he's probably got some kind of rights, but it's true that she can get the rest of us out if she wants to. But Robin doesn't want to stay anyway. Who would want to stay under a threat like that? In fact, everybody wants to leave. Even Morgan. It looks like that relationship is over, because what she really did was force him to choose between her and the group, and he chose the group. I could have predicted that, couldn't you?"

"So you're telling me that the whole group has broken up? And lost the farm?"

"They've lost the farm, but the group hasn't broken up. They've just got to start over, find another farm, maybe buy one if they make enough from their music. I'll be leaving in a couple of weeks anyway to go back to the Hammond, but the others want to stick together however they do it. Even if they have to rent a caravan and live in that for a while."

"Three people in a caravan? Are they serious?"

"They don't intend to give up. Not without a fight. And when I finish at the Hammond I'm definitely going to join them. I only have one more year. I could leave now, but if I want that solo career that Robin's talking about I've got a much better chance as a Hammond graduate. The industry will take me a lot more seriously, and the

Hammond Music Department have contacts. Robin won't hear of me dropping out. He's ever so sweet. I love him to bits."

"I think he's a good man. They're all good people. They deserve to make it..."

"I'm sorry about all that work you did in the reference library. It looks like it was wasted."

"Maybe not. Not if they can find another farm. I'll think of it as a training exercise. Next time I'll know exactly what I'm doing. I'll be almost like a professional engineer. Nothing's going to be wasted."

"I'm sure you're right. I'd better go now. This is Eileen's phone, and there'll be another row if she comes in and catches me. There's a horrible atmosphere here now. You can imagine the foul mood she's in. I think maybe it's made the rest of us even closer though. Maybe something good will come out of it. I hope it will."

"What's going to happen to her? Is she going to live on the farm by herself?"

"I suppose so. That's her problem. I don't feel sorry for her. Do you?"

"A little bit. She's made a mess of things, but we all do that from time to time. She must be very unhappy. Unhappy people lash out and do nasty things. Don't be too hard on her."

"You're just as sweet as Robin. Sweeter, even. I love you to bits too. And I miss you. I hope you can get back before school starts again. I don't think I can smuggle you into the dorm."

"I'll try."

"And I hope you're wrong about your dad. He's a lovely man too. Give him my love when you see him. Tell him to get well – the world needs people like him."

"I'll tell him. I love you, sweetheart."

"I love you too. Always."

Chapter Thirty-seven
Farewell to Belfast

Danny's mother and his Aunt Maud literally cried on each other's shoulders for a good ten minutes when she arrived. The two sisters sat on the big sofa in the front lounge and talked nonsense about how much they had always loved each other and how they should never have gone to live in different cities. Danny began to wonder if anybody ever remembered the past as it really was, good bits, bad bits, in-between bits, and all the great dull stretches when very little really happened. Perhaps, he thought, each of us spends a lifetime creating a comforting fantasy to believe in when we grow old.

In the evening a few friends of his mother – really little more than acquaintances – visited to offer their sympathies, and to deliver the ubiquitous Mass Cards, even though his father had made it pretty clear that he wasn't a Catholic. Some of his former patients and their relations, including Mr Whittaker, came to offer their sympathy too. The violin was not mentioned.

Danny had no wish to socialise. He excused himself early and spent most of the evening in his bedroom. Emotionally numb, he re-played the old Kingston Radio tapes, and listened for a while to live transmissions from Radio Free Belfast. Between the highly one-sided news bulletins and rousing partisan rhetoric they played Republican songs from the 1920s and 30s, such as *Kevin Barry*, *The Foggy Dew* and *The Rifles of the IRA*. There wasn't much pretence now that it was a Northern Ireland Civil Rights Association station. He felt a flicker of pride at the strength and quality of the signal. That good old 807 power valve was still doing its job very well indeed.

He was surprised to hear Bernie's unmistakable voice, telling people that the IRA was protecting them from far worse atrocities than the ones that the Protestant paramilitaries were actually committing, and that the British were on the point of granting Northern Ireland its freedom under the pressure of the ever-intensifying IRA bombing campaign. In reality he had seen very little about the Northern Ireland bombing campaign in the British press – things that were happening on the streets of America and France were stealing far more of the headlines.

He heard stories from various commentators of what the Republicans claimed were completely innocent Catholics of all ages lifted by the British Army and imprisoned without lawyers or trials or contact with their families or loved ones. Even if only a quarter of it was true, it occurred to Danny that the British were doing exactly what Big Jim had said they would do; over-reacting, creating martyrs, hardening the attitudes of the Catholic population against them, strengthening the position of the IRA. It might take a bit longer than the couple of years Jim had estimated, because the media battle wasn't being won, but things seemed to be moving in the direction he had predicted. He would live to see Ireland re-united.

He went downstairs when he was fairly certain that all the guests had gone and the two women were on the point of going to bed. The shelves and surfaces in the front lounge had become festooned with Mass Cards and bunches of the traditional large white lilies that the Irish people seemed to associate with funerals. His mother and her sister were still on the sofa where he had left them, but silent now, nursing cups of tea that Kitty had made for them, an old photo-album closed on his mother's knee. To his alarm he noticed two bottles of sherry on the coffee table next to some of the flowers, but they were unopened and there were no glasses in sight.

"Danny. Where were you?" she greeted him. "Why didn't you come down and talk to the people?"

"Sorry, Ma. Sorry, Aunt Maud. I didn't feel much like talking."

"You haven't eaten anything. You must be hungry."

"No, I'm not hungry. Has Joyce phoned?"

"No. Have you told her about your father? Is she coming to the funeral?"

"I left a message for her. She's in a concert with The Diggers this weekend. She probably isn't in Wales at all. Probably hasn't got the message yet."

"She's a lovely girl. Your da was very fond of her." She motioned for Danny to sit, which he did. "Danny, your auntie and I have been talking… about the future. I know you have friends here in Belfast, and your school is here, but there's nothing for me, and nobody to look after me."

Danny knew exactly what was coming. He had been thinking about it upstairs.

"What your Aunt Maud has offered, and it's a very kindly offer, is for the two of us to move in with her in Birmingham, and she'll keep an eye on me and see that I get the right help and the right medical care that I need. I'm not very well as you know, and the truth is, I'm never going to be well again. I know it's a bit selfish, to take you out of your school..."

"No, Ma. You're right. There's nothing for either of us here. The city's a war zone. It's going to get worse and worse. My only real friend here is Bernie, and I'll be leaving St. Benedict's at the end of the year anyway. All the people I know will be going somewhere else. It's a good time to change schools. I can finish my 'A' levels in Birmingham. It won't make any difference. I'll be fine."

An image of the map that he had been studying upstairs flashed into Danny's mind. Birmingham was about eighty or ninety miles from Chester and the Hammond School. It shouldn't take more than a couple of hours on the train. Mid-Wales was a similar sort of distance. He could think of worse places to live than Birmingham.

His mother seemed surprised. "You don't mind, then? You're okay about it?"

"Yes. It's fine. Let's do it. Every minute we stay here the house is worth less. In a year or two you won't be able to give away a house in Belfast – even out in this part. It's the sensible thing to do."

She stretched out a feeble arm in an invitation to kiss or embrace. Danny merely held her hand momentarily and released it. "You're a good boy," she told him. "A really good boy."

The funeral cortege left from their front door the following morning. His father had asked to be cremated, perhaps because it was something about which the Catholic Church was ambivalent, believing that it must surely hinder the Almighty in his task of resurrecting the bodies of the faithful on the last day. Danny's father had chosen Carnmoney Crematorium, on the slopes of Carnmoney Hill in the grounds of the large cemetery near the ancient Carnmoney Presbyte-

243

rian Church, which of course had been Roman Catholic before the Reformation, and close to the small Jewish Cemetery on the Church Road. Danny recalled a conversation in which his mother had talked him out of leaving his body to medical science or offending Uncle John by insisting on a completely secular ceremony. These arrangements represented a careful compromise in which each had given a little ground to the other.

The crematorium was quite a long way from where they lived, out in the country in the opposite direction to the city, so they had a drive through lush green farmland and wooded hillsides before pulling in to the spacious car park in the crematorium grounds and disembarking one by one from the long line of vehicles.

It was only at this point that the mourners got a good look at one another. Danny estimated that there must be about fifty cars and perhaps twice that number of people in total attending the ceremony. One individual stood out at once, both to him and the two women. "That priest in the black robe over there," his mother asked excitedly, "It must be your Uncle John. Will you run over and see if it is?"

Danny had only met his Uncle John once when he was very young, and was uncertain if he would be able to identify him. His mental image was of a feeble-minded and superstitious old windbag, a danger to children and the unsophisticated because of his determination to convert everybody he met to a belief in fundamentalist Roman Catholic dogma. It didn't really line up with other people's impressions of the priests of the Society of Jesus, but it was an image that had been pounded into Danny's brain by years of exposure to his father's sarcastic contempt for his older brother. Could John have journeyed all the way from Ecuador, his last known address, for his brother's funeral? Danny doubted it. "I'll go and see," he told his mother, and walked towards the tall, slightly stooped figure.

"Uncle John?" he enquired, standing behind the figure. The man turned around and Big Jim Harrison beamed down at him.

"Good god!"

"Not quite," he smiled. "Excuse the fancy dress. How are you, Danny?"

"I'm fine. What are you doing here?"

244

"I always admired your father. I told you so. We go back a long way. I've come to say goodbye, the same as everybody else." He took Danny's hand. "I'm really sorry that you've lost your father. He was a great Irishman and a great human being. He'll never be forgotten by the people who knew him. He was my hero, and many other people's as well. I mean it." He released Danny's hand. "Can we have a little talk? Let's sit over there." He indicated an empty bench away from the crowd, by the side entrance to the little crematorium church. Danny walked over with him and they sat down.

"Things seem to have got pretty nasty here," said Danny, trying not to draw anyone's attention to his lightly disguised companion.

"I'm worried about the way things are going. Every day it gets harder to keep the movement together. All kinds of jostling for position going on. I try to keep my eye on the ball but it isn't easy. Radio Free Belfast is thriving, as I'm sure you know. It's been a great help."

"I've heard it. I heard Bernie giving a political speech. That's something I never thought I'd hear."

"Bernie's okay. He's coming on. A lot more mature than he used to be."

"You know, Jim... No, I won't say."

"Won't say what, Danny?"

Danny felt disloyal, but he couldn't back out now. "Just a feeling. Nothing really... but, I wonder about Bernie sometimes. There's a side to him that makes me a bit uneasy. Something I can't put my finger on."

Jim nodded. "Those kind of instincts are what keep you alive. Never ignore them. Thanks for the tip."

"Actually, Jim. There's something I have to tell you. My mother wants to move to Birmingham, to live with her sister. She wants to sell the house in Belfast. It looks like I won't be living here much longer."

Jim's face lit up. "Really? Birmingham? That's a coincidence."

"Is it? Why?"

"We've got a fully operational Active Service Unit in Birmingham. It's the only English city where we've got one, even though there are a lot more Irish in London. I'll get you an introduction.

They may need your help from time to time. Or they may be able to help you. And when you get to know them, there's something you can do for me."

Danny felt his spirits sink as he listened to Big Jim. He had the uncomfortable feeling that his period of extended leave was coming to an end. "What's that?"

"Just keep your eyes and ears open. Like you always do. The Birmingham people get their orders from Dublin. I don't have a great deal to do with them. I'd like to know what you think of them. What kind of feelings you get from them. Keep me up to date with the gossip. That kind of thing."

Danny nodded. "How big is the unit?"

"Tiny. Three people. They have a rented flat in Northfield. There would be room for you to move in if you wanted to leave home."

Danny thought about what it would be like living with his mother and his aunt. Not a barrel of laughs, he decided. "Well," he said, "I can always meet them and see how we get on."

Chapter Thirty-eight
The Birmingham Group

Danny pulled his collar together against the drizzle. He gave the outside of the house a cursory inspection in the failing light of the autumn evening. It was a red brick semi-detached, built to the same general pattern and probably much the same age as the one he had lived in in Belfast. He pushed the doorbell and waited. After a few moments a light came on in the hallway and a woman's voice with an Irish accent, muffled by the thickness of the door, asked him who he was.

"I'm Danny Gallagher. I think you're expecting me."

There was a clicking of locks and the door opened. A thin, serious-looking woman in her mid thirties stood inside. Her dark brown hair was cropped short and she wore baggy green slacks and a loose white top that reached well below her waist. Heavily-framed spectacles gave her the appearance of a stereotype librarian or school-mistress. It seemed to Danny that she had gone out of her way to make herself unattractive. She motioned him in without speaking and he followed her up the stairs to the front lounge of what seemed a spacious if very untidy first floor flat. A scruffy red-haired man of about the same age as the woman was slumped on a sofa reading a newspaper with an open can of beer at his feet. "This is Danny Gallagher," she announced as he looked up from the paper.

"Jeez! He's a young 'un, isn't he? Hello there, Danny. I'm Rinty." His accent was from Ireland's rural south, Danny guessed either Cork or Kerry. He let go of the paper, which joined the beer on the floor. Beaming a smile he stood up and shook Danny's hand. "This auld bag here is Jessie. And you'll meet Seamus in a minute. Seamus is the official boss. But I wouldn't take that too seriously. Are you really the fellow that does the bombs? You look about twelve."

"I'm eighteen. My birthday was last Sunday."

"Well, it's all the same to us. Young or old, it's your skills that matter. They say you designed the ones we've been using and the course that we've all had in assembling the hardware. Is that a fact?"

"Yes. Was everything all right?"

"Well, we've assembled and delivered a couple of them, and they both worked fine. But did you hear about the new stuff that's coming in?"

"No. What new stuff?"

"Sit down and have a drink. Seamus'll tell you all about it when he comes back. He's making himself a cup of tea in the kitchen."

"I'll sit down, but I don't drink."

"Very wise. I'm tryin' to give it up myself. Isn't that right, Jessie?"

On cue, Seamus came in carrying a mug which he placed on the table, and looked Danny up and down. He was a bit older than the other two, a difference that was accentuated by the fact that he was neatly dressed in well-polished black brogues, dark grey trousers that had a distinct crease, and a cream shirt with a stiff collar that seemed to cry out for a tie. His eyes were small and sunken, his hair well-combed, thick, black and greasy. As soon as Danny laid eyes on him he knew that he had seen him somewhere before. His mind flailed around furiously trying to remember where.

"Danny," he said without warmth, "good to see you. The Belfast commander speaks very highly of you."

Danny took his proffered hand and shook it. It felt rather limp. "Good to see you too. I hope I can be of some use to you here."

Seamus sat down before he spoke. "I hope so too. But first, let's get to know each other a little bit." He waited for Danny to sit before he continued. "We're a very small cell, as you can see, just the three of us. We've been given the task of moving the bombing campaign on to the British mainland. It's the only way we're going to get the attention of the British press. You could blow the whole of Northern Ireland out of the sea and they wouldn't give a damn over here. The high command in Dublin understands that now. So we've got to bring the campaign to them right here, where they live. One explosion on the mainland is worth twenty in Northern Ireland."

"I see. But the rules of engagement remain the same, don't they? Attacks on property, not personnel. Adequate warnings. Military, commercial and industrial targets."

"Of course. We aren't barbarians."

"And this new stuff that Rinty mentioned?"

"Plastic explosives. The latest thing, all the way from Czechoslovakia. Lighter and more powerful than gelignite. Safer to handle, and it detonates so quickly that containment isn't necessary. You can mould it like clay, and it's waterproof and almost impossible to set off accidentally. You could throw a lump of it in the fire and it wouldn't explode. It needs a special type of detonator, more powerful than the one you use with gelignite. It's the perfect explosive, just about. Expensive, but you get your money's worth. Haven't they spoken to you about it?"

"No. Not a word. Have you got it here now?"

"Not yet. It's coming by sea, on a small boat to an unofficial landing stage. We'll be told when it's time to go and collect it. It could be a week, could be a month. But we know it's coming."

"It sounds like you know all there is to know about it. Why do you need me?"

He shrugged. "I suppose we don't, strictly. You've already given us everything we really need. But you may be able to work out the details for us. Exactly how much to use, the optimum shape for the charge. That sort of thing."

"I'll do what I can. But from what you've said, I don't think those details will be very critical."

"We've got some plans that may involve a different kind of timer. Something that can run for days or even weeks. Would that be straightforward?"

Danny hesitated. "I wouldn't like to say off the top of my head. I can research it for you. Why would you need a timer like that?"

He touched the side of his nose. "Sorry, Danny, I can't say. That kind of information is distributed on a 'need to know' basis." He addressed Jessie. "Any chance of a cup of tea for our guest?" She left to deal with his request. "I hear you're living with your mother and your aunt. We've got a room here that we don't use if you want it. This place is bigger than it looks."

"I'm not sure. Can I think about it?"

"Of course. Your aunt's place isn't far from here anyway."

Danny felt comfortable with Rinty, but the other two seemed inscrutable, lacking in warmth. Maybe they had been in Birmingham longer. The first thing he had noticed about English cities was that social interaction was initially more distant. People didn't say hello or good night when they passed on the street or chat to each other on buses. There was less eye contact, fewer informal exchanges. English cities were bigger and more impersonal. Maybe that was all he was picking up. He would need to give the idea of moving in more time. "I wouldn't mind taking a look at the room though," he added with a pleasant smile.

Compared to the Gothic grandeur of the Harrods building that Danny had just walked past, London's cathedral to retail commerce, seven stories high and covering a five-acre site, with its stunning window displays, each one a work of art, shaded by their trademark line of green awnings, Christies sales rooms and offices were positively modest. Just an understated plain black shop front with plate glass windows each side of the entrance, through which a number of inner doors and counters could be seen. Groups of dark-suited customers and attendants, all of whom seemed to be male, stood around talking. The building radiated the good taste and self assurance generated by centuries of unbroken tradition.

He gathered the courage to go in and was greeted by a dark-suited doorman who had the voice and presence of a prince. "Good morning, sir. How may I help?"

Danny swallowed and produced a letter from his inside pocket. "I wrote a letter," he said, feeling totally inarticulate. "I have an appointment with a man named Mr Malkov. To look at this." He held out the violin case.

The attendant took the letter and glanced at it once before returning it. "This way, sir."

He led Danny past the chatting groups of people to one of the inner doors and knocked. It was immediately opened by a small immaculately dressed gentleman with receding grey hair and sideburns. He wore a waistcoat and a fob watch on a chain, and looked to Danny like an extra in a Charles Dickens film. Danny noticed that he was wearing white gloves. "Mr Gallagher to see you, Mr Malkov."

"Good morning," said the little man. "Please sit down." The room was small and contained only a table surrounded by a number of chairs and bearing an old-fashioned office intercom. The attendant left, closing the door quietly behind him.

Danny sat opposite Malkov and placed the violin case on the table. "I've got all the documentation," he said, reaching into his shoulder bag and placing a large envelope on the table as Malkov opened the case. Malkov ignored the envelope but removed the instrument from its case and examined it closely, saying nothing. He took out the bow and examined that too. He produced an eye glass and examined both even more closely. Finally, he put the instrument back on top of its case. "I think I need a second opinion," he said pleasantly. He touched a button on the intercom. "Is Mr Crothier free for a moment?" There was a squawk of a distorted human voice from the machine. "Thank you."

In a few moments another man joined them. He was taller and had long delicate hands, again shielded in white gloves. He wore a neat blue tie and a spotless three-piece black suit that would have done credit to an undertaker. "Would you please take a look at this, Mr Crothier. Tell me what you think."

The newcomer lifted the instrument, turned it around in his hands, stared into the two holes in its front. "This is genuine," he said quietly, "without question."

"Thank you, Mr Crothier." The taller man left.

"Do you have any idea of the value of this instrument?"

"Well, I believe it's a good one."

"Yes, Mr Gallagher. It's a good one. It was made in the second half of the 17th century by a man named Nicolo Amati, who was the grandson of Andrea Amati, the teacher to Antonio Stradivari & Andrea Guarneri. It's of a pattern known as the 'Grand Amati'. The body is slightly larger than that of his earlier violins. Many concert performers prefer them. The condition is superb. Do you want to offer this instrument for auction at Christies?"

Danny hesitated. "Just what kind of money are we talking about?"

"I would be very surprised if it failed to realise one hundred thousand pounds. That's probably a conservative estimate."

Danny was glad that he was sitting down. He could live on that comfortably – for about a hundred years. It would pay for his father's house about ten times over. He said nothing for a long time. Finally, Malkov spoke. "Is there anything else you would like to know, Mr Gallagher?"

"I'm sorry, Mr Malkov. I was thinking. The thing is, I don't trust myself to do the right thing with that kind of money. Do you think I could make a special arrangement with Christies, about the dispersal of the money after the sale?"

"Of course. What kind of arrangement do you have in mind?"

"I want to keep my own name out of it. I know you take a commission, and there are expenses, but when all that's taken care of, I would like the balance to be divided in two and sent to two different accounts. Half to the Yehudi Menuhin School in Surrey. I would like the note to say that it's from The Diggers, which is a folk music trio. It should say that it's a donation to the work of the school in memory of Gerrard Winstanley, who would have been a neighbour of theirs about the time this violin was made. And the other half I would like to go to The Diggers themselves. The note should be signed with my father's name, Kieran Gallagher, and that one should say..." He thought for a moment. "How about, 'Please buy yourselves a farm and keep the change'?"

"If you can wait a moment I'll get someone to write down your instructions. It will be our pleasure to carry them out."

Chapter Thirty-nine
Leaving Home

"I'm not strong enough for stairs any more," Danny's mother complained, pausing to catch her breath half way up the steps to the front door of her sister's modest maisonette. "We need to look for a bungalow, or something on the ground floor. By the time I get to your front door I'm worn out."

Maud, who was carrying a bulging shopping bag in each hand, hurried up past her and put them down by the door to search for the key in her shoulder bag. "It's only one flight. Hardly anything at all. I've been here for more than fifteen years now. I know all the neighbours. It's a good area. You should see some parts of Selly Oak. I'm lucky to have this place. You don't know what it's like trying to find somewhere to live over here."

"But I don't mind chipping in. I'll have quite a bit from the sale of the Belfast house when it comes through."

"Quite a bit? How much do you think a bungalow would cost, anywhere within ten miles of here – assuming there was one?"

She struggled up to her sister's side and paused to catch her breath again before she spoke. "You made this place sound like paradise in your letters. I wasn't poor in Belfast. Not really. Why should I be poor here? Why shouldn't I have what I want? What I need, because of my health?"

Maud abandoned the search of her shoulder bag. "Damn. I think I came out without the key." She pushed the doorbell.

"I'm serious, Maud. I want a bigger place. A place that's on the ground floor. I've put up with stairs for long enough. This place is no good for me."

Danny's shape appeared behind the frosted glass and he opened the door. His mother addressed Maud, ignoring him. "You've still got your health and your strength, thank god. You don't know what it's like to feel weak all the time."

The two women pushed past Danny, continuing their increasingly heated conversation. "You knew exactly what my place was like when you agreed to come over here. It's got three good-sized bedrooms. In Belfast, one of your rooms was just a box-room. I don't think this is small. If you thought it wasn't good enough why did you come here?"

"I came to be with you, not because of where you lived. I assumed that when Kieran's money came through we could get somewhere really nice. I don't see what you've got against it."

"Use your common sense. If you sink all Kieran's money into a house, what are you going to live on when you get old and maybe need a domestic, or even a nurse? I won't be young either, you know. There's only so much I can do for you. Even now. I've got to go to work. I can't wait on you hand and foot."

"Well, thanks very much. Showing our true colours now, are we? I have absolutely no desire to become a burden. Isn't that what I'm saying? Isn't it all the more reason to live in a place where I can keep my independence, where I'll be able to do my own shopping, get in and out when I need to…?"

Danny could see things veering towards unpleasantness. He intervened. "I think I may be able to help."

Maud looked at him coldly. "You? How?"

"Well, if I moved out – into a place of my own – the two of you could look for a smaller place on the ground floor. Just two bedrooms. That wouldn't cost so much and it wouldn't be so hard to find."

"Don't let Maud push you out," his mother protested. "We can easily stay together. We're a family. I don't want you to leave home."

"I'm almost eighteen, Ma. I'm not going to live at home for ever anyway, am I? And I wouldn't go far. In fact, I know some people in Northfield who've got a room to let. It's only a couple of miles away."

His mother was surprised. "How did you meet them? We've only been in Birmingham a few weeks."

"They're Irish. Friends of Bernie's."

His mother paused and glanced at her sister. "We all leave home sooner or later," said Maud.

Danny was pleased that his aunt seemed to approve of the idea. It was the reaction he had expected. After years of living alone it must have been hard enough for her to cope with her sister moving in, let alone a nephew that she barely knew, and didn't get on with particularly well. He could see all the old tensions that his father had spoken about surfacing again in the relationship between Maud and his mother. The myth of their sweet sisterly devotion was about to be shattered. He was happy that he had somewhere else to go. He had no wish to play the role of resident referee in an on-going sororal cat-fight.

Danny's first task was to bring some semblance of tidiness to the Northfield flat. The mess, he realised, was confined mainly to the sitting room and the kitchen, these being the two rooms that Rinty mostly used. Rinty sat around in the evenings watching TV, reading the paper or chatting; leaving cups, plates, beer-cans and every imaginable species of litter in piles behind him. In the kitchen he liked to attempt to cook, which he did badly, and piled up the sink, draining board and work-surfaces with dirty cutlery and utensils. Jessie tried to wash them but never fully caught up with the task, so that usually individual items had to be washed as they were needed. Danny was surprised at her tolerance. She also presumably tidied and cleaned the bedroom that they shared, which Danny didn't enter, but he noticed that it looked quite presentable any time the door was open.

The door to Seamus' room was never open – in fact it was seldom unlocked. The reason Seamus gave was that it contained confidential papers relating to the Volunteers, and if ever the house was raided the lock might give him an extra minute or two to destroy them. He was a secretive kind of man, Danny considered it likely that the papers were a fiction, that he simply didn't trust people to respect his privacy.

Danny arranged his own room the way he liked it, with a table in front of the window to serve as a work bench, and a cork notice board on the wall where he could pin things. His books, and a single communications receiver that he had taken with him from Belfast, as well as some personal pictures, he arranged on a shelf unit by the bed. He had a good-sized wardrobe and a chest of drawers. The room was fine.

Seamus handed over for safe keeping a single box of gelignite and two complete sets of pipes, timers and components to assemble bombs. These Danny stored neatly in cardboard boxes by one of the walls. It all felt chillingly like old times in Belfast. But from the point of view of physical comfort, there was nothing that he lacked.

The atmosphere in the flat was more serious and more distant than Danny was used to. Rinty could be light-hearted when Danny got him on his own, but that was seldom, and when either of the others were around their presence seemed to inhibit this side of his character. Their evening conversations were either very serious – politics, or Irish history, or whatever the current news story happened to be – or very trivial: football, pop music, shows on the TV, strange English people they worked with or had seen on the bus. They never talked about their former lives, or anything the least bit personal. Danny found it quite difficult to get to know them or form a clear impression of the kind of people they were. He wondered if the reason they avoided the personal area was that they saw him as a schoolboy (although he had yet to register with any local school or college), somebody too young to be engaged with seriously.

Danny had in his possession a sealed letter from St Benedict's addressed to the headmaster of whatever school or learning institution he chose to register with in Birmingham. He had of course steamed it open and read it very carefully. It was written by his Form Master, typed out (with a few mistakes which were corrected in ballpoint) by the school secretary and counter-signed with a note by Father Walsh. The language in which it was framed was inflated and pretentious, full of clever innuendo and euphemism. Danny was very familiar with this kind of language, his father could switch it on whenever he wished for comic effect. As he read, Danny mentally translated the letter into plain English.

What it said was that Danny was a rather ordinary student, the son of a very clever physician father, but a dim and pathetic mother whose genetic contribution had probably consigned his talents to the centre ground. His father was an atheist and had destroyed the boy's religious faith, leaving him generally confused and easy prey to purveyors of socialism and other socio/philosophical aberrations. In most things where aptitude could be measured on a scale of one to ten he was likely to score something in the region of five. The exception was his inability to learn a foreign language, which was seemingly absolute. He did however possess a near clinically obsessive level of concentration in certain narrow areas of science that interested him, particularly radio and electronics, and they had him ear-marked for an electrical engineering career of some description. Unusually for a boy of generally scientific bent, he was able to string a few words together in an English essay. Father Walsh had added a handwritten comment to the effect that if they didn't expect too much of him they might be pleasantly surprised, although he doubted it.

While Danny had to admit that it was a generally fair and balanced assessment of his abilities, it didn't greatly motivate him to carry on with his 'A' level studies.

Away from family influence, with nobody to impress or to nag, he allowed himself to drift along, spending a lot of his time in his room, reading, or playing around with the communications receiver, not bothering to visit any schools or discuss his future with any of the educational gurus who would have been happy to advise him.

He had completed the first year of the Northern Ireland syllabus, in Birmingham the syllabus would be different, and he wasn't sure he could walk straight into the examination year even if he wanted to. Indeed he knew that if he wanted to go on with the subjects he had been studying he would have a lot of catching up to do – he hadn't opened a schoolbook during the whole of the summer holidays. But mainly he was finding it difficult to care.

He decided that what he needed was at least a year completely away from school work. A year or so doing something practical on the Digger's new farm. He could return to his 'A' levels later, or study at night school, if he felt it was going to serve any useful purpose. The auction of the violin wouldn't take place for almost two months, and it would be a couple of weeks after that before the money would be released, then there would be the whole business of finding and buying a farm. He didn't think the actual purchase would be happening until about Christmas time, when of course Joyce would be free again and they could go and help the group to move into the new farm together. He wrote a detailed letter explaining the plan to her, attributing the gift to his father, and she answered in a tone of awe and delight at the dying doctor's generosity. A few days later he received a similar letter of appreciation from Robin and the others.

He answered the letters – it was a great feeling to share in their joy, even at a distance. He started to write a separate letter to Eileen, but abandoned it when he realised that he didn't know what it was that he wanted to say.

Now he had something really wonderful to look forward to. As a result of the wind that Mrs Whittaker's violin was going to give to the Diggers' sails there was every chance that he would one day find himself living with Joyce and the others in a model Diggers community in Wales, helping to run a Centre for Alternative Technology. He could think of no more worthwhile project to which to devote his life, and no happier circumstances in which to live. The fulfilment of this vision became his holy grail. Nothing else mattered. He began to structure his life around it.

Thanks to the Bank of Ireland savings account that Big Jim had set up for him, and the £25 that was deposited into it every week, money was not a problem. Allowing the others to assume that his school term had started, he left the flat at the same time each weekday morning and spent his days in the Birmingham Central Library on the aptly named Paradise Circus, researching small scale energy and food production, and to a lesser extent the writings of Winstanley and other utopian theorists. When he went to join them on the new farm he would have a bit more insight into the philosophical side of their ideas, as well as the necessary competence and expertise to tackle any engineering problem that was likely to arise.

Then, at the end of his third week in the new flat, Seamus knocked on his door in the early evening. "Danny," he said, "we've had our phone call. We've got to drive down to a little bay on the Isle of Thanet tonight. The shipment has arrived."

Chapter Forty
Active Service

They assembled in the lounge for their briefing. Seamus was unusually animated. He got the three of them to sit down, but remained standing himself.

"Okay. This is the big one. It's taken more than a year to set this up and I wouldn't like to tell you how much it's cost. After tonight, we join the senior league. These are the finest explosives money can buy. Compared to these, the sticks of gelignite are just fire crackers.

"It's packed in boxes of one-and-a-half kilograms each. That's just over three pounds. Each box is a bit smaller than a shoe box and there are fifty of them. A total of seventy-five kilograms. The weight of one and a half bags of cement. There's another box containing the special detonators. Not very much of a load, but I'm taking no chances. I've hired two small cars. Not vans, cars, so that if somebody looks into the windows they won't see anything. We're using two cars, so that if either of us gets stopped and searched, or if one of us is involved in an accident, we only lose half the shipment, not the whole of it. It's very unlikely to happen, but it's a possibility and we have to allow for it. The cars won't be traceable back to us – they've been hired in false names with forged documents.

"We're going to drive in convoy." He turned to Rinty. "You're going to follow me. Just keep close behind, I won't go very fast. You don't need to know the exact location, you just follow me. We'll make one toilet stop about half way, and have a bite to eat if we need it. It's quite a long way, and we're going to avoid the motorways and big main roads. They're full of police patrols and cameras. We won't be there much before first light. Remember we aren't in a hurry. We aren't going to be breaking any rules of the road. I hope you're sober, Rinty. How many have you had tonight?"

"Me?" He looked hurt. "One can. I swear to God. One can. Isn't that right, Jessie?" She didn't answer.

"You're coming with me, Danny. You're going to be the navigator. We'll be using the back roads, and I haven't been to this little bay before, so it'll be useful if you can do the map reading."

Danny nodded. He realised that this was the first actual IRA military operation that he had been on. He felt his heart beat a little faster at the thought.

Seamus was very quiet for the first part of the journey, as Danny had expected. They drove through mostly residential areas, sticking religiously to the speed limits, while the car with Rinty and Jessie tailgated them impatiently, always trying to press closer than Seamus found comfortable.

"He's a right hothead, that one," Seamus said at last. "You tell him to calm down and take it easy, but it doesn't make the least difference. He's up our arses all the time trying to make us go faster. I wish you were a driver, I'd be a lot more comfortable with you behind me."

Danny felt quite flattered. "I try to carry out instructions," he said, wondering if it was always true. "They're an odd couple, aren't they? Him and Jessie. I wonder sometimes what keeps them together."

"I try not to wonder about other people's lives. The way they get on is their own business."

It was a bit of a conversation stopper. Danny abandoned his attempt at small talk with Seamus. He decided it was the wrong time – Seamus was tense and wanted to concentrate on the task in hand. At their brief shared meal stop in a lorry drivers' café the conversation with Seamus was equally terse, but Rinty tried to make a couple of jokes that in the circumstances fell flat. Jessie barely spoke. Danny resigned himself to the prospect of zero social interaction until those boxes were safely back in Northfield.

They took a narrow unmade road out of Herne Bay and quickly left the street lights behind. In the total darkness of the overcast autumn night Seamus slowed the car to a walking pace, the headlights picking up nothing beyond the two neglected hedges that fringed the track. They descended slowly, to a place where the track divided, and

Danny told Seamus to take the less travelled one to the left. Around the next bend, they were suddenly driving over a gravelly beach with the dark and brooding sea beside them and a small fishing vessel with a light in one of its port holes tied up at a crumbling wooden jetty in front of them. Seamus switched off the headlights and drew to a gentle halt by the shore end of the ancient structure. "Well done, Danny," he said quietly. "Good navigating."

Danny acknowledged with a nod as Seamus climbed out, telling him to wait. The second car pulled up alongside and its lights died too. Seamus signalled them to wait also while he made his way to the boat.

At first Danny found the total silence and almost total darkness rather restful. Minutes went by. He began to notice faint clicking noises as the hot engine cooled down. More time passed. Now he began to feel a bit fidgety. He opened his door and went to the driver's window of the other car, which Rinty rolled down. "He's been in there a long time," he said. "Do you think everything's all right?"

Rinty shrugged. "He gets jumpy at times like this. He's a very cautious man. He's probably getting the captain to tell him what his mother's maiden name was, or something like that. He'll be okay."

Right on cue, Seamus came stamping back across the stones. "Those bastards are trying to pull a fast one," he snapped. "Forty-four fucking boxes. Not fifty. Six short. Maybe they think because we're Irish we can't count up to fifty."

Rinty climbed out to join the two of them. "Forty-four. It's still a lot. It's not too bad. Maybe they ran into some kind of problem."

"I was on the phone to them six hours ago. If there was a problem why didn't they tell me then?"

"Well," Rinty mused, "maybe some of the boxes got nicked on the journey. Or maybe it's just a communication problem. The guys over there don't even speak English."

"My contact in Czechoslovakia speaks better English than you."

"No great accomplishment." Rinty laughed at his own joke.

"You may think this is funny, Rinty. I don't. I'm stopping the final payment until it's sorted out. Let's get the stuff loaded, and as soon as we see a phone box we stop so that I can talk to Dublin."

"Ach, take it easy, Seamus. Sure we had lots of wee hiccups when we were buying the gelignite."

"Don't you tell me to take it easy. This whole operation was set up by me. It goes on my record. When people make an agreement I expect them to stick to it. Who the hell do they think they are? If I can't trust them to deliver the agreed amount, can I trust them that what they have delivered isn't shit?"

"I think if it was shit you would have got your full fifty boxes," Danny put in, immediately wishing that he had kept out of the conversation.

"The kid's got a point there," said Rinty.

"I won't be happy till I've seen some of this stuff do its job. As soon as we get home, Danny, after we've had a sleep, I want you to assemble a bomb with the new explosive and one of the new detonators. We'll plant it tomorrow night."

"Are you sure you're not rushing into it?" Rinty urged. "Why the big hurry?"

"I told you why. Because we don't know if we're dealing with trustworthy people. I want to see this stuff blow the crap out of somewhere before Dublin parts with another penny to the Czechs. Come on, we've got boxes to load."

As Seamus had predicted, the sun had risen before the two cars pulled in again at the door of the Northfield flat. Wearily, they carried the boxes upstairs and piled them by the wall in Danny's bedroom. The box of detonators completed the collection.

"Forty-four boxes is a hell of a lot of plastic explosive," Danny said in a half-hearted attempt to console Seamus when he saw the height of the pile. "I don't think we'll miss that extra six."

Seamus didn't comment. "Time to get a bit of sleep," was all he said. "Tonight we go bombing."

Danny felt a jolt of excitement when he heard Seamus say "Tonight we go bombing". Despite the number of hours he had been awake he didn't feel at all sleepy, and he wanted to see what their new purchase looked like. When the others left he carefully opened one of the boxes and took out a few of the individually-wrapped packages of what looked like beige-coloured modelling clay. He amused himself by pressing it into interesting shapes. He made a human head, and a bird with extended wings. Eventually he gave himself over to the task of stuffing it into one of the capped-off pipes, and before long had assembled a complete bomb, lacking only the final connections to the battery. It would save time later, he thought. At last he began to feel a little tired. He put the device away, brushed his teeth, and, closing his curtains carefully against the daylight, went to bed.

Unaccustomed to sleeping in the daytime, when Danny woke up he had no impression of how much time had passed. He opened one of the curtains to reveal an almost dark sky, suggesting that it was early evening. He could hear the rattle of utensils outside and realised that the others were already up, and Rinty was attempting to cook a meal. He was considering the idea of a quick shower when Seamus knocked on his door and asked if he could come in. When he did Danny noticed that he was carrying a large metal paint tin by its handle. It bore the label of a well-known manufacturer and a legend to the effect that it was "brilliant white".

"I was just going to get up," Danny explained. "I think I slept a bit longer than I intended."

"No problem. I just wanted to talk about the bomb."

"It's okay. It's ready. I put it together when I got in." Danny produced the familiar black steel cylinder and laid it on the bed.

"You should have waited. That's not what we want."

Danny looked puzzled.

"No. We want to take advantage of the fact that you don't need containment with plastic explosives. That means a much lighter casing. In fact, this." He held out the paint tin.

"You want to assemble it in that. Yes, that can be done, but don't forget, the pipe serves two purposes. Containment, plus making it difficult or impossible to disarm. If somebody gets smart and looks inside that, they'll see what's going on at a glance. All they'll have to do is cut any of the wires and the thing will be rendered harmless."

"They won't look inside."

There was an awkward silence.

"You mean, no warning?"

263

Seamus didn't answer. Instead he continued issuing his instructions. "And there's something else." He rattled the tin. It seemed to be full of small metal objects. "There's a few pounds of assorted scrap iron in there. Nuts and bolts, nails, screws, rivets, stuff like that. That stuff stays. Distributed as evenly as possible."

For a moment neither of them spoke. Danny broke the silence. "You're talking about an anti-personnel weapon. An anti-personnel weapon planted without a warning."

"The pipe bomb would be no different. The casing of that would fragment and create a lethal spray too. This way it's just a lot lighter, and easier to disguise. And a lot more powerful of course. The final effect is exactly the same."

Danny was shocked into silence.

After a few moments Seamus spoke again. "So? What are you waiting for?"

"I'm not doing it. I'm not having anything to do with that device."

There was another silence. When he spoke again, Seamus spoke very quietly.

"You're not having anything to do with that device? Who the hell do you think you are?"

"The first thing I asked you about when I came here was the rules of engagement. Jim Harrison was absolutely clear about them right from the outset. This is not what I agreed to do."

"Jim Harrison? You may not have noticed, but this isn't fucking Belfast. Jim Harrison doesn't give the orders here. I'm the commander of this Active Service Unit, and I'm telling you to assemble that bomb in accordance with my instructions. I'm not asking for your bloody opinion. I'm not interested in arguing with you. The rules of engagement have changed. Now carry out my order."

"If you do this you throw away all the support of the ordinary Irish public, and the American public too. The people who contribute money to the IRA when they come around with the hat in the pubs. The people who defend our actions internationally. You make it impossible for the trade unions or anybody on the ordinary left to sympathise with the Republican cause. It's insane. It's not just immoral, it's stupid."

"Is that it? Have you finished?" Seamus seemed unnaturally calm. He bent down and checked the contents of one of Danny's large cardboard boxes. Removing some of the items it contained, he tossed in one of the new detonators, followed by one of the boxes of plastic explosives, and finally the paint tin that he had been carrying. "I'll make my own bloody bomb. The Dublin people warned me I'd have this kind of trouble with you. I haven't time to continue this conversation now. We'll talk again in the morning. We're all going on this mission and we won't be back tonight, in case we lead anybody back to the house. Keep the door locked and don't let anybody in." He lifted his box and left, not bothering to close Danny's door behind him.

For Danny, the day/night cycle had been reversed. For the remainder of the night he stayed in his room, wide awake, listening for a long time to the murmur of voices from the lounge, then the slamming of doors as the three of them left. At about 11.00 pm he heard the low-pitched rolling thunder-clap of a distant large explosion, followed shortly by the familiar far-away wailing of the sirens of emergency vehicles. After that the silence became absolute and he was alone with his thoughts.

At about 6.00 am he drifted into a shallow fitful sleep, from which he awoke feeling groggy and poorly rested about four hours later. He treated himself to his long-delayed shower, put on his clothes and with some apprehension made his way towards the lounge to await the return of his flat-mates.

Chapter Forty-one
Endgame

Danny had walked into the lounge and closed the door behind him before he noticed Bernie in the soft chair on the opposite side of the fireplace. He was sitting casually with his legs crossed, wearing an unnecessarily heavy overcoat and toying with his gun. "Hello Danny," he greeted him in a quiet tone. "Long time no see."

"Yes. Long time. An unexpected pleasure."

"Why don't you sit down?" He used the gun as a pointer. Danny obeyed, sitting down opposite him in the matching soft armchair. Bernie did not lower the gun. "What do you think of Birmingham?"

Danny shrugged. "Too big. Too impersonal. Too flat. Too much traffic."

"I can't say I've fallen in love with it myself – but I won't be staying very long."

Danny raised his hand in a vague gesture of helplessness. "I would offer you a drink..."

"No. That's okay. I'm on duty."

"This is an official call then?"

"I'm afraid so." Bernie kept the gun pointed straight at Danny's chest, but both of them took pains to ignore its presence. Bernie paused as though to collect his thoughts. "I'm surprised at you, Danny. I thought you would have better judgement. Trying to influence IRA tactical policy single-handed. Disobeying a direct order. Did you really think we could turn a blind eye? Did you think there would be no consequences?"

"I didn't think about what would happen at all, to be honest. You're right. Bad judgement. I would never make a politician."

"And I hope you realise you've put me in a very embarrassing position. Even if Jim Harrison was still around to protect you, he couldn't get you off this one."

"Isn't Jim still around? What happened? Where did he go?"

Bernie hesitated. "It was an unfortunate business. Three days ago. Accidental discharge of a firearm."

I'm… sorry to hear that."

"I was sorry too. I liked Jim. We all did. He was a very popular commander. But he was a bit of a dinosaur. Nothing could move forward while he was still there. The new commander of the Belfast Brigade isn't much older than us."

"Is that so? What's he like?"

Bernie searched for the right words. "A Dublin man. Not university like Jim, very working class. Hot on discipline. More of a soldier than a politician, I would say."

"I think I know what you mean. I suppose there are going to be big changes then."

"Yes. Quite right. Big changes." He looked down at the gun. "He… doesn't want you around any longer either, Danny. Not after last night."

"I guessed that. So you've come all the way from Belfast just to kill your old friend?"

"Not just for that. I was in England already, as it happens, on another errand. Visiting some other people that he doesn't want around any more. I've got a little list."

"That's a line from a Gilbert and Sullivan comic opera. Did you realise?"

"No, I'm afraid I didn't. I suppose you could say that I've neglected the opera, what with one thing and another…"

"Sorry, I just thought it was funny. Who else is on this list then? Anybody I know?"

"Connor Laverty and his old man Liam. Somebody we knew at St. Benedict's contacted us – told us he'd seen Connor in the bars around the Southampton docks a couple of times. I need to check it out, might be nonsense, but I think it could well turn out to be right. Liam was a dock worker in Belfast originally, you know."

"Sounds like a very promising lead. But are they really worth the trouble? What's the point?"

"Liam's a deserter. We've got to set the right example. And if we retire Liam but not Connor, he's going to come looking for revenge, isn't he? And he knows who some of us are. Wouldn't be very clever." He toyed with the gun. "So, aren't you wondering why I haven't pulled this trigger yet?"

"Oh, I thought you just wanted to catch up on the news. Have a last chat about old times. The gun isn't empty again, is it?"

"No, not this time."

"I don't think it was the first time either, at the Civil Rights march. I think there were two bullets in it originally. And the reason whoever gave the order only gave you two was because he was afraid you might get carried away. Can I tell you some of the theories I've come up with, sitting there in that little bedroom on my own?"

Bernie nodded. "Please do."

"I more or less guessed a long time ago that you were the Belfast hit man. I think you shot that priest that I told Jim about right at the beginning. Sheelagh's dad too. And you were supposed to kill Connor when he got out of gaol, but you were too slow getting there. You were on that bank raid as well, weren't you? It was you who shot that girl in the hand. You knew it was a girl that had been shot before anybody else did. Before it was on the news."

"She was going for the silent alarm. It would have got us all caught. They wouldn't need radio to send a car out from York Road Police Station. Anyway, you flatter me. I'm not the only person in the IRA with a gun. I'm just one of a whole bunch whose job it is to do the organisation's dirty work for them from time to time. 'Hit man' isn't what we're called. 'Special Operations Officer' is the term we use. What you call things is very important nowadays, you know. Why did you think I had that particular role?"

"Mainly the stuff I saw all the times I've been in your bedroom. All those cowboy books and war comics – 'graphic novels', I believe they call them now. As you say, we've got to get the name right. I noticed that the pages with the bloodiest scenes were always marked and dog-eared. That's what you get off on, isn't it? Violence and pain and killing. All that kind of thing. That's the equivalent of porn for you. It's probably why you joined the Volunteers. Am I right?"

Bernie shrugged. "I wasn't the first teenager to like action stories."

"No, but you found a way to make them real, didn't you? That was a stroke of luck. But there were a couple of things about your career that niggled me right along."

"Oh? What things?"

269

"I don't think Jim Sullivan gave the order to fire into the crowd at the Civil Rights march. Or the order to shoot Sheelagh's dad. Maybe some of the other ones didn't come from him either. I think you've been working for two masters. Stirring things up in Belfast. Am I right?"

Bernie said nothing.

"Something else too. When I first met Seamus here, I was sure I'd seen him somewhere before. Not spoken to him, just seen him. I racked my brains for a while trying to remember where it was. Then it came back to me. The day we went down to the ferry terminal in Belfast to see Joyce off on her way to England – there was this tall man in a dark suit that you said looked like a plain clothes policeman? Remember? That was Seamus."

"So what?"

"Well, obviously I started asking myself why he was there. At first I thought maybe you were right, maybe he *was* a plain clothes policeman under deep cover. Maybe he infiltrated the Dublin organisation and got sent over here to run the Birmingham cell. But it didn't ring true. He must have been quite senior in Dublin to be given this much responsibility, he must have been there for years. And if he was a cop, I think the authorities would have swooped by now. They wouldn't stand idly by and let the Birmingham unit carry out two bombing missions. No, I think he has to be genuine, in the sense that he really is Dublin IRA. So I wondered if he might have been snooping, but snooping for the IRA. Maybe either you or I were under some kind of investigation. But that didn't really make sense either. He just stood there at the ferry terminal, he made no attempt at concealment. There was nothing secretive about him. So I think the explanation was much simpler. I think he just came up from Dublin to have a chat with you. He was simply waiting for the chance to take you quietly to one side and have a talk. He probably did it after the rest of us left. And during that talk, I think he recruited you into this alternative IRA that Jim talks about. I think you and he have been working pretty closely together ever since. Am I warm?"

A broad smile spread across Bernie's face. "You're a clever little bastard, aren't you? Your father's son. Let's just say I like to be on the winning side. We call ourselves 'provisional' inside the family.

Not 'alternative'. The Provisional IRA. And we're getting bigger and stronger every day. Make no mistake, Danny, we're the future of the movement. Jim Harrison and the old fogies that he represents, all that pussyfooting around, it's going the way of the dodo. The time has come to move on. We'll be taking a firm line from now on.

"I would have asked you to come with us, but I knew you wouldn't. You're just a younger version of Jim Harrison, aren't you? All that bullshit about ethics and media image and rules of engagement. Do you really think you can win this contest playing by Queensbury rules? Do you think England's going to give us our freedom because we blow up an empty building on some deserted high street? Poppycock. Not in a million years. The English are laughing at the IRA, we've given them no reason to take us seriously. If you want England to make concessions your campaign has to be hurting them. Bodies and funerals – widows and mothers on TV crying their eyes out. Real hurt. And if you haven't got the stomach for it, then you shouldn't be in the Volunteers. That's all there is to it.

"We're going to win, Danny, and when we do nobody's going to give a damn how we did it – what the rules of engagement were or how much blood we spilled. Those kind of things will never be mentioned again. Not once we've won. We'll be terrorists one minute and ministers and foreign secretaries and god-knows-what the next. The red carpets will be rolled out for us, the same as when the old IRA became the government in the south in 1922. That's how it works. If you want to win you've got to play by the real rules, not the ones you would like to apply.

"But none of it affects you, does it? You won't be around to see the changes."

For a few tense moments neither of them spoke, then Bernie laid the pistol down on his lap. "I'm not going to do it, Danny." He was speaking so quietly now that Danny had to strain to make out the words. "I'm going to sit here and you're going to leave, and I'm going to tell the Commander and everybody else that you were gone before I got here. Do you want to know why?"

Danny nodded. "Yes. I do. Why, Bernie?"

"Because you're Joyce's number one man and you always have been, whether she admits it or not, and it would break her heart if I pulled this trigger – and I don't want to break Joyce's heart. I'm telling you because I want you to know what a lucky bastard you are. And if you ever see Joyce again you can thank her and tell her that she's the reason you're still walking around on the surface of this shitty little planet."

"You really think I'm her number one man? Top of the list? I'd love to believe that. That's what I always wanted more than anything else in the world. Anyway, I'll thank her, like you said... and will I give her your love?"

"You're taking the piss now, aren't you?"

"No, Bernie. I'm being serious. She's what makes us blood brothers, remember? But I don't suppose I'll ever see her again now. You've got a better chance than I have. You give her *my* love if you see her. All of it. Tell her she's the reason I *want* to be walking around on the surface of this shitty little planet. The only reason."

There was a pause.

"Go and collect your stuff, Danny. Your passport, any money you've got, your toothbrush, whatever you want to keep. And empty out that Bank of Ireland savings account before the Dublin people block it."

"Thanks, Bernie. I appreciate it."

"This is the one and only chance you're going to get. Go very far away and buy yourself a new identity. They'll come after you – it might not be soon, but they will come. Don't imagine that you're off the hook. Now hurry up. If the others come back before you're gone I'll have no choice but to pull this trigger."

"I really appreciate it, Bernie."

Danny hurried through to his own bedroom where the boxes of plastic explosive were piled almost to the ceiling. He collected a few things from the drawers into a canvas shoulder bag. The last item was the framed picture of Joyce from his bedside table, which he wrapped in a clean shirt and placed at the top. Then he zipped up the bag and left it on the bed while he lifted the partly assembled pipe bomb that he had been working on and cleared a small space for it at the base of the boxes of explosives. He wound the mechanism of the timer, adjusted it carefully and clicked the little switch to the 'armed' position. Finally, he screwed the end cap into position. As he stood up to collect the shoulder bag and return to the lounge he could just hear the timer's faint ticking.

"Okay, Bernie. I've got everything I need. I won't forget this. I owe you a big one. Till we meet again, comrade." He held out his hand and Bernie took it.

"Till we meet again... blood brother." Bernie remained in his chair and picked up the gun again. He looked down at it, seemingly engrossed in his thoughts.

Danny made a hasty departure, turning the key in the mortice lock of the front door from the outside before jogging briskly down the road and around the corner. When he felt he had put a reasonable distance between himself and the house he slowed down and looked around him. It was a pleasant morning, sunny and still. The streets were empty of people, all he saw was a delivery van turning in from the main road and a black cat that watched his passing from beneath a parked car.

When the explosion came it was undoubtedly the loudest sound that he had heard in his entire life. The effect of the shock wave was like being hit in the centre of the stomach with a sledge hammer. He staggered but did not fall. Glass from the windows above him showered down like an abrasive snow. He wiped it from his hair and shoulders and stood still for a moment. It was only when he started to walk again that he realised the world had become totally silent. He had no footfalls, there was no birdsong or rumble of distant traffic from the dual carriageway. He deliberately crunched the powdered glass beneath his shoe and heard nothing. He had become a ghost moving through a world that was only partly real.

The thought that his eardrums might never recover crossed his mind, then a darker realisation – a ghost was something very close to what he had indeed become. Any attempt to communicate with Joyce, or even with his mother, would sooner or later convey to the IRA the fact that he had survived the explosion. Would make it clear, indeed, that he had *engineered* the explosion. If Connor and Liam merited 'retirement' for mere desertion, what greater effort would they assign to the removal of someone who had crossed them in the way that he had? Danny Gallagher had indeed died in the explosion. Now somebody else was walking down a suburban back street of Birmingham, a man reborn, without a history or a name, without family, friends or lovers. Without any clear reason for carrying on with his life.

He had become a murderer, not just of some stranger but of his best friend Bernie, and maybe even of innocent bystanders. And yet he felt nothing. It was puzzling how he could be so calm and detached. Maybe the guilt for that crime belonged to the Danny who had died, and with rebirth came a new account with the Recording Angel, or maybe he was merely numb and the full reality of it would hit him later. He didn't think so though. If anything he felt less guilt now than he had before. He had finally taken a stand, tried to put things right, to make some kind of amends. As a result maybe Connor and Liam and one or two other people would live a little bit longer. The dirty bombing campaign on the mainland would suffer at least a minor setback too.

Of course nothing would really change. They had the technology now, as Seamus had pointed out. Danny wasn't needed any more. He wondered if there was any way they could ever know for sure that he hadn't died in the explosion, or that Bernie had. What were the chances that they would recover human remains from an explosion as big as that, and the inferno that would follow it?

Thinking it over, Danny realised that his chances of creating a new identity for himself were in fact relatively good. He would head for the Southampton docks next, and try to find Connor and Liam Laverty. He would warn them that the Volunteers were on to them, and that he was on the run himself. Liam could have the pleasure of saying I told you so. Maybe they could all buy a passage on a cargo ship to somewhere far away – somewhere warm and fun-loving, where simple people lived simple lives and didn't worry about religion or politics or trying to build utopias that would always disappoint.

Perhaps what he had done hadn't been the best option available to him; if he had known that Bernie would be there in the morning perhaps he should have… He left the thought hanging, uncompleted. Thinking about what might have been was a pointless activity.

As he continued down the street and around the corner on to the main road, he realised that he was beginning to hear again. Sounds were distant and attenuated but he could tell that his eardrums had survived and begun the process of recovery. The world was becoming real again.

And that world right then seemed to Danny like a pretty rocky field in which to plant your dreams. The money from the violin might keep the spark alive a little bit longer for The Diggers, but he could no longer bring himself to believe that they were going to achieve anything in the long term. He thought about them, and all the others: his father, Big Jim, Connor, Liam – even Sheelagh and her father – all blundering around with the best of intentions, trying to create something a bit better than the heartbreaking world in which they found themselves, all headed for defeat and disappointment. Maybe trying to build a perfect society was like trying to build a Perpetual Motion machine. At first glance it looked like it ought to be possible, but it wasn't, because the notion violated a fundamental natural principle. Maybe there was another natural principle that stopped us from creating that ideal human society. The more he thought about it the more the idea appealed to him. He even came up with a name for it – The Principle of Conservation of Human Misery. One thing was certain, he had blown his own chance of saving the world. He would be doing pretty well now just to save himself.

He waved down a taxi, the first time his ingrained thriftiness had permitted him to do such a thing, and sat at the back behind the driver.

"Did you hear that bloody explosion?" the man asked as soon as he had closed the door. "Unbelievable, wasn't it? I wonder what's gone up this time. There were people killed in that pub last night. IRA bastards! Sorry mate, not Irish yourself are you?"

"As a matter of fact I am. But I agree. Total bastards, the IRA. Can you take me to the nearest Bank of Ireland, please, then to New Street Station. I presume that's where you catch the train for Southampton?"

"That'll be the place. I'll have to charge you both the meter time and the parking if I wait for you at the bank."

"No problem."

He took the bag from his shoulder and placed it on the seat beside him. He took out Joyce's picture and looked at it. It was the one they had used at the radio station, taken when she was just coming up to her fifteenth birthday, showing only her head and bare shoulders. It was the most beautiful face Danny had ever seen or could ever imagine. She had signed it across the bottom in black marker, "To my love Danny" and her name, ending in the traditional line of "Xs" that represented kisses. When he closed his eyes he could see her clearly, in her yellow summer dress, waving to him from the crowded deck of *The Manxman* and performing her sweet little curtsy, with the fairytale castle perched on its rock in the middle of the bay behind her.

A tear fell on the glass and trickled down to the edge of the frame.

Epilogue

"So, what have you been doing with yourself all these years, Seamus?"
"I'm a lawyer by training. Did I ever tell you that? I went into a
law firm in Birmingham after… our brief association. Practiced there
ever since, pretty much. Retired a couple of years ago. I've spent
those two years looking for you, mainly."

"How boring for you. I'm sorry it took so long. You never… got
caught then?" It was a question that didn't require an answer. Danny
looked down at the angular shape beneath the printed fabric. "Is it
another of the old Makarovs?"

"Goodness, no. You *are* out of date. We've changed several
times since those." He removed the sarong to reveal a gleaming
silver handgun. "These are Italian. The Beretta 92 series. Some of
them can carry a 20-round magazine."

"Amazing."

Once again, the conversation tailed off into silence Seconds
passed. "I lost my command after that little prank of yours, you know."

"Again, I can only apologise. But then, we didn't win, did we?
You were never going to get a government job out of it."

"No, I suppose not. Funny old life, isn't it? In fact, being fair to
you, what you said that night turned out to be correct. Blowing
people up wasn't the way forward."

Danny shrugged. "Oh well. We all made a lot of bad decisions
back then, didn't we?"

Seamus looked him in the eye for a long time. "You know," he
said at last, "I've imagined this moment almost every day of my life
since I came back and found half the street demolished in Northfield.
Now that the moment has come, I can't seem to muster any feeling.
Any hatred. Odd, isn't it?"

Danny paused to consider. "Maybe we're both a bit old for this
kind of thing."

"Maybe we are." With slow deliberation he released the cock-
ing lever of the automatic and slipped it into his pocket. "Why don't
we go and have a drink instead?"

"You're forgetting – I don't drink."

Merilang Press Books
www.merilang.com

You may be interested in other books from Merilang Press:

Books for Adults

Sun on the Hill
Poems from Wales by Daffni Percival

Letters from My Mill
by Alphonse Daudet, translated by Daffni Percival

The Short, the Long and the Tall
Short stories by Andrew McIntyre

The Rainbow Man and other Stories
Short stories by David Gardiner

The Other End of the Rainbow
Short stories by David Gardiner

Solid Gold
An anthology of the best prose from 5 years of *Gold Dust* magazine, edited by David Gardiner

Children's Books by Daffni Percival

And Thereby Hangs a Tail
Memoirs of a border collie puppy as he grows up and learns to be a 'good sheepdog' as his mother told him
1st edition (colour), 2nd edition (black & white)

A Sheepdoggerel Anthology
A collection of animal poems with a preponderance of collies

The Rainbow Pony
A bedtime story for young children – small card book

Also by David Gardiner:

Sirat
A science fiction novel about the first emergence on earth of
electronic consciousness (iUniverse, 2000)